Nuclear Energy Regulation, Risk and The Environment

Analyzing the impact and benefits of nuclear energy on environment, this book examines nuclear treaties in relation to environmental protection, highlights legal framework on non-proliferation and denuclearization, explores treaties on nuclear safety and nuclear security, discusses legal regimes on management of nuclear wastes, assesses the third-party liability regime and discusses the role of IAEA, EURATOM and NEA in regulating nuclear energy. It explores nuclear energy in the context of climate change and sustainable development. This book also examines the international legal framework on notification, assistance and emergency preparedness in the event of nuclear accidents, considers legal aspects of decommissioning of nuclear power plants and the main legislative trends on nuclear energy use in selected countries. It also addresses regulatory responses to nuclear energy in the wake of the Fukushima power plant nuclear accident in Japan.

Abdullah Al Faruque, Professor, Department of Law, University of Chittagong, Bangladesh

Routledge Research in Energy Law and Regulation

Regulation in the European Electricity Sector
Maciej M. Sokolowski

Law and Green Energy Policies
Roy Partain

Nuclear Energy Regulation, Risk and The Environment
Abdullah Al Faruque

Local Content Oil and Gas Law in Africa
Lessons from Nigeria and Beyond
Pereowei Subai

Nuclear Energy Regulation, Risk and The Environment

Abdullah Al Faruque

Routledge
Taylor & Francis Group
LONDON AND NEW YORK

First published 2019
by Routledge
2 Park Square, Milton Park, Abingdon, Oxon OX14 4RN

and by Routledge
52 Vanderbilt Avenue, New York, NY 10017

First issued in paperback 2020

Routledge is an imprint of the Taylor & Francis Group, an informa business

British Library Cataloguing-in-Publication Data
A catalogue record for this book is available from the British Library

Library of Congress Cataloging-in-Publication Data
Names: Faruque, Abdullah al, author.
Title: Nuclear energy regulation, risk and the environment / Abdullah Al Faruque.
Description: New York, NY : Routledge, 2018. | Series: Routledge research in energy law and regulation | Includes bibliographical references and index.
Identifiers: LCCN 2018028654 | ISBN 9780815375357 (hbk)
Subjects: LCSH: Nuclear energy—Law and legislation. | Environmental law. | Liability for nuclear damages. | Radioactive waste disposal—Law and legislation. | Nuclear industry—Risk management. | Nuclear facilities—Law and legislation. | Nuclear power plants—Safety regulations
Classification: LCC K3990 .F37 2018 | DDC 343.09/25—dc23
LC record available at https://lccn.loc.gov/2018028654

ISBN 13: 978-0-36-758519-8 (pbk)
ISBN 13: 978-0-8153-7535-7 (hbk)

Typeset in Galliard
by Apex CoVantage, LLC

Dedicated to
my daughter
Naira

Contents

Preface

Energy plays a central role in defining human well-being. Energy is essential for fulfilling human needs, to maintain industries, to expand technology, and to sustain economic growth. Access to reliable, affordable, economically viable, socially acceptable and environmentally sound energy services is crucial in achieving sustainable development. Many countries are using nuclear energy as an alternative to fossil fuels and for security of supply and as an important element of their transition to a low carbon economy. Apart from generating commercial electricity, nuclear reactors are used in government-sponsored research and development programs, universities, hospitals and industry; in science and engineering experimental programs; at nuclear weapons production facilities; and in some countries by the military services. Rising demand for energy, energy security, lessening dependence on fossil fuels, climate change mitigation and diversification of security of supply are the main reasons for the increasing use of nuclear energy. One of the pressing challenges for the international community is how to secure an adequate supply of energy without causing any further damage to environment. The increasing popularity of nuclear energy can be attributed to its capacity to address these concerns, reconciling the goals of energy security and environmental protection. Regulation of nuclear energy has technical, environmental, economic and social dimensions as it should be technically sound, environmental friendly, economically viable and cost effective as well as socially acceptable in a given country. Nuclear energy regulation has developed as a separate branch of international energy law and consists of numerous multilateral treaties, principles, technical standards, and guidelines that deal with the risk associated with use of nuclear energy. International regulation of the peaceful use of nuclear energy is still evolving with advancement of scientific knowledge and the changing perception of risk factors.

The book analyzes the impact of nuclear energy on the environment and its benefits, identifies risk factors in the nuclear industry, examines nuclear treaties in relation to environmental protection, addresses the theoretical relationship between environmental law and nuclear energy law, explores the legal framework on non-proliferation of nuclear weapons and denuclearization, highlights the legal regime on management and trans-boundary movement of radioactive wastes, analyzes the legal regime on nuclear safety and security, assesses the third-party liability regime under nuclear treaties, and discusses main legislative trends on the environmental approach to nuclear energy use. It also examines nuclear energy in the context of climate change, nuclear accidents and their environmental effects, international regulation of nuclear risks, and the legal regime on nuclear safety. It examines regulatory responses to nuclear energy undertaken worldwide after the Fukushima nuclear power plant accident of March 2011. It also highlights on regulatory challenges in the decommissioning of nuclear power plants, and explores linkages between sustainable development and use of nuclear energy.

The chapters have been structured and designed to be logically consistent and coherent. The chapters address the principles, contemporary issues, customary international law and multilateral treaties relating to nuclear energy and the environment. Discussion of the relevant principles and provisions of treaties are followed by analysis of the institutional role and responsibility regarding standard setting in nuclear safety, regulation of various kinds of risk, developing nuclear liability and national regulatory framework on nuclear energy.

Chapter 1 explains the importance and significance of nuclear energy, examines risk factors in the use of nuclear energy, the public perception of such risk and the evolution of nuclear energy law. The chapter also locates nuclear energy in the context of sustainable development and evaluates the role of nuclear energy in addressing climate change. In particular, it discusses the Paris Agreement on Climate Change 2015, and its relevance to the use of the nuclear energy. It also examines three accidents: Three Mile Island 1979, the Chernobyl accident in 1986, the Fukushima accident in 2011, and their effects on the environment.

Chapter 2 examines the theoretical relationship between international law and environmental law. It identifies the provisions on nuclear energy in environmental instruments and analyses the application of principles of environmental law in nuclear treaties. In this context, it discusses many important principles of environmental law which are applied in the field of nuclear energy. It is argued that the relationship between environmental law and nuclear energy law is still evolving and environmental law has impacted the nuclear energy law as many nuclear activities are subject to international environmental law and many environmental law principles have been integrated into international nuclear energy law.

Chapter 3 contains analysis of multilateral treaties on non-proliferation of nuclear weapons and denuclearization. It also focuses on the effectiveness of the Treaty on Non-Proliferation of Nuclear Weapons the Comprehensive Test Ban Treaty, and highlights different regional treaties on denuclearization. In this regard, it also highlights analyzes decisions of the ICJ in nuclear test cases, the 1996 Advisory Opinion on the Legality of the Threat or Use of Nuclear Weapons, and the Marshall Island cases on compensation for nuclear damage. It is noted that despite some weaknesses of the NPT, it has helped to curtail the nuclear proliferation as NPT ratification significantly enhances greater transparency resulting from application of the IAEA safeguard, facilitating exchange of information by the IAEA and reducing uncertainty about a state's behavior. On the other hand, the regional treaties on denuclearization complement the global non-proliferation regime as the geographical scope of the nuclear free zone has expanded considerably since the 1970s. Treaties on denuclearization and non-proliferation of nuclear weapons contain implementation mechanisms which are mainly based on compliance measures such as verification, exchange of information, consultations, and submission of annual reports to the treaty bodies established at the regional level. These compliance measures ask for a non-confrontational, cooperative and problem-solving approach.

Chapter 4 addresses both soft law and hard law instruments on the management of nuclear wastes. It highlights the IAEA's 1990 Code of Practice on the Trans-boundary Movement of Radioactive Waste, the Joint Convention on the Safety of Spent Fuel and Radioactive Waste Management 1997, EU Directives and the IAEA Standards on management of nuclear wastes. Although responsibility for the management of nuclear waste rests primarily with the concerned states, national regulatory frameworks must incorporate international standards developed by the IAEA and the Joint Convention. However, the current international legal regime is silent about liability that may arise from damage caused by the underground repositories for spent nuclear fuel and high-level radioactive waste which may remain hazardous for thousands of years.

Chapter 5 addresses the issues of nuclear safety and nuclear security. Regarding safety, it discusses the provisions of relevant treaties such as the Convention on Nuclear Safety 1994, and the IAEA Safety Guidelines. In relation to nuclear security it analyzes the Convention on the Physical Protection of Nuclear Material 1980, the Convention for the Suppression of Acts of Nuclear Terrorism 2005, and the protocols to the Four Geneva Conventions of 1949. The effectiveness of the Convention on Nuclear Safety 1994 has also been examined.

Chapter 6 identifies the regulatory issues and challenges of decommissioning nuclear installations. It also highlights the cost factor in decommissioning, radiation protection in decommissioning, aspects of safety and security, and management of wastes in the decommissioning process of nuclear installations. It is observed that decommissioning a nuclear facility poses many challenges regarding safety, liability, public interest and environmental protection which should be addressed in the regulatory framework of a country.

Chapter 7 deals with liability regimes for third parties under nuclear treaties. In particular, it discusses the principles relating to third-party nuclear liability under the Paris Convention on Nuclear Third Party Liability 1960, the Vienna Convention on Civil Liability for Nuclear Damage 1963, the Joint Protocol Relating to the Application of the Vienna Convention and the Paris Convention 1988, the Convention on Supplementary Compensation for Nuclear Damage (CSC) 1997, the Vienna Protocol 1997 and the Paris Protocol 2004. It is observed that although the current liability regime is much improved from its earlier version, its effectiveness is limited due to sparse participation of states. The international nuclear liability regime is also criticized for being extremely patchy and complicated.

Chapter 8 addresses the issues of notification, emergency preparedness and response to a potential or actual nuclear accident. In this regard, it analyzes the provisions and examines the effectiveness of the Convention on Early Notification of a Nuclear Accident 1986; and Convention on Assistance in the Case of Nuclear Accident or Radiological Emergency 1986. Despite some limitations, these two Conventions have been widely accepted and set standards on notification of nuclear accidents and the obligation on states to provide assistance; such standards have contributed to the overall improvement of nuclear safety by reducing the likelihood of trans-boundary harm.

Chapter 9 explores the institutional framework of regulation of nuclear energy at the global and regional levels. It analyses the role of the IAEA, NEA, EURATOM and ICRP in setting nuclear safety standards, radioactive waste management, technology transfer, technical assistance in developing and formulating regulatory frameworks and providing the necessary infrastructure for the peaceful use of nuclear energy. It is found that the IAEA has made a profound contribution in setting international standards on the use of nuclear energy, developing a liability regime, establishing safety and security norms for nuclear installations and developing an oversight mechanism for ensuring the peaceful use of nuclear energy. The IAEA's role in developing nuclear law – in the form of both soft law (code, recommendations) and hard law (multilateral treaties) has been enormous and has created many new norms under international law. However, not all nuclear states have fully incorporated the treaties or soft law norms in their national regulatory framework.

After the Fukushima accident, it was realised that the current international nuclear regulatory system needed to be more effective and that the IAEA should be strengthened to enforce the international legal rules. Its ability in terms of the oversight and monitoring of nuclear installations should be increased in view of the growing number of states using nuclear energy.

While the mandate of the IAEA is different from that of the NEA, there are technological areas of interest common to both organizations. Both organizations are interested in the safe operation of reactors, waste disposal and protection of the public from radioactive exposure, and in carrying on research and studies. EURATOM has greatly contributed to the development of Europe's nuclear industries, ensuring security of supply, and guaranteeing high standards of public safety.

Chapter 10 looks at legislative trends in nuclear energy and analyzes the extent to which national laws have taken an environmental approach to nuclear energy. In particular, it explores the national legal framework of two developed countries and two developing countries on nuclear civil liability, management of nuclear wastes, nuclear safety and decommissioning. It also discusses the provision of environmental protection under the nuclear energy laws of these countries.

Chapter 11 provides an overview of regulatory responses at global, regional and state levels after the Fukushima Daichi nuclear accident. In particular, it considers regulatory responses adopted in the USA, EU, Japan and some other countries. It observes that many countries have improved safety requirements for nuclear power plant improvements, identified the need to develop and enhance knowledge of external hazards in the safety analysis, and taken measures to improve emergency preparedness since the accident.

Concluding remarks have drawn together the findings of the previous chapters, provided some insights into the future of nuclear energy and identified areas of possible reforms of the international legal framework on nuclear energy.

The writing of most of this book was completed during my stay (January to December 2017) in Australia as a Visiting Fellow of the Centre for Environmental Law of Macquarie University. I am grateful to Dr Shawkat Alam, Professor at the Macquarie Law School and Director of the Centre for Environmental Law of Macquarie University, for giving me this opportunity as Visiting Fellow, and for his constant cooperation in the writing this book. I am grateful to Dr Roy Baker, Lecturer at the Macquarie Law School, the staff of Macquarie Law School and the library of Macquarie University for their excellent support and assistance in finding relevant source materials for this book and providing research facilities. I would also thank my wife Najnin Begum and my son Monmoy for their encouragement for the completion of this book.

Abbreviations

AEC	Atomic Energy Commission
AERB	Atomic Energy Regulatory Board
AFCONE	African Commission on Nuclear Energy
ALARA	As Low as Reasonably Achievable
ASSET	Assessment of Safety Significant Events Team
BAEC	Atomic Energy Commission
BAERA	Bangladesh Atomic Energy Regulatory Authority
CLND	Civil Liability for Nuclear Damage Act
CNRA	Committee on Nuclear Regulatory Activities
CRPPH	Committee on Radiological Protection and Public Health
CSC	Convention on Supplementary Compensation for Nuclear Damage
CSNI	Committee on the Safety of Nuclear Installations
CTBT	Comprehensive Nuclear Test-Ban Treaty
CTBTO	Comprehensive Nuclear Test-Ban Treaty Organization
DAE	Department of Atomic Energy
DOE	Department of Energy
EEZ	Exclusive Economic Zone
EIA	Environmental Impact Assessment
EIADR	The Environmental Impact Assessment for Decommissioning Regulations
ENO	extraordinary nuclear occurrence
EPA	Environment Protection Agency
EPA	Environmental Protection Agency
ERDA	Energy Research and Development Administration
EU	European Union
EURATOM	European Atomic Energy Community
GHG	Green house Gas
HLW	High Level Waste
IAEA	International Atomic Energy Agency
ICJ	International Court of Justice
ICRP	International Commission on Radiological Protection
IDC	International Data Centre

ILO	International Labour Organization
INES	International Nuclear Event Scale
LLWPA	The Low-Level Radioactive Waste Policy Act of 1980
MIT	Massachusetts Institute of Technology
NDA	Nuclear Decommissioning Authority
NDMA	National Disaster Management Authority
NEA	Nuclear Energy Agency
NNWS	Non-Nuclear Weapon States
NPCB	Nuclear Power Company of Bangladesh
NPCIL	Nuclear Power Corporation of India Ltd
NPPs	Nuclear Power Plants
NPT	Non-Proliferation Treaty
NRC	Nuclear Regulatory Commission
NSC	Nuclear Safety Commission
NWTRB	US Nuclear Waste Technical Review Board
NWFZ	Nuclear Weapon Free Zone
OECD	Organization for Economic Cooperation and Development
ONR	Office for Nuclear Regulation
OSART	Operational Safety Review Team
OSPAR	The Convention for the Protection of the Marine Environment of the North-East Atlantic
RADWASS	Radioactive Waste Safety Standards
RAPAT	Radiation Protection Advisory Team (RAPAT)
RECA	Radiation Exposure Compensation Act
RWMC	Radioactive Waste Management Committee
SDR	Special Drawing Right
SEANWFZ	Southeast Asian Nuclear Weapon-Free Zone
SNF	Spent Nuclear Fuel
SNI	Sensitive Nuclear Information
SPNFZ	South Pacific Nuclear Free Zone Treaty
TRU	Transuranic Waste
UAE	United Arab Emirates
UN	United Nations
UNCLOS	United Nations Convention on Law of the Sea
UNFCCC	United Nations Framework Convention on Climate Change
USSR	Union of Soviet Socialist Republics
WAMAP	Waste Management Advisory Programme
WATRP	Waste Management Assessment and Technical Review Programme
WHO	World Health Organization

Cases

Nuclear Tests Case (Australia v France) (1973) ICJ Rep 257
Nuclear Tests Case (New Zealand v France) Admissibility, Judgment [1974] ICJ Rep 457
Legality of the Threat or Use of Nuclear Weapons, Advisory Opinion (1996) ICJ 226 (July 8).
Republic of the Marshall Islands v United States, 79 F. Supp. 3d 1068, 1072 (N.D. Cal. 2015).
Peoples Union for Civil Liberties v Union of India 2 SC 476

International instruments

1996 Protocol to the London Convention on the Prevention of Marine Pollution by Dumping of Wastes and other Matter 1972
Agreement between Spain and Portugal on Co-operation in Matters affecting the Safety of Nuclear Installations in the Vicinity of the Frontier 1980
Agreement Governing the Activities of States on the Moon and Other Celestial Bodies of 1979
Antarctic Treaty 1959
Brussels Supplementary Convention 1963
Civil Liability Convention (CLC) 1992
Comprehensive Nuclear Test-Ban Treaty (CTBT) 1996
Convention concerning the Protection of the World Cultural and Natural Heritage, 1972
Convention for the Protection of the Marine Environment of the North-East Atlantic (OSPAR Convention), 1992
Convention for the Suppression of Acts of Nuclear Terrorism 2005
Convention on Access to Information, Public Participation in Decision-Making and Access to Justice in Environmental Matters 1998
Convention on Assistance in the Case of Nuclear Accident or Radiological Emergency 1986
Convention on Civil Liability for Oil Pollution Damage resulting from Exploration for and Exploitation of Seabed Mineral Resources 1977
Convention on Early Notification of a Nuclear Accident 1986
Convention on Environmental Impact Assessment in a Trans-boundary Context 1991(Espoo Convention)
Convention on International Liability for Damage Caused by Space Objects 1972
Convention on International Trade in Endangered Species of Wild Fauna and Flora 1973
Convention on Nuclear Safety 1994
Convention on Supplementary Compensation for Nuclear Damage (CSC) 1997
Convention on the Conservation of Migratory Species of Wild Animals 1979
Convention on the Physical Protection of Nuclear Material 1980
Convention on Third Party Liability in the Field of Nuclear Energy 1960
Convention relating to Civil Liability in the Field of Maritime Carriage of Nuclear Material 1971

Denmark–Federal Republic of Germany Agreement relating to Exchange of Information on Construction of Nuclear Installations Along the Border 1977

France–Belgium Agreement on Radiological Protection concerning the Installations of the Nuclear Power Station of the Ardennes 1967

France–Switzerland Agreement on the Exchange of Information in case of Accidents which could have Radiological Consequences 1979

IAEA Code of Practice on the Trans-boundary Movement of Radioactive Waste 1990

ILO Convention (No. 115) Concerning the Protection of Workers against Ionizing Radiations 1960

International Convention on Civil Liability for Oil Pollution Damage 1969

International Convention on Liability and Compensation for Damage in connection with the Carriage of Hazardous and Noxious Substances by Sea

Joint Convention on the Safety of Spent Fuel and Radioactive Waste Management 1997

Joint Protocol Relating to the Application of the Vienna Convention and the Paris Convention 1988

London Convention on the Prevention of Marine Pollution by Dumping of Wastes and other Matter 1972

Paris Convention on Nuclear Third Party Liability 1960

Rio Declaration on Environment and Development 1992.

South Pacific Nuclear Free Zone Treaty 1985 (Treaty of Rarotonga)

Stockholm Declaration on Human and Environment 1972

Treaty Banning Nuclear Weapon Tests in the Atmosphere, in Outer Space and Under Water 1963

Treaty Declaring Africa a Nuclear Weapon-Free Zone 1995 (Treaty of Pelindaba)

Treaty for the Prohibition of Nuclear Weapons in Latin America 1967 (Treaty of Tlatelolco)

Treaty on a Nuclear-Weapon-Free Zone in Central Asia (CANWFZ) 2006

Treaty on Non-Proliferation of Nuclear Weapons 1968

Treaty on the Prohibition of the Emplacement of Nuclear Weapons and other Weapons of Mass Destructions on the Seabed and the Ocean Floor and in the Subsoil thereof (Seabed Arms Control Treaty) 1971

Treaty on the Southeast Asia Nuclear Weapon-Free Zone 1995 (Treaty of Bangkok)

UN Convention on International Watercourses 1997

United Nations Convention on the Law of the Sea Convention 1982 (UNCLOS)

UN Security Council Resolution 1540 on Nuclear Terrorism 2004

Vienna Convention on Civil Liability for Nuclear Damage 1963

Statutes and regulations

UK

Energy Act 2004
Energy Act 2013
Health and Safety at Work etc Act 1974
Ionising Radiations Regulations 1985
Ionising Radiations Regulations 1999
Nuclear Industries Security Regulations 2003
Nuclear Installation Act 1965
Nuclear Installations (Liability For Damage) Order 2016
Nuclear Safeguards Act 2000
Radiation (Emergency Preparedness and Public Information) Regulations 2001
Radiological Protection Act 1970

USA

Atomic Energy Act of 1954
Energy Policy Act 1992
Energy Reorganization Act 1974
Low-Level Radioactive Waste Policy Act of 1980 (LLWPA)
Low-Level Radioactive Waste Policy Amendments Act of 1985
National Environmental Policy Act (NEPA) of 1969
Nuclear Waste Policy Act of 1982
Nuclear Waste Policy Amendments Act of 1987 (NWPAA)
Price-Anderson Act 1957
Radiation Exposure Compensation Act (RECA) 15 October 1990
Uranium Mill Tailings Radiation Control Act 1978

Bangladesh

Bangladesh Atomic Energy Regulatory Act 2012
NSRC Regulations 1997

Nuclear Power Plant Act 2015
Nuclear Safety and Radiation Control Act 1993

India

Atomic Energy (Radiation Protection) Rules 2004
Atomic Energy (Safe Disposal of Radioactive Wastes) Rules 1987
Atomic Energy Act 1962
Civil Liability for Nuclear Damage Act 2010

1 Nuclear energy in context

Introduction

The linkage between energy and the environment is well established and undeniable as the use of any energy source has some effect on the environment *albeit* the degree of effect may vary depending on the particular form of energy used. The symbiotic relationship between energy and the environment can be further explained by the fact that use of non-renewable sources such as fossil fuels can emit carbon dioxide, which contributes to global warming. The international community is increasingly pursuing energy security and sustainable development through deployment of cleaner, more efficient and low-carbon energy technologies. Thus, in the energy sector, reduction of greenhouse gas emissions remains a main factor in choices about energy options for electricity generation. Although reduction of greenhouse gas emission is not the main driving force in current use of nuclear energy by the States, it's potential role in promoting sustainable energy source will be of central importance in the coming decades.[1]

The environmental aspects of nuclear power plants and the facilities of the associated fuel cycle are not very different from any other large-scale industrial activity. However, the radioactive materials that are part of the various fuel cycle operations, particularly those radioactive materials generated during the operation of nuclear reactors, have to be strictly controlled.[2]

The growing global demand for energy, the issue of combating climate change and the gradual decline of dependence on fossil fuels has warranted a renewed emphasis on nuclear power. Nuclear energy is currently contributing about 17 per cent of the total global electricity production. Nuclear material and technology is also useful for medicine and agriculture. The justification for a nuclear revival has been based largely upon two policy priorities: climate change mitigation and security of energy supply.[3] Nuclear energy is often considered a clean

1 Evelyne Bertel and Joop Van de Vate, 'Nuclear Energy & The Environmental Debate: The Context of Choices' (1995) 4 *IAEA Bulletin* 2.

2 Ms Hagen, 'Nuclear Power, Man, and the Environment' (1982) 24(2) *IAEA Bulletin* 3.

3 Peter D. Cameron, 'The Revival of Nuclear Power: An Analysis of the Legal Implications' (2007) 19(1) *Journal of Environmental Law* 71–87.

non-renewable energy source in terms of emissions. From an emission standpoint nuclear energy is more environmentally friendly than coal, oil or gas. The importance of nuclear energy is increasing since it is capable of meeting a significant portion of the energy needs of a country. Thus, nuclear power should be considered as one of the significant options for meeting future world energy needs at low cost and in an environmentally acceptable manner. Nuclear energy has assumed growing significance as emission-free energy in an era of serious concern about global warming.[4] In order to improve public perception of the nuclear industry, the issue of safety and waste management need to be further developed and addressed and the industry must continue to pursue a policy of non-proliferation of nuclear weapons.

Risk factors in nuclear energy

Although nuclear technology is currently applied in diverse areas of human activity, such as medicine, nuclear research, agriculture and food preservation, the main risk stems from the generation of nuclear energy from the nuclear power plant. The nuclear power plant is the main part in the nuclear fuel cycle chain, and it is the place where the fission process occurs.[5] Other parts of the nuclear fuel cycle include the transportation of nuclear materials and the management and transportation of spent fuel and nuclear waste.[6] Thus, the sources include all types of nuclear facilities, such as power reactors, research reactors, nuclear fuel cycle facilities, etc, as well as medical, research and industrial sources, and defence-related sources where appropriate. After the Fukushima nuclear power plant accident, public concern about nuclear energy has increased significantly. There are widely varying perceptions of the risks and benefits of nuclear energy. The catastrophic nature of the risk of exposure from a nuclear power plant that can potentially bring great destruction and untold human suffering to humanity and the environment makes this risk unacceptable to humanity.[7] The opposition to nuclear power plant has been expressed in the following ways:

First, the long-term disposal of radioactive wastes remains a major challenge for the international community. A nuclear power plant creates spent nuclear fuel at the reactor site. Spent nuclear fuel is considered high-level waste that has many potential negative effects on the environment. The resulting waste from use of nuclear energy can last thousands of years and can pose some danger to present

4 Daniel C. Rislove, 'Global Warming V. Non-Proliferation: The Time has Come for Nations to Reassert their Right to Peaceful Use of Nuclear Energy' (2007) 24(4) *Wisconsin International Law Journal* 1069–1098.

5 Elena Molodstova, 'Nuclear Energy and Environmental Protection: Responses of International Law' (1994) 12(1) *Pace Environmental Law Review* 193.

6 Ibid, 200.

7 Luis E. Rodríguez-Rivera, 'The Human Right to Environment and the Peaceful Use of Nuclear Energy' (2007) 35(1) *Denver Journal of International Law and Policy* 173–192.

and future generations. No state has found a solution to the problem of long-term disposal of nuclear waste.

Second, a major concern of nuclear energy is the long-term effects of radiation on the people living near or working in a nuclear power station. Although nuclear power plants emit low levels of radiation into the environment, long-term exposure to low-level radiation can be a health risk. While sources of ionizing radiation are essential to modern health care, they can be detrimental to living organisms if the production and the use of radiation sources and radioactive material are not covered by measures to protect individuals exposed to radiation.[8] Ionizing radiation and radioactive substances have a permanent effect on the environment and the risks associated with radiation exposure can only be restricted, not eliminated entirely.[9] Radiation protection from nuclear energy has become an important concern from the perspective of both human and environmental health.

Third, every operating nuclear power plant poses some risk of a severe or large-scale accident. But the risk of such accident is extremely low or insignificant. The nuclear industry estimates the chances of a severe reactor accident to be about one for every 10,000 reactor years of operation.[10]

Fourth, nuclear power plants may not emit carbon dioxide during operation, but high amounts of carbon dioxide are emitted in activities related to building and running the plants. The process of mining the uranium which is used in nuclear power plants also releases high amounts of carbon dioxide into the environment. The mining needed to extract uranium may itself have some negative environmental impacts. Some carbon dioxide emissions occur in various stages of the nuclear fuel chain – mining, milling, transport, fuel fabrication, enrichment, reactor construction, decommissioning and waste management. Uranium mining and milling of uranium mill tailings have radioactivity and this remains after uranium is extracted by milling.[11] Another type of radioactive waste consists of tailings generated during the milling of certain ores to extract uranium or thorium. These wastes have relatively low concentrations of radioactive materials but they remain for long period of time.[12] Thus, uranium mill tailings can adversely affect public health.[13] Nuclear fuel is a kind of enriched uranium but plutonium is a by-product of nuclear power generation. Apart from uranium, which is the primary source of supply for nuclear energy production, plutonium from spent fuel and re-enriched tails from processing residues, stockpiles and ex-military weapons is a secondary source of supply.

8 Carlton Stoiber, Alec Baer, Norbert Pelzer, Wolfram Tonhauser, *Handbook on Nuclear Law* (Vienna, International Atomic Energy Agency 2003) 45.

9 Ibid.

10 Karl S. Coplan, 'Inter-civilizational Inequities of Nuclear Power Weighed against the Intergenerational Inequities of Carbon Based Energy' (2006) 17 *Fordham Environmental Law Review* 227.

11 Environment Alert Bulletin, 'Nuclear Waste: Is Everything Under Control?', see http://www.grid.unep.ch/products/3_Reports/ew_nuclear.en.pdf, accessed 27 August 2018.

12 Radioactive Waste, see https://www.nrc.gov/reading-rm/doc-collections/fact-sheets/radwaste.pdf, accessed 3 July 2018.

13 Radioactive Waste Disposal: An Environmental Perspective, EPA. See https://www.epa.gov/sites/production/files/2015-03/documents/000003ob.pdf, accessed 26 July 2018.

Fifth, nuclear power has higher overall lifetime costs compared to natural gas and coal. The nuclear reactpr is more expensive to build than conventional fossil fuel units. Thus, nuclear energy may be the most expensive way to produce electricity.

Sixth, the illegal trade in nuclear material and the proliferation of nuclear weapons is another global concern. Many countries are aspiring to nuclear energy and any increase in the number of states with nuclear energy capacity increases the likelihood of nuclear proliferation through weaponization of civilian nuclear energy materials. The current international legal framework is not fully adequate to eliminate the risk of such proliferation and to meet the security challenges of the expanded nuclear energy programme.

Seventh, transportation of radioactive material raises another public concern over the environmental impacts of such transport. Transport of nuclear fuel to and from nuclear power plants requires adequate packaging and regulatory measures to protect humans and the environment from the hazards of exposure to radiation. The volume of transportation of radioactive material is increasing rapidly and will continue to increase with the growth of the nuclear power industry.[14]

Eighth, potential terrorist and cyber-attacks and sabotage on nuclear power plants pose additional risks.[15] There is a fear that nuclear weapons or enriched uranium or plutonium may reach terrorist groups who can make small and unsophisticated nuclear bombs. The possibility of diversion of nuclear material through terrorist acts cannot be ruled out.[16] Furthermore, risks posed by human error and natural disasters can also be significant.[17]

Finally, there are unknown and unpredictable safety and environmental risks associated with nuclear energy production that may have long-term consequences.[18] Use of nuclear energy also raises public health concerns with regard to uranium mining and reactor safety, as well as transport and disposal of nuclear waste.[19] Some epidemiologists point out the statistically significant increase of cancer among workers in the nuclear fuel cycle and people living close to nuclear waste reprocessing plants.[20] Some public health scholars suggest that nuclear

14 J.U. Ahmed and H.T. Daw, 'Environmental Impacts of the Production and Use of Nuclear Energy: A Summary of the United Nations Environment Programme Study' (1980) 22(2) *IAEA Bulletin* 27.

15 Jeffrey Donovan, 'IAEA's Amano Calls for Strengthened Computer Security in a Nuclear World' (IAEA 2015).

16 Essam E. El-Hinnawi, 'Review of the Environmental Impact of Nuclear Energy' (1978) 20(2) *IAEA Bulletin* 39–40.

17 Adam Arnold, 'The Quest for Sustainable Energy Security: Germany's Nuclear Scrutiny vs. "All of the Above"', (2015) 15 *Sustainable Development Law and Policy* 26, 26.

18 Regina S. Axelrod, 'Democracy and the Global Nuclear Renaissance' in Regina S. Axelrod and Stacy D. VanDeveer (eds.), *The Global Environment: Institutions, Law and Policy* (4th edn, Sage Publications 2015) 325.

19 Mass. Inst. of Tech., 'The Future of Nuclear Power' (2003).

20 Carlos Alvarez-Dardet, 'Nuclear Waste as a Public Health Challenge' (2001) 55 *Journal of Epidemiology and Community Health* 449.

power plants expose people to 'low-level ionizing radiation, with increased health risks attendant to this exposure'.[21] Harvard and MIT scholars have stressed that modern reactor designs can achieve a very low risk of serious accidents but have admitted that, although technological progress has made nuclear reactors safer, they are not totally risk free and the risk of a reactor leak or other kind of accident can never be dismissed completely.[22] Thus, nuclear technology is seen as 'inherently hazardous' given its potential for large-scale damage to human health and the environment.[23] Although nuclear risk *per se* has a low probability that is difficult to estimate, its foreseen damages are of an extreme magnitude in the event that it occurs.[24] In other words, whereas the risk of a nuclear catastrophe is low, its impact on public health remains unknown.[25] Risks posed by nuclear energy production are very difficult or even impossible to quantify.[26]

Although since the Chernobyl accident the nuclear power industry has strengthened its safety practices and standards, some risks are inherent in nuclear energy. The scope of nuclear risk is now broader than merely the risk of nuclear accident.

Nuclear accidents and their environmental effects

The major accidents at nuclear power plants have resulted in severe environmental contamination. Safe use of nuclear energy remains a great challenge for the international community. Despite the efforts of the current international nuclear safety regime, in the history of nuclear power operation there have been many accidents, the most serious of which include the accident at Three Mile Island in March 1979, and the accident at Chernobyl in April 1986.

Three Mile Island accident 1979

The Three Mile Island accident occurred on 28 March 1979 near Middletown, Pennsylvania in which the nuclear reactor partially melted down. A combination of personnel error, design deficiencies, and component failures was responsible for the

21 Richard W. Clapp, 'Nuclear Power and Public Health' (2005) 113 *Environmental Health Perspective* 720.

22 See Richard Anderson, 'Nuclear Power: Energy for the Future or Relic of the Past? BBC News (27 Feb. 2015), available at http://www.bbc.com/news/business-30919045, accessed 3 July 2018.

23 John G. Palfrey, 'Energy and the Environment: The Special Case of Nuclear Power' (1974) 74 *Columbia Law Review* 1375, 1382.

24 Evelyne Ameye and Inigo Igartua Arregui, 'National Nuclear Third Party Insurance Pools Revisited from a European Union Competition Law Perspective' (2012) 30 *Journal of Energy and Natural Resources Law* 265, 266.

25 Damian Carrington, 'Unsure about Nuclear Power? Here are the Five Questions you must Answer to Decide', *The Guardian*, 21 April 2011.

26 Valentina Vadi, 'Energy Security v. Public Health? Nuclear Energy in International Investment Law and Arbitration' (2015–2016) 47 *Georgetown J. of International Law* 1069, 1114.

Three Mile Island accident. This was the most serious accident in US civilian nuclear power plant-operating history, although its small radioactive releases had no detectable health effects on plant workers or the public. But this incident led to sweeping changes involving emergency response planning, reactor operator training, human factor engineering, radiation protection, and many other areas of nuclear power plant operations.[27] It also caused the NRC to tighten and heighten its regulatory oversight. All of these changes significantly enhanced US reactor safety.[28]

NRC's regulations and oversight became broader and more robust, and management of the plants was scrutinized more carefully. The major changes that have occurred since the accident include upgrading and strengthening of plant design and equipment requirements; identifying the critical role of human performance in plant safety; enhancing emergency preparedness, integrating NRC observations, findings, and conclusions about licensee performance and management effectiveness into a periodic, public report; expanding performance-oriented as well as safety-oriented inspections; and the use of risk assessment to identify vulnerabilities of any plant to severe accidents and expanding NRC's international activities to share enhanced knowledge of nuclear safety with other countries in a number of important technical areas.[29]

Chernobyl accident 1986

The Chernobyl accident occurred on 26 April 1986 during the testing of a turbo-generator in the fourth unit of the Chernobyl Nuclear Power Plant situated in Ukraine, which at the time of the accident was part of the former Soviet Union. The accident had caused a significant increase in radioactivity levels in the former Soviet Union and some European countries. The accident was particularly important in demonstrating the potential international effects of a nuclear power plant incident. In fact, in the light of the accident's significant trans-boundary consequences, the safety of nuclear power plants has assumed an international dimension. It was recognized that while each state operating a nuclear power plant bears full and unequivocal responsibility for safety, for each state the maintenance of safety is an international responsibility.[30] The devastating consequences of Chernobyl incident of 1986 prompted the international community to take strong regulatory measures to address the issues of notification and assistance in the event of a nuclear accident and to ensure safe and peaceful uses of nuclear energy. As a result, two multilateral treaties were adopted – the Convention on Early Notification of a Nuclear Accident 1986 and the Convention on Assistance

27 'Backgrounder on the Three Mile Island Accident', available at https://www.nrc.gov/reading-rm/doc-collections/fact-sheets/3mile-isle.html, accessed 3 July 2018.

28 Ibid.

29 Ibid.

30 Johan Rautenbach, Wolfram Tonhauser and Anthony Wetherall, 'Overview of the International Legal Framework Governing the Safe and Peaceful Uses of Nuclear Energy: Some Practical Steps' (2006) OECD Paper 13.

in the Case of Nuclear Accident or Radiological Emergency 1986. The Chernobyl accident also led to institutional reform within the IAEA as it undertook an expanded programme of nuclear safety and radiological protection. The reform also resulted in strengthening the IAEA Incident Reporting System and the International Nuclear Information System.

Fukushima Daiichi nuclear power plant accident 2011

The accident at the Fukushima Daiichi nuclear power plant in Japan occurred as the result of a severe earthquake and subsequent tsunami on 11 March 2011. The tsunami led to flooding of the plant and damage to equipment which resulted in an extended station blackout, failure of the cooling system and consequent melting of the cores, and releases of radioactive material to the surrounding region. A series of accidents was reported in the following weeks, including hydrogen explosions and leakage of cooling water. After the 11 March earthquake and the following tsunami, the plant stopped generating electricity. The accident caused contamination of the environment with potential long-term consequences. The Fukushima disaster combined a natural catastrophe with man-made errors.[31] The supplier, 'General Electric', had been criticized for designing a plant that was vulnerable to earthquake and risk of flooding. The design of the power plant contributed to the accident.

According to the IAEA Report on Reactor and Spent Fuel Safety in the Light of the Accident at the Fukushima Daiichi Nuclear Power Plant, the tsunami factor was not sufficiently taken into account by the operator. Moreover, the Nuclear and Industrial Safety Agency of Japan confirmed in its Report of March 2012 that most communications facilities became unavailable due to loss of electric power. This significantly obstructed contact with the central control room, which caused considerable delay in restoring the situation. The scope of immediate fallout was so vast it included an area as large as Chicago. The most contaminated area, the ten miles immediately around the plant, will likely be uninhabitable for hundreds of years. Plants, crops, livestock, and water in the region all were contaminated with radioactive materials. Radioactivity released from the nuclear power plant also affected the marine environment of the Pacific Ocean.

These three accidents increased public fear and the distrust of nuclear energy increased significantly, with increasing demand for the strengthening of the safety regulation of nuclear power plants around the world.

Public perception of nuclear energy, risk assessment and management

Safety and security are important aspects of the operation of nuclear reactors. Current resistance to nuclear energy is mainly due to public fear of the potential

31 See Michael G. Faure and Liu Jing, 'Compensating Nuclear Damage in China' (2013) 11 *Washington University Global Studies Law Review* 781–816.

damage that could result from an accident at a nuclear installation or during the transport of nuclear material. Setting up a nuclear power plant in any country can generate concerns and attract criticism from a wide range of people owing to fear or the threat of being exposed to unusual levels of radiation.[32] Much of the public fear about nuclear power plants arises from the perceived danger of radiation which is invisible in nature, potential military use of nuclear energy, risks of accident and production of ultra-hazardous wastes that can have a negative effect on the environment if not managed safely. The calculations used to assess nuclear risk in both the military and the civilian use are fallible and as such the calculation of risk is extremely complicated due to the small quantity of available data and the problem of identifying every variable associated with risk.[33]

Public perception of risk and scientific analysis of such risk are important elements that should be taken into account in the decision-making process relating to nuclear energy. Risk assessment and risk management are an integral part of nuclear power design, construction and operation. Assessing public perception of any proposed nuclear power plant is critical for its acceptance due to the opposition and protest from local communities and other civil society groups, such as environmentalists, that may arise at later stages of the operation. In general, technical risk assessment involves the identification of a hazard associated with a substance or activity, and the likelihood of that hazard's occurrence.[34] Since any nuclear energy project may pose serious threats of serious or irreversible damage to the environment and human health, environmental risk evaluation has become a key issue of analysis of any nuclear energy project.[35] Although negative environmental impact is not unique to nuclear energy, any potential negative environmental impact must be identified, comprehensively assessed and managed. Assessment and evaluation of risk is a necessary mechanism for the nuclear industry in identifying the negative consequences of nuclear activity and is an instrument for decision-making.[36] Risk assessment and management of nuclear-related activities should be deeply ingrained in legal, regulatory and institutional framework on nuclear energy and continuously updated to protect the workers and the public from routine radiation, to reduce the risk of serious nuclear accidents to the lowest possible level.[37]

32 Misam Jaffer, 'Impact of Nuclear Power Plants', 26 March 2011, available at http://large.stanford.edu/courses/2011/ph241/jaffer2/, accessed 3 July 2018.

33 Sidney D. Drell, George P. Shultz and Steven P. Andreasen, 'Reducing the Global Nuclear Risk' (2012) Policy Review, available at https://www.hoover.org/research/reducing-global-nuclear-risk, accessed 3 July 2018.

34 Jane Holder and Maria Lee, *Environmental Protection, Law and Policy: Text and Materials* (2nd edn, Cambridge University Press 2007) 16.

35 Miriam Alfie Cohen and Adrian de Garay, 'Risk society and the precautionary principle', in Jamie Benidickson, Ben Boer, Antonio Herman Benjamin and Karen Morrow (eds), *Environmental Law and Sustainability after Rio* (Cheltenham, Edward Elgar 2011) 85.

36 Ibid.

37 Christopher E. Paine, 'The Nuclear Fuel Cycle, Global Security, and Climate Change: Weighing the Costs and Benefits of Nuclear Power Expansion' (2009–2010) 44 *University of Richmond Law Review* 1047, 1049.

Thus, public acceptability of nuclear energy requires an understanding of risk perception and the development of processes and institutions that involve greater participation by the public in the decision-making process. Nuclear regulatory bodies can play an important role in reducing risk perception and increasing confidence through undertaking stakeholder consultation and awareness programmes about nuclear energy. Sound management of nuclear wastes, efficient processes for the nuclear fuel cycle, and use of effective and secure technologies for nuclear reactors are some of the key issues that must be addressed in order to reduce the perception of risk. The reduction of nuclear risks requires every level of the nuclear enterprise and related military and civil organizations to embrace the importance of safety and security as an overarching operating rule.[38] Independent regulations of the nuclear industry and incorporation of independent peer review into all aspects of the nuclear enterprise are also crucial to setting and enforcing the safety and security rule.[39]

Significance of nuclear energy

Significance of nuclear power can hardly be over emphasized due to the growing energy demand and the mounting challenge of climate change. In comparison to fossil fuel energy, nuclear energy has many advantages. First, diversification of energy sources and reducing dependence on fossil fuel is one of the driving factors for nuclear energy. Second, it can enhance security of supply of energy without causing significant environmental harm. The traditional and non-renewable fuel can cause environmental pollution. Nuclear power as a non-renewable energy simultaneously reduces pollution and enhances energy security and it can advance both objectives.[40]Agenda 21 states that developed countries need to promote renewable sources of energy and more efficient modes of transformation. Agenda 21 further proposes that "A comprehensive approach to human settlements development should include the promotion of sustainable energy development in all countries." It is expected that nuclear energy will be considered as most viable option amongst the renewable energy in foreseeable future as it produces remarkably little environmental pollution and greenhouse gas emissions. It is also considered as one of the ways to reduce dependence on coal, oil and natural gas. Recently, climate change concerns of burning of fossil fuel have rejuvenated commercial and civilian nuclear energy use in both developed and developing countries.[41] In particular, in terms of required land area, the performance of a nuclear power plant is essentially independent of its location. Therefore, NPPs require a

38 Drell, Shultz and Andreasen (n 33).

39 ibid.

40 Lincoln L. Davie, 'Beyond Fukushima: Disasters, Nuclear Energy, and Energy Law' (2011) *Brigham Young University Law Review* 1937.

41 John Moens, 'The Nuclear Power and the Environment', available at http://www.nuclearfiles.org/menu/key-issues/nuclear-energy/issues/health-environment/moens_nuclear_power_environment.html, accessed 13 July 2018.

much smaller land area compared with wind and solar technologies.[42] It is also well established that the health effects from nuclear power plant construction and operation are consistently low and are much lower than fossil fuel alternatives.[43] The amount of energy produced from nuclear reaction is huge compared to the energy produced from other primary resources. Advances in nuclear reactor technology have substantially improved the underlying economics and safety profile of nuclear power. Although the capital costs of building nuclear installations have risen substantially in recent years, nuclear power can still be cost-competitive relative to other renewable energy sources such as windmill or solar energy in terms of the base-load generation of electricity. Nuclear energy costs are relatively stable and less vulnerable to changes in fuel prices generation than coal or gas fired.[44]

Evolution of nuclear energy law

Nuclear energy law draws its sources from three different category of legal instruments: multilateral treaties that deal range of issues on regulating nuclear energy, non-binding standards and technical norms developed by the IAEA and bilateral agreements on nuclear cooperation, technology transfer, notification and assistance. Evolution of nuclear energy law can be categorized in three fairly distinct phases.[45] The first phase, beginning in the late 1940s and 1950s, is marked by adoption of some international instruments for the promotion of the peaceful use of nuclear power. In this phase, nuclear energy is seen as diversification of energy sources and it provided European and the USA as an alternative source of energy apart from coal and oil. Nuclear energy was developed to tackle the general shortage of 'conventional' energy in the 1950s and as a means of achieving energy independence.

The second phase developed after the Chernobyl accident in 1986 and Three Mile Island is seen as enhanced protection of safety and security of nuclear power installations as well as increased liability for damage to third party. This period has been viewed 'the use of law as a source of constraint amid renewed concerns about safety.' According to one commentator, these nuclear accidents brought to an end the positive attitude towards nuclear power that had been seen for several decades. Since these accidents, international community witnessed a significant growth in the number of international treaties, national laws and regulations and establishment of institutions to address the issue of safety, health and the environment. These legal development mainly dealt with safety of nuclear installations

42 Ibid.

43 Climate Change and Nuclear Power, (IAEA, Vienna 2016) 52, available at https://www-pub.iaea.org/MTCD/Publications/PDF/CCANP16web-86692468.pdf, accessed 13 July 2018.

44 Kais Saidi and Mounir Ben Mbarek, 'Nuclear Energy, Renewable Energy, CO2 Emissions, and Economic Growth for Nine Developed Countries. Evidence from Panel Granger Causality Tests' (2016) 88 *Progress in Nuclear Energy* 364–374.

45 Cameron (n 3) 72.

and increased liability for nuclear operator. While the newly developed legal instruments dealing with nuclear liability are innovative in respect of the considerable extension of the scope of damage covered and the increased amount of compensate, those dealing with nuclear safety adopted innovative approach in respect of compliance which is based on 'incentive' rather than 'legally binding' commitments.[46] Consequently, these legal developments made the cost of nuclear power became more expensive and the nuclear industry became highly regulated in all of the developed countries.[47]

In the third or most recent phase, the issues of climate change mitigation, nuclear waste disposal and public participation and consultation in case of construction of new nuclear power plant and waste disposal figure prominently.[48] Recently public acceptance and consultation for a new generation of nuclear power stations has appeared to be significant trend in nuclear industry and in particular, management and governance of nuclear waste in many countries require deliberative decision involving range of stakeholders.

Energy security and the outlook for nuclear energy

Nuclear energy is seen as a diversification of energy supply and emerged as an independent source of energy during the 1960s. The oil crises of the early 1970s with consequent oil price hike caused acute anxiety about the security of the oil supply among the Western states, giving impetus to governments to initiate programmes of nuclear power plant construction to reduce the high degree of dependence on imports.[49] Since then nuclear energy has become an important source of renewable energy around the world. Today there are some 440 nuclear power reactors operated in 30 countries. In addition, some countries, such as Bangladesh, Belarus, the United Arab Emirates, Thailand, Turkey and Poland are currently constructing their first nuclear power plants to meet growing energy demand and increase energy security. Some other countries are operating research and other reactors. It is predicted that worldwide electricity consumption will increase substantially in the coming decades, especially in the developing world, to meet the needs of economic growth. Current forecasts suggest that electricity demand is increasing twice as fast as overall energy use and is likely to rise by more than two-thirds to 2040.[50] All major international reports on future energy supply suggest an increasing role of nuclear energy alongside growth in all other

46 Dr Nathalie L.J.T. Horbach, 'Nuclear Safety and Liability Conventions', in Nathalie L.J.T. Horbach (ed.), *Contemporary Developments in Nuclear Energy Law: Harmonising Legislation in CEEC/NIS* (The Hague, Kluwer Law International 1999) 5.

47 Cameron (n 3) 76.

48 Cameron (n 3) 72.

49 Cameron (n 3) 73.

50 'World Energy Needs and Nuclear Power', World Nuclear Association, http://www.world-nuclear.org/information-library/current-and-future-generation/world-energy-needs-and-nuclear-power.aspx, accessed 13 July 2018.

forms of low-carbon power generation for a sustainable energy system.[51] Nuclear power capacity worldwide is increasing steadily, with over new 59 nuclear power reactors are under construction in 17 countries. Some countries have phased out nuclear energy following the Fukushima incident due to public opposition, and Germany has abandoned its nuclear industry. The importance of nuclear energy is increasing as radiation releases from nuclear facilities are very small in routine operation and a significant threat to worker and public health may occur only under accident conditions. The potential hazards from nuclear accidents and the probability of such accidents can be further reduced by technological improvement, training of manpower, emergency preparedness, and effectiveness of regulatory measures.[52]

The role of government in nuclear energy

Because of the significant risks involved in nuclear energy it is subject to a very high degree of regulation at both national and international levels. Given the unique safety and security concerns of nuclear energy, the scale of the required investment and infrastructure and the long time frame required to realize its large potential benefits, governments are to play a key role in the development of nuclear industry.[53] Historically, nuclear industry is a highly regulated area and the state has a profound role and responsibility for the safety and security of its nuclear power plants. Government should adopt effective legislation, and establish an independent regulatory body which can ensure nuclear safety and contribute in building confidence in nuclear energy. Independent regulatory bodies should be in place in countries having nuclear reactors for ensuring that nuclear energy activities are carried out in compliance with high safety and radiation protection regulations. Governments should arrange adequate resources for regulatory bodies and vest them with necessary power and authority so that they can function independently, competently and fulfil their responsibilities properly. While the prime responsibility for safety rests with the operator of the facility, an independent regulator is essential to monitor the operator's performance against accepted standards. It must have the authority and means to implement safety measures, including the ultimate authority to shut down the plants in the event of an emergency. Governments should formulate policies, processes and procedures for the siting, construction, design and approval of nuclear installations, including waste management facilities. Governments have also a role in ensuring that the public is adequately informed about nuclear energy policy and there is adequate opportunity for public participation in the decision-making process relating to nuclear energy.[54] Governments with nuclear reactors should

51 Ibid.
52 'Nuclear Energy in a Sustainable Development Perspective' (NEA, OECD, 2000) 9.
53 'Government and Nuclear Energy' (NEA, OECD, 2004) 14.
54 Ibid 10.

also ratify international Conventions and adhere to international safety norms in order to bring national nuclear legislation into conformity with international safety standards.

Nuclear energy in the context of sustainable development

Sustainable development in relation to energy acknowledges the links between energy access, fulfilling basic needs, and poverty alleviation.[55] The United Nations 2030 Agenda for Sustainable Development identifies universal access to electricity as a key development priority and a prerequisite for sustainable economic growth. Sustainable development depends on the long-term availability and environmentally sound production of fuel and affordable, clean, low-carbon and reliable energy source. In recent years, the goals of energy policy have been shifted towards sustainability. In order to achieve sustainable development, access to sustainable energy is a fundamental prerequisite.[56] Nuclear energy is treated as one of the sustainable energy options and strategies in many countries. The main challenge in achieving sustainable energy is to strike an appropriate balance between pursuing energy security and protecting the environment through deployment of cleaner, more efficient and low-carbon energy technologies. The core idea of sustainability-based energy policy is to advance three objectives: economy, environment and equity, by ensuring security of supply and promoting the environmental goals of better ecological protection.[57] Nuclear energy is not an exception. The sustainability criteria of nuclear energy can include a range of factors such as the economic, social and environmental dimensions of nuclear power plant operation, and risk assessment. Agenda 21 noted that 'energy is essential to economic and social development and improved quality of life'[58] and observed that 'all energy sources will need to be used in ways that respect the atmosphere, human health and the environment as a whole'.[59]

The performance of nuclear energy against criteria for sustainable development is relevant in two areas: the efficient use of natural resources and the limited environmental impacts.[60] In terms of efficiency, unlike other fuel cycles involving depletable natural resources for energy (coal, oil, gas), uranium can be recycled, reprocessed and used again as nuclear fuel.[61] Uranium is more abundant and

55 Stephen R. Tully, 'The Contribution of Human rights to Universal Energy Access' (2006) 4 *Northwestern University Journal of International Human Rights* 518.

56 David Hodas, 'International Law and Sustainable Energy: A Portrait of Failure' in Jamie Benidickson, Ben Boer, Antonio Herman Benjamin and Karen Morrow (eds.), *Environmental Law and Sustainability after Rio* (Cheltenham, Edward Elgar 2011) 257–278.

57 Ibid.

58 Para 9.9 of Agenda 21, https://sustainabledevelopment.un.org/content/documents/Agenda21.pdf, accessed 13 July 2018.

59 Ibid.

60 Ferenc L. Toth, 'Nuclear Energy and Sustainable Development' (2014) 74 *Energy Policy* S1–S4.

61 Ibid.

more efficient as a fuel, and the reserves of uranium are also widely distributed across the world.[62] This ample resource base, and the scope for improving the efficiency of their use make nuclear energy a serious potential contributor to sustainable energy development.[63]

In view of current reserves of uranium, which are large enough to support nuclear fuel production for decades, and its potential to be recycled and reprocessed, nuclear energy is consistent with the objectives of sustainable development related to the effective use of natural resources and their preservation for future generations.[64] Abundance of uranium also provides diversity and security of fuel supply. Furthermore, the capacity for the recycling of nuclear fuel is a unique feature that distinguishes it from fossil fuels which, once burned, are largely dispersed into the environment in gaseous or particulate forms.

The role of nuclear energy in addressing climate change

Nuclear power is a low-carbon technology both in absolute terms and relative to other electricity generation technologies. The full technology chain for nuclear energy includes uranium mining, milling, conversion, enrichment, fuel fabrication, reprocessing, conditioning of spent fuel, interim storage and final disposal of radioactive waste, including the construction of the final repositories, as well as power plant construction, operation and decommissioning. The greenhouse gas (GHG) emissions associated with downstream activities, such as decommissioning and waste management, are also very low. Nuclear power plants do not emit air pollutants such as nitrogen oxides (NOx) and sulphur dioxide (SO_2). Nuclear power (a) represents a well-established technology for generating electricity that produces no carbon or other climate-relevant emissions; (b) is amenable to significant scaling-up and thus can provide large amounts of power; and (c) uses a natural resource (uranium), which is relatively abundant. Reduction of GHG emissions remains a driving force and this issue is likely to be the main factor in choices of energy options for electricity generation during the coming decades. Nuclear energy is considered one of the significant options for reducing carbon emissions since nuclear power plant operation emits no or negligible amounts of carbon dioxide. Such negligible emission occurs in various stages of the nuclear fuel chain – mining, milling, transport, fuel fabrication, enrichment, reactor construction, decommissioning and waste management.[65] Nuclear energy's potential role in reducing GHG emission and in electricity generation

62 Ibid.
63 Ibid.
64 'Nuclear Energy in a Sustainable Development Perspective' (n 52) 8.
65 'Reducing Climate Change Impact', http://www.iaea.org/newscenter/news/2009/climatechange.html, accessed 13 July 2018. The 'nuclear fuel cycle' refers to the entire program from the mining and milling of uranium, through the manufacture of fuel elements for the reactor, transport and reprocessing of irradiated fuel, to the management of wastes produced in all steps of the cycle.

will be of central importance in coming decades.[66] This has been reflected in a Massachusetts Institute of Technology (MIT) study, which finds that there are only a few realistic options for reducing carbon dioxide emissions from electricity generation:

- increasing efficiency in electricity generation and use;
- expanding use of renewable energy sources such as wind, solar, biomass, and geothermal;
- capturing carbon dioxide emissions at fossil-fueled electric generating plants and permanently sequester the carbon; and
- increasing use of nuclear power.[67]

The International Energy Agency captures the world's profound sustainable energy and climate change challenges in the following words:

> The world's energy system is at a crossroads. Current global trends in energy supply and consumption are patently unsustainable – environmentally, economically and socially. ... It is not an exaggeration to claim that the future of human prosperity depends on how successfully we tackle the two central energy challenges facing us today: securing the supply of reliable and affordable energy; and effecting a rapid transformation to a low-carbon, efficient and environmentally benign system of energy supply. ... Preventing catastrophic and irreversible damage to the global climate ultimately requires a major decarbonisation of the world energy sources.[68]

Despite the realization that nuclear energy is a most valuable tool available to counter global climate change, it has been ignored in the international legal framework on climate change. For example, neither the United Nations Framework Convention on Climate Change (UNFCCC) 1992 or the Kyoto Protocol 1997 mentions nuclear energy. Nuclear energy was specifically excluded from the joint implementation and clean development mechanism designed to help implement the Kyoto Protocol on climate change. The Kyoto Protocol asks the parties to cooperate in the development and transfer of, or access to, 'environmentally sound' technologies, practices and processes relevant to climate change. In order to achieve the goal of emissions reduction, parties shall implement or elaborate on policies and measures that include: enhancing energy efficiency; increasing the use of 'renewable' forms of energy; CO_2 sequestration; and 'advanced and environmentally sound technologies'.

66 Bertel and de Vate (n 1).

67 *Future of Nuclear Energy*, An Inter-disciplinary MIT study, Massachusetts Institute of Technology, Massachusetts, (2003) http://web.mit.edu/nuclearpower/pdf/nuclearpower-summary.pdf, accessed 13 July 2018.

68 IEA, World Energy Outlook 2008, 37, available at https://www.iea.org/media/weoweb site/2008-1994/WEO2008.pdf, accessed 13 July 2018.

According to Article 3 of the Kyoto Protocol, developed countries are to refrain from using emission reduction units generated from nuclear facilities to meet their commitments. It appears from this provision that developed countries should emphasize other renewable energy resources, such as wind, solar and hydroelectricity. But any rational regime that claims relevancy in addressing global climate change should include nuclear energy as a proven strategy of GHG emission mitigation.[69] It is even claimed that given the tremendous benefits that nuclear energy can bring in combating climate change, the Kyoto Protocol was mistaken in excluding nuclear energy from its compliance mechanisms.[70]

The Paris Agreement aims to limit the increase in the global average temperature to well below 2°C above pre-industrial levels and pursue efforts to limit it to 1.5°C. Without significant efforts to limit future GHG emissions from the energy sector, the expected global increase in energy production and use could well trigger 'dangerous anthropogenic interference with the climate system'.[71] Low-carbon technologies, renewable sources of energy such as nuclear energy, will play the principal role because they can provide low-carbon electricity to satisfy the increasing demand for modern energy services. According to an IAEA report, 'Any exemption, limitation, restriction or exclusion of any of these technologies would undermine the economic rationale of cost efficiency and would increase mitigation costs and delay actual emissions reduction'.[72]

By 2030, the transition in line with the 2°C target will require more than doubling low-carbon investments. GHG emissions from the energy sector can be mitigated if states adopt strong supporting policy measures. Some of the measures suggested to achieve this goal include developing and strengthening national mitigation targets as formulated from Intended Nationally Determined Contributions under the Paris Agreement; reducing risks faced by investors in low-carbon technologies; supporting innovation and technology transfer to enhance the deployment of low-carbon technologies; closing inefficient coal power plants; and implementing policy incentives which serve the joint purposes of sustainable development.[73]

In fact, use of nuclear energy can be a valuable way to achieve the objectives of the 2015 Paris Agreement which aims to reduce current emission rates to the lowest levels. Further improvements in nuclear technology in the future can also reduce nuclear CO2 emissions which are already among the lowest. These very low CO2 emissions on a life cycle of nuclear power makes it an important technology option in addressing climate change mitigation in the future.[74]

69 Timothy J.V. Walsh, 'Turning Our Backs: Kyoto's Mistaken Nuclear Exclusion' (2003) 16(1) *Georgetown International Environmental Law Review* 147–170.

70 Ibid.

71 Article 2 UNFCCC.

72 'Climate Change and Nuclear Power' (Vienna, IAEA 2016) 4.

73 Ibid, 15.

74 Ibid, 21.

2 Theoretical relationship between international nuclear law and environmental law

Introduction

Like any other large scale industrial activities, nuclear power plants have environmental aspects. Nuclear law was developed after the Second World War as a distinct branch of international law to guide and regulate the development of nuclear activities for civil use. However, nuclear energy law intersects with international environmental law in many ways. The relationship between the two branches of law can be explained in the following ways.

First, many international environmental law instruments regulate nuclear activities. Expanding the horizon of environmental law embraces numerous fields, including nuclear activities.[1] Access to information regarding nuclear matters, concepts of transparency and stakeholder involvement are relatively recent in the nuclear field and are examples of the effect that the development of international environmental law has had on nuclear law and nuclear activities.[2]

Second, many important principles of environmental law have been integrated into nuclear treaties to deal with environmental concerns of nuclear operation. The principles of environmental law – both substantive and procedural in nature – have been increasingly incorporated into international nuclear law treaties. The initial focus of nuclear law was on radiation protection and third-party liability for damage caused by nuclear activities to protect people and property, without explicitly referring to environmental protection. Traditional nuclear law was thus dominated by an anthropocentric approach which focuses on protecting people and property rather than the environment.[3] The nuclear accidents in Chernobyl and at Three Mile Island led to the development of an enhanced prevention and protection culture, resulting in the adoption of important nuclear safety Conventions and the second generation of nuclear third-party liability Conventions. This new generation of liability Convention led to a growing emphasis

1 P. Bourdon, 'The Growing Interrelationship Between Nuclear Law and Environmental Law' (2015) 33(2) *NEA News*, 15–18.
2 Ibid.
3 Sam Emmerechts, 'Environmental Protection under Nuclear Law: Still a Long Way to Go' in *International Nuclear Law: History, Evolution and Outlook* (2010) NEA, OECD, 123.

on environmental protection in the field of nuclear activities.[4] Thus, modern nuclear law as a specialized branch of law aims to ensure that nuclear activities are carried out in a manner that is safe for both the public and the environment. The relationship between environmental law and nuclear energy law is still evolving. Environmental law applies to the nuclear field both directly and indirectly: directly, by making nuclear activities subject to international environmental law, and indirectly by introducing environmental law principles and the concept of environmental protection into international nuclear law.[5]

Nuclear energy in environmental instruments

Environmental regulation of nuclear energy can be found in several environmental soft law instruments and treaties. For example, Principle 26 of the Stockholm Declaration on Human and Environment 1972, which is a non-binding document, refers explicitly to nuclear power. It states that man and his environment must be spared the effects of nuclear weapons and all other means of mass destruction. The 1972 London Convention on the Prevention of Marine Pollution by Dumping of Wastes and other Matter prohibits the dumping at sea of high-level radioactive wastes, including nuclear wastes. The main objective of the London Convention is to prevent indiscriminate disposal at sea of wastes that could be liable for creating hazards to human health; harming living resources and marine life; damaging amenities; or interfering with other legitimate uses of the sea. In 1996, states adopted a Protocol to the London Convention which replaces the Convention for those countries that ratify the Protocol. The Protocol has come into force. Under the Protocol all dumping is prohibited, except for possibly acceptable wastes on the so-called 'reverse list'.[6] The Protocol moves the emphasis from sea dispersal to precautionary and preventative action on land.

The Law of the Sea Convention 1982

UNCLOS 1982 required States Parties to minimize to the fullest possible extent the release of toxic, harmful or noxious substances, especially those which are persistent. UNCLOS contains specific provisions on the right of innocent passage for ships carrying nuclear or other inherently dangerous or noxious substances.[7] The coastal state may require foreign ships exercising the right of innocent

4 Sam Emmerechts, 'Environmental Law and Nuclear Law: A Growing Symbiosis', available at https://www.oecd-nea.org/law/nlb/nlb-82/091_110_ArticleEmmerechtsSam.pdf, accessed 4 July 2018.

5 Lincoln L. Davie, 'Beyond Fukushima: Disasters, Nuclear Energy, and Energy Law' (2011) *Brigham Young University Law Review* 123.

6 Convention on the Prevention of Marine Pollution by Dumping of Wastes and Other Matter, IMO, available at http://www.imo.org/en/OurWork/Environment/LCLP/Pages/default.aspx, accessed 4 July 2018.

7 Articles 22 and 23 UNCLOS.

passage through its territorial sea to use designated sea lanes. In particular, tankers, nuclear-powered ships and ships carrying nuclear or other inherently dangerous or noxious substances or materials may be required to confine their passage to such sea lanes.[8] It also provides that foreign nuclear-powered ships and ships carrying nuclear or other inherently dangerous or noxious substances shall, when exercising the right of innocent passage through the territorial sea, observe special precautionary measures established for such ships by international agreements.[9]

The Convention for the Protection of the Marine Environment of the North-East Atlantic (the OSPAR Convention) 1992

The OSPAR Convention is the mechanism by which 15 governments and the EU cooperate to prevent and eliminate pollution and protect the maritime area against the adverse effects of human activities so as to safeguard human health and to conserve marine ecosystems. This Convention prohibits dumping of radioactive wastes into the sea. It contains precautionary and 'polluter pays' principles.

Convention on Environmental Impact Assessment in a Trans-boundary Context 1991(Espoo Convention)

The Convention on Environmental Impact Assessment in a Trans-boundary Context includes many fields of environmental regulation including nuclear activities. The Convention obligates the States Parties to take all appropriate and effective measures to prevent, reduce and control significant adverse trans-boundary environmental impact from proposed activities. In order to achieve this goal, the party of origin of an activity shall ensure that an environmental impact assessment is undertaken prior to a decision to authorize or undertake a proposed activity. The Convention includes nuclear activities in those industrial hazard activities likely to entail trans-boundary consequences. Under the Convention, nuclear power stations and other nuclear reactors must submit to the procedure of an environmental impact assessment, with the exception of nuclear research installations. In Kiev on 21 May 2003, a Protocol to the Espoo Convention was adopted on Strategic Environmental Assessment, expanding the obligations of the Contracting Parties. This Protocol aims to establish a new procedure providing for a high level of environmental protection by evaluating the likely environmental impacts, including health effects. The procedure comprises of the determination of the scope of an environmental report and its preparation, the carrying out of public participation and consultations, and the report shall contain the results of the public participation and consultations in a plan or programme. Trans-boundary consultation with concerned authorities shall be held for projects listed in Annex I to the Protocol, which includes decision-making related to production and

8 Article 22 UNCLOS.
9 Article 23 UNCLOS.

conversion of fissile and fertile materials with limited power. More elaborately, the Espoo Convention applies to projects including nuclear facilities and activities such as nuclear power stations and nuclear reactors (except research reactor) and installations designed solely for the production or enrichment of nuclear fuel, for the reprocessing of irradiated nuclear fuel or for the storage, disposal and processing of radioactive waste.[10] The Kiev Protocol 2003 under the Espoo Convention requires States Parties to evaluate the consequences of their 'plans and programmes' that are likely to have significant environmental effects in a broad range of sectors including nuclear energy. The Kiev Protocol requires public participation at a very early stage in the decision-making process. Under the Kiev Protocol, parties planning to develop a nuclear programme shall ensure that all relevant stakeholders – the public, national, regional and local environmental and health authorities, and other Contracting Parties likely to be affected by the trans-boundary impacts of the plan – are consulted.

Such trans-boundary consultation on nuclear energy was carried out by Ukraine for the first time in April 2017, when the Ukrainian Government, which is a Party to this Convention, invited neighbouring governments to participate in consultations regarding the lifetime extension of nine of its nuclear reactors. This trans-boundary consultation took place due to increasing demand of environmental activists and civil society groups who had been calling on Ukraine to recognize its obligations under the Espoo Convention. In the practice of trans-boundary consultations on nuclear issues, this is only the start of a test for public participation and transparency in Europe's nuclear sector.[11]

The Aarhus Convention on Access to Information, Public Participation in Decision-Making and Access to Justice in Environmental Matters 1998[12]

The Aarhus Convention entered into force in 2001. This Convention contains the most detailed requirements for public participation in decision-making relating to environmental matters. Among other things, it requires States Parties to implement public involvement in decisions on specific development activities listed in Annex 1.[13] The list of specific activities includes nuclear power stations and other nuclear reactors, including the dismantling or decommissioning of such power stations or reactors.[14] This is also the main international instrument

10 Annex 1 Espoo Convention.

11 Ana-Maria Seman, 'Nuclear Trans-Boundary Consultations are a Test for Public Participation and Transparency Across Europe' (30 May 2017) available at https://www.opendemocracy.net/od-russia/ana-maria-seman/nuclear-transboundary-consultations-are-test-for-public-participation-and-transparency-across-europe, accessed 4 July 2018.

12 The 1998 UN Economic Commission for Europe Convention on Access to Information, Public Participation in Decision-Making and Access to Justice in Environmental Matters, June 25, 1998, UN Doc. ECE ICE P/43(1998).

13 Article 6.

14 Annex 1 to the Convention.

that grants the public the right to access environmental information. The Aarhus Convention also requires public authorities to possess and update environmental information relevant to their functions, to ensure an adequate flow of information to public authorities about proposed and existing activities that may significantly affect the environment and to disseminate immediately and without delay all information that could enable the public to take preventative or mitigating measures in the event of an imminent threat to human health or the environment.[15] Under the Convention, public authorities have a duty to make information available to the public when requested and the Convention lays out time frames for responding to these requests. Thus, requests for information on the environmental impact of nuclear projects are often covered by the Aarhus Convention as such information may be classified as 'environmental'.[16] For example, public authorities will be under an obligation to inform the public of radiation levels on its territory in case of accident or outside its territory and should not keep this information confidential. The Convention also provides that in the event of an imminent threat to human health or the environment, all information held by public authorities which could enable the public to take measures to prevent or mitigate harm arising from the threat must be disseminated without delay.[17] Article 4 creates a presumption in favour of information disclosure and public authorities can deny a request for information only on the basis of a list of specific grounds for refusal.

The public authority may refuse to disclose information which would impair the ability of a person to receive a fair trial, or would adversely affect national defence or public security. The government should establish a publicly accessible database to provide information on a range of activities including water, energy and other resources.[18] According to the Convention, the public should be able to

15 Article 5 of the Aarhus Convention.

16 The 'environmental information' under the Aarhus Convention includes any information in written, visual, aural, electronic or any other material form on: (a) the state of the elements of the environment, such as air and atmosphere, water, soil, land, landscape and natural sites including wetlands, coastal and marine areas, biological diversity and its components, including genetically modified organisms, and the interaction among these elements; (b) factors, such as substances, energy, noise, radiation or waste, including radioactive waste, emissions, discharges and other releases into the environment, affecting or likely to affect the elements of the environment referred to in (a); (c) measures (including administrative measures), such as policies, legislation, plans, programmes, environmental agreements, and activities affecting or likely to affect the elements and factors referred to in (a) and (b) as well as measures or activities designed to protect those elements; (d) reports on the implementation of environmental legislation; (e) cost-benefit and other economic analyses and assumptions used within the framework of the measures and activities referred to in (c); and (f) the state of human health and safety, including the contamination of the food chain, where relevant, conditions of human life, cultural sites and built structures inasmuch as they are or may be affected by the state of the elements of the environment referred to in (a) or, through those elements, by any of the matters referred to in (b) and (c).

17 Emmerechts, 'Environmental Protection under Nuclear Law: Still a Long Way to Go' (n 3) 132.

18 Article 5(9) of the Convention.

participate in the decision-making of a project, plan, policy or programme relating to the environment.[19] This also includes nuclear projects which may produce a negative environmental effect.

Incorporation of principles of environmental law in nuclear law

Some of the important principles of environmental law such as the precautionary principle, principle of preventive action, the polluter pays principle and the principle of cooperation have been incorporated in the nuclear energy related treaties.

Principle of prevention of harm

The principle is implicitly or explicitly endorsed in many treaties that regulate activities that create a risk of trans-boundary pollution. These treaties cover the following subject matters: the marine environment; the management of high seas fisheries; the protection of rivers; nuclear energy; atmospheric pollution; climate change; ozone layer; waste management; toxic substance; and biodiversity. The principle of harm prevention is contained in the Latin maxim *sic utere tuo ut alienum laedas* – use your own property in such a manner as not to cause harm to the property of another. The principle has been derived from arbitral and judicial decisions. In the *Trail Smelter Arbitration* (1941) it was held that no state has the right to use or permit the use of territory in such a manner as to cause injury to the territory of another. The *Corfu Channel* case *(UK v Albania)* (1948) confirmed every state's obligation not knowingly to allow its territory to be used for acts contrary to the rights of other states.

The principle has been embodied in the Stockholm Declaration 1972 and the Rio Declaration 1992. According to Principle 21 of the Stockholm Declaration and 2 of the Rio Declaration 1992, states have sovereign rights to exploit their own natural resources pursuant to their own national policies but they have a responsibility to ensure that activities within their jurisdiction and control do not cause damage to the environment of other states (trans-boundary harm) or of areas beyond the limits of national jurisdiction (high seas, outer space, Antarctica).

The main objective of this principle is to avoid environmental harm and reduce the risk of harm. A trans-boundary harm may result from a trans-boundary movement across several boundaries, causing detrimental effects in several states, or it may also result from an act which causes harm in and beyond national jurisdiction or control. There are four elements of trans-boundary damage: first, the physical relationship between the activity concerned and the damage caused; second, human causation; third, a certain threshold of severity that calls for legal action; and fourth, trans-boundary movement of the harmful effects.[20]

19 Article 6 of the Convention.

20 Xue Hangin, *Transboundary Damage in International Law* (New York, Cambridge University Press 2003) 36.

States find themselves bound by a due diligence requirement to prevent trans-boundary pollution. However, customary law does not specify what diligent conduct entails or what concrete measures states are required to take in order to fulfil their duties under the Rio Declaration.[21] The obligation to prevent trans-boundary harm is subject to variety of interpretations as to what preventative actions may be required of a state, as well as what amount of damage is to be prevented.[22] Not all trans-boundary damage necessarily gives rise to international liability. It is applicable only in those cases where trans-boundary damage crosses a certain threshold of severity.

Most environmental treaties require States Parties to comply with some sort of due diligence requirement (EIA, consultation, monitoring sources of potential trans-boundary harm). A state which complies with all such requirement may not be held liable, 'however devastating the harm may be'.[23]

Examples of treaties relating to harm prevention and liability include the 1972 Convention on International Liability for Damage Caused by Space Objects, the 1992 Civil Liability Convention (CLC) and the 1992 Fund Convention, the 1969 International Convention on Civil Liability for Oil Pollution Damage, and the International Convention on Liability and Compensation for Damage in Connection with the Carriage of Hazardous and Noxious Substances by Sea. This principle has been incorporated in the Nuclear Liability Conventions, which will be discussed in detail in Chapter 8 of this book.

The principle of 'no harm' was re-stated in the case of *Legality of the Threat or Use of Nuclear Weapons* (1996)[24] and accepted by both parties (Hungary and Slovakia) in the *Gabčikovo* case.[25]

Breach of the principle entails the state responsible to pay compensation. The principle has been crystallized into a rule of customary international law and norm of *jus cogens.* This principle imposes not an absolute duty to prevent all harm, but rather an obligation to minimize detrimental consequences of permissible activities.

The preventative principle has long been used in nuclear law to promote the exercise of caution so as to prevent all kinds of damage that might be caused by the use of nuclear technology and to minimize adverse effects resulting from nuclear incidents. In the realm of nuclear law, this principle was initially focused on avoiding personal injury and property damage rather than environmental damage.[26] But the Chernobyl accident demonstrated that an accident at a nuclear

21 P. Birnie and A. Boyle, *International Law and the Environment* (2nd edn, Oxford University Press 2002) 113.

22 A. Nollkemper, *The Legal Regime of Transboundary Water Pollution: Between Discretion and Constraint* (London, Martinus Nijhoff and Trotman 1993) 31.

23 A. Boyle, 'Codification of International Environmental Law and the International Law Commission: Injurous Consequences Revisited' in A. Boyle and D. Freestone (eds.) *International Law and Sustainable Development* (Oxford, Oxford University Press 1999) 139.

24 ICJ Rep 241, para. 29.

25 (1997) ICJ Rep 7 at 41.

26 Emmerechts, 'Environmental Protection under Nuclear Law: Still a Long Way to Go' (n 3) 137.

facility, regardless of the location, can have severe trans-boundary consequences on environment and as such this principle has been included in subsequent liability Conventions to prevent environmental damage. Since Chernobyl there have been several attempts to address the trans-boundary impact of nuclear radiation release or nuclear activities. The 1998 Agreement on Environmental Cooperation with the Dismantling of Russian Nuclear-Powered Submarines withdrawn from the Navy's service in the Northern Region is an example of bilateral agreement between Russia and Norway for the prevention of potential trans-boundary harm that may be caused by Russia's dilapidated nuclear submarines. Under the Agreement, Norway has provided assistance for the dismantling of decommissioned nuclear submarines and the handling of spent reactor fuel from submarines and nuclear ice-breakers and other solid and liquid radioactive waste.[27] Russia's decommissioned nuclear submarines and 2100 spent fuel rods were stored at the Northern Fleet's former service bases at Andreyev Bay, which is about 45 kilometres from the Norwegian border. This was a great concern for Norway as they posed a greater risk of radioactive pollution and hazards to health in Norway. The Russian-Norwegian cooperation agreement on nuclear safety presents a mechanism for preventing and mitigating the trans-boundary impact of nuclear activities.

The 'polluter pays' principle

The 'polluter pays' principle has emerged as one of the main instruments of protection of the environment. This principle requires that the 'costs of pollution should be borne by the person responsible for causing the pollution and consequential costs'.[28] The polluter pays principle is an economic rule of cost allocation which is based on the theory of externalities. It requires the polluter to take responsibility for the external costs arising from his pollution. In all cases, the principle involves intervention by the public authorities. There are two ways to ensure that prices reflect the true cost of production and consumption: taxation that corresponds to the estimated economic value of the environmental damage, and regulatory standards to prohibit or limit the damage associated with an economic activity.[29] It means that the polluter has primary responsibility for environmental harm and is directly accountable in national law.[30] The main function of the polluter pays principle is to internalize the social costs borne by the public authorities for pollution prevention and control.[31]

27 Cooperation with Russia on nuclear activities and the environment in the High North, Report No. 11 (2009–2010) to the Storting, the Ministry of Foreign Affairs of Norway, available at https://www.regjeringen.no/contentassets/dcb69db75e6a4b40ac3897088e601579/en-gb/pdfs/stm200920100011000en_pdfs.pdf accessed 4 July 2018.

28 Philippe Sands and Jacqueline Peel, *Principles of International Law* (3rd edn, Cambridge: Cambridge University Press 2012) 228.

29 Nicolas de Sadeleer, *Environmental Principles: From Political Slogans to Legal Rules* (Oxford University Press 2002) 21.

30 Ibid 24.

31 Ibid 35.

This principle is implemented through the imposition of an environmental liability system. The premise of the principle is based on the rules governing civil liability for environmental damage. The principle expects polluters to bear the costs of measures carried out by public authorities with respect to potential and actual environmental damage.[32] It is now widely applied in the environmental regulations of many developed countries as a mechanism for internalizing the economic costs of pollution control, clean- up and protection measures. Its increasing popularity among developed countries can be attributed to its flexibility and effectiveness of achieving environmental and economic efficiency, to obviate the problem of over-regulation and under-enforcement associated with direct regulation.[33]

The polluter pays principle has been integrated into many nuclear treaties. The price of nuclear energy should cover the full social costs so that taxes or fees are used to encourage greater efficiency. This principle is applied in nuclear liability Conventions through incorporation of channelling of liability for third-party damage by the operator of the nuclear installation. The third-party liability Conventions impose strict liability on the operator of the plant for nuclear damage and require it to provide cover for costs of damage, mainly in the form of insurance.

Precautionary principle

The precautionary principle is based on uncertainty of risk. Precaution does not posit a perfect understanding of any given risk: it is sufficient that a risk be suspected, conjectured or feared. Thus, it aims at ensuring anticipatory preventative action in response to uncertainty.[34] The question is no longer merely how to prevent assessable, calculable and certain risks, but rather how to anticipate risks suggested by possibility, contingency, plausibility and probability.[35] Decision-making processes must henceforth take all risks into account, whatever their degree of certainty. This principle has been formulated in Principle 15 of the Rio Declaration.[36] It calls for action when there is scientific uncertainty about the precise degree of risk or the magnitude of potentially significant or irreversible environmental harm. It obviates the principle of burden of proof.

Given the inherent risk factors involved in nuclear energy and nuclear wastes, this principle is applied in the nuclear industry to assess risks of ionizing radiation and radioactive wastes. In order to comply with legal requirements during the licensing process, a risk assessment of the nuclear installation and facility is

32 H. Smets, 'The Polluter Pay Principle in the Early 1990s' in Luigi Campigio et al (eds.), *The Environment After Rio: International Law and Economics* (Springer 1994) 136–137.

33 J.B. Opschoor and Hans B. Vos, *Economic Instruments for Environmental Protection* (Paris, OECD 1989) 24.

34 Nicolas de Sadeleer (n 29) 91.

35 Ibid 93.

36 'Where there are threats of serious or irreversible damage, lack of full scientific certainty shall not be used as a reason for postponing cost effective measures to prevent environmental degradation.'

conducted to facilitate risk management activities. The principle has been incorporated in many instruments, including several environmental instruments. In relation to radioactive waste management, Agenda 21 recommends that states should not promote or allow the storage or disposal of high-level, intermediate-level or low-level radioactive wastes near the marine environment unless such storage or disposal poses no unacceptable risk to people and the marine environment or does not interfere with other legitimate uses of the sea.[37] The International Commission on Radiological Protection advocates a precautionary approach to radiological protection by arguing that even small radiation doses may produce some deleterious health effects.[38]

Principle of cooperation

Global environmental problems warrant a global solution on a multilateral basis. Solution of environmental problems thus requires the support of a network of international organizations and states. The global nature of environmental problems requires that states follow a comprehensive and effective set of norms, rules and methodologies in carrying out their commitment to environmental protection.[39] The concept of a duty upon states to cooperate finds support in various international agreements, decisions of international courts and tribunals, and resolutions of international organisations. The general principle was formulated in Principle 24 of the Stockholm Declaration[40] and Principle 27 of the Rio Declaration. Principle 27 of the Rio Declaration lays down that states and people shall cooperate in good faith in the field of sustainable development. Cooperation requires exchange of information, notification and consultation. The international dimension of nuclear energy and of the potential trans-boundary effects of its activities underscores the necessity of international cooperation in this field and the need for cooperation has been stressed in many nuclear treaties. The IAEA cooperates extensively with the states having nuclear programmes to ensure safety and security of nuclear installations both bilateral and multilateral framework.[41] Many bilateral nuclear energy agreements have been concluded among states to promote cooperation in the peaceful use of nuclear energy. These agreements are typically called 'Nuclear Energy Cooperation Agreements' and refer to bilateral treaties which provide the framework for cooperation between two states in the peaceful uses of nuclear energy, including nuclear trade and collaboration.

37 Agenda 21, Chapter 22, sub-section (5)(c).

38 International Commission on Radiological Protection (ICRP), 1990 Recommendations of the International Commission on Radiological Protection, ICRP Publication 60 (Elsevier Science 1991).

39 Shawkat Alam, *Sustainable Development and Free Trade* (London, Routledge 2008) 25.

40 Principle 24 of the Stockholm Declaration provides: 'International matters concerning the protection and improvement of the environment should be handled in a co-operative spirit by all countries, big or small, on an equal footing.'

41 Emmerechts 'Environmental Protection under Nuclear Law: Still a Long Way to Go' (n 3) 138.

Reference to protection of environment is found in some bilateral Nuclear Energy Cooperation Agreements. Such reference to environmental protection can be found either in the preamble or the operative part of a treaty. For example, the 2017 Agreement between Japan and India on cooperation in the peaceful uses of nuclear energy only commits to environmental objective in its preamble.[42] Some other bilateral treaties make express provisions for environmental protection in their operative parts. For example, under the Agreement for cooperation between the USA and the United Arab Emirates concerning peaceful uses of nuclear energy adopted in 2010, the Parties shall consult to identify the international environmental implications arising from nuclear energy development activities and shall cooperate in protecting the international environment from radioactive, chemical or thermal contamination arising from peaceful nuclear activities and in related matters of health and safety.[43] Similarly, Article 11 of the Agreement for cooperation between the USA and India concerning peaceful uses of nuclear energy provides that the Parties shall cooperate in following the best practices for minimizing the impact on the environment from any radioactive, chemical or thermal contamination arising from peaceful nuclear activities and in related matters of health and safety.[44]

Principle of intergenerational justice

The principle of inter-generational justice has emerged as an important strategy for conservation of natural resources in view of the growing threats of environmental degradation and resource depletion arising out of the current consumption pattern. This principle is inextricably linked with the notion of sustainable use of natural resources, and the notion of trusteeship. It is one of the core elements of sustainable development. This principle, in brief, requires that each generation should ensure that successor generations do not fall below the level of welfare that they themselves had reached.[45] It denotes environmental protection, pollution control and a whole range of other environmental measures agreed to at the international level, fulfilling responsibilities towards future generations. Responsibilities of the present towards future generations arise in the field of the environment, natural resources and sustainable development. Concern over future generations has been increasingly reflected in recent years in bilateral and multilateral agreements, declarations and resolutions. The 1972 Stockholm

42 The Agreement can be found at http://www.mofa.go.jp/files/000202920.pdf, accessed 4 July 2018.

43 Article 14 of the Agreement, available at http://www.nti.org/media/pdfs/StateandUAEPeacefulNucJan2009.pdf?_=1316627912, accessed 4 July 2018.

44 Agreement for cooperation between the USA and India concerning peaceful uses of nuclear energy, available at https://2001-2009.state.gov/r/pa/prs/ps/2007/aug/90050.htm, accessed 4 July 2018.

45 See Edith Brown Weiss, *In Fairness to Future Generations: International Law, Common Patrimony and Intergenerational Equity* (Transnational Publisher 1989).

Declaration of the UN Conference of the Human Environment recognized for the first time intergenerational justice to protect and improve environment.[46] The second principle of the Stockholm Declaration advocates the safeguarding of the natural resources of the earth for the benefit of present and future generations. From the 1972 Stockholm Conference onwards, many international environmental Conventions refer to the rights of future generations. The 1972 Convention concerning the Protection of the World Cultural and Natural Heritage, the 1973 Convention on International Trade in Endangered Species of Wild Fauna and Flora and the 1979 Convention on the Conservation of Migratory Species of Wild Animals all acknowledged concerns for future generations.

There are two intergenerational aspects of use of nuclear energy: First, use of uranium for nuclear energy generation may lead to depletion of uranium which is a finite resource, and consequently future generations will have less access to it. The second intergenerational aspect in nuclear energy is the fact that nuclear waste can exist for a long period of time and consequently the safety and security of future generations can be affected negatively if wastes are not properly disposed of. The latter is a fundamental condition if future generations are to enjoy equal opportunities.[47] Objection to the idea of disposing of the waste in geological repositories is based on long-term uncertainties for future generations. In addition to the depletion of a non-renewable resource, the remaining long-lived radiotoxic waste adds another intergenerational dimension to the problem. In the last decades, the long-term concerns about waste have triggered a debate on how to deal with radiotoxic waste in an equitable way. The IAEA has laid down several principles of Radioactive Waste Management, in which concerns about future generations were expressed in terms of the 'achievement of intergenerational equity'.[48] It was asserted that nuclear waste should be managed in such a way that it 'will not impose undue burdens on future generations'.[49]

Article 1 of the Convention on Spent Fuel Management recognizes the intergenerational implications of nuclear waste, and provides that Parties must aim to avoid imposing 'undue burdens' on future generations, including burdens that are greater than those permitted for present generations. One leading environmental authority notes that this appears to be 'the strongest provision on intergenerational equity in any environmental treaty'.[50]

46 Principle 1 of the Declaration states: 'Man … bears a solemn responsibility to protect and improve the environment for present and future generations.' Principle 2 of the Stockholm Declaration says that 'Natural resources of the earth including the air, water, land, flora and fauna … must be safeguarded for the benefit of the present and future generations'.

47 Behnam Taebi, *Nuclear Power and Justice between Generations: A Moral Analysis of Fuel Cycles* (2010) 14, available at http://www.janleenkloosterman.nl/reports/thesis_taebi_2010.pdf accessed 4 July 2018.

48 Principles of Radioactive Waste Management Safety Fundamentals, IAEA 1995.

49 Ibid.

50 Birnie and Boyle (n 21) 464.

Principle of prior notification and consultation

When activities have the potential to damage the environment outside a state's border, the acting state is obliged to give potentially affected states prior notification of the plans, and then engage in consultation or discussions of the plans with them and possibly even to negotiate in good faith alternatives to the plans.[51] The principle of prior notification has been incorporated in many environmental instruments and treaties, such as the Rio Declaration 1992,[52] the 1982 Law of the Sea Convention, and the 1997 UN Convention on International Watercourses. The duty to notify states of possible trans-boundary harm is an emerging principle of international environmental law.

The principle of prior notification and consultation with neighbouring states is also applicable in the case of construction of nuclear power plants. In particular, the construction of nuclear power plants in border area is an example of where notification and consultation must be in place to avoid trans-boundary impact of nuclear operation. Article 17 of the 1994 Nuclear Safety Convention and Article 13 of the 1997 Joint Safety Convention impose obligations on Parties to consult with other Parties if a nuclear installation or facility is constructed in their border areas and if they are likely to be affected by that proposed installation or facility.

Several bilateral treaties have been concluded to address the obligation to consult, exchange of information and notification arising out the construction of nuclear power plants in border areas. Examples of such bilateral treaties include the France-Belgium Agreement on Radiological Protection concerning the Installations of the Nuclear Power Station of the Ardennes 1967; Denmark-Federal Republic of Germany Agreement relating to Exchange of Information on Construction of Nuclear Installations Along the Border 1977; Agreement between Spain and Portugal on Co-operation in Matters affecting the Safety of Nuclear Installations in the Vicinity of the Frontier 1980; and the France-Switzerland Agreement on the Exchange of Information in case of Accidents which could have Radiological Consequences 1979.

Principle of environmental impact assessment

Environmental Impact Assessment (EIA) is the important modality of the precautionary principle. It is a process of integration of environmental consideration in the decision-making process. EIA as a national instrument shall be undertaken for proposed activities that are likely to have significant adverse impact on the environment. Access to information and public participation are two main requirements of EIA as it is widely recognized that environmental issues are best

51 Ved P. Nanda and George Pring, *International Environmental Law and Policy for the 21st Century* (New York, Transnational Publishers 2003) 55.

52 Principle 19 of the Rio Declaration states: 'States shall provide prior and timely notification and relevant information to potentially affected States on activities that may have a significant adverse transboundary environmental effect.'

handled with the participation of all concerned citizens. Agenda 21 calls on all states to ensure that 'relevant decisions are preceded by environmental impact assessments'. EIA is a formal study process used to predict the environmental consequences of a proposed major development project. A sound EIA should be based on an analysis of comprehensive baseline data about existing environmental and socio-cultural conditions of the proposed project, and should assess the full range of possible environmental and socio-cultural impacts that could result from the operation of a project and identify measures to mitigate adverse impacts; and suggest alternatives to the proposed project after comparing environmental costs with economic and social benefits. Thus, EIA predicts and evaluates the potential impacts of a project on the environment, identifies alternatives and mitigation measures by using its findings in planning and decision-making. In this way, the EIA provides a risk assessment by analyzing information, assumptions and base line data in order to estimate the probability of harm to the environment by the operation of the proposed project. The scope of an EIA may vary considerably, depending on the anticipated scale and significance of environmental effects of the operation under consideration and the location of the project. The EIA helps to prevent environmental damage by identifying and assessing the potential environmental effects of project activities before they are undertaken and by suggesting mitigation measures of anticipated negative impacts through an environmental management plan on the basis of information gained through the EIA.[53]

There is a growing consensus that timely and broad-based stakeholder involvement is as vital an ingredient for effective environmental assessment as it is for project planning, appraisal and development in general.[54] EIAs that successfully involved a broad range of stakeholders have tended to lead to more influential environmental processes and consequently to development that delivered more environmental and social benefits.[55] It also helps to address relevant issues, including those perceived as being important by other sectoral agencies, public bodies, local communities and other affected groups.[56]

EIAs are used increasingly as the primary tool for stakeholder involvement in the nuclear energy development and have become an essential instrument in preventing negative environmental effects that could arise from the implementation of a nuclear project.[57] Requirement of EIA has been implicitly incorporated in the Nuclear Safety Convention 1994. Article 17 of the Nuclear Safety Convention asks the States Parties to ensure that appropriate procedures are established

53 Carole Klein Chesivoir, 'Avoiding Environmental Injury: The Case for Widespread Use of Environmental Impact Assessments in International Development Projects' (1990) 30 *Virginia Journal of International Law* 517–518.

54 Ross Huges, 'Environmental Impact Assessment and Stakeholder Involvement' (London, International Institute for Environment and Development 1998).

55 Ibid.

56 Ibid.

57 Emmerechts, 'Environmental Protection under Nuclear Law: Still a Long Way to Go' (n 3) 134.

for evaluating all relevant site-related factors likely to affect the safety of a nuclear installation for its projected lifetime and the likely safety impact of a proposed nuclear installation on individuals, society and the environment. Similarly, Article 8 of the Joint Convention requires the States Parties to ensure that before construction of a spent fuel management facility, a systematic safety assessment and environmental assessment be carried out; and before the operation of a spent fuel management facility, updated and detailed versions of the safety assessment and of the environmental assessment shall be prepared. Thus, the Joint Convention deals with the issue more specifically. However, the Nuclear Safety Convention is silent about the point in time when such environmental impact assessments need to be conducted.

Public participation in the environmental decision-making process

Public participation in environmental issues generally includes the right of the stakeholder to be involved in the decision-making process relating to environmental matters.[58] Public participation has been incorporated in environmental law through the concept of sustainable development, of which public participation is a central tenet.[59] International environmental laws are also increasingly making provisions for public participation. Public participation in environmental matters can produce many benefits. It can improve environmental decision-making and encourages sound business practices for sustainable development.[60] According to some authors, the public participation in environmental matters may have two kinds of benefits: first, from the process-based perspectives the benefits of public participation are the following: raising public awareness and educating the public; giving the public an opportunity to express its concerns; fostering a sense of empowerment in participants; strengthening local communities and other groups; reducing conflicts among competing interests; facilitating governmental accountability; increasing public acceptance of decisions reached and contributing legitimacy to decisions. From the substantive-based perspectives public participation is desirable because it can make the decisions substantively 'better', more equitable, more environmentally protective, more reflective of local needs and more reflective of public values.[61]

58 See Najnin Begum and Rakiba Nabi, 'Public Participation in Environmental Decision Making in Bangladesh: To What Extent is the Existing Regulatory Framework Effective (2011) 51(1) *Indian Journal of International Law* 67–84.

59 George (Rock) Pring and Susan Y. Noe, 'The Emerging International Law of Public Participation Affecting Global Mining, Energy and Resources Development', in Donald N. Zillman, Alastair R. Lucas and George (Rock) Pring (eds), *Human Rights in Natural Resource Development* (Oxford, Oxford University Press 2002) 13.

60 Susan Casey-Lefkowitz et al, 'The Evolving Role of Citizens in Environmental Enforcement' (1996) 11 *National Environmental Enforcement Journal* 40.

61 Begum and Rakiba (n 58) 22.

The evolving principle of public participation in environmental matters is also echoed in the Rio Declaration of 1992. Principle 10 of the Rio Declaration of 1992 lays down that environmental issues are best handled with the participation of all concerned citizens, at the relevant level and at the national level, and each individual shall have the opportunity to participate in decision-making process.[62] The 1998 Aarhus Convention on Access to Information, Public Participation in Decision-Making and Access to Justice in Environmental Matters[63] contains the broadest and most detailed requirements to date for public participation in decision-making. Among other things, it requires states to implement public involvement in decisions on specific development activities, including metals production and processing facilities, other mineral industry developments, mining projects, energy sector facilities (such as refineries, large power plants, and nuclear plants), chemical plants, waste disposal and incineration facilities, dams and large water projects, pipelines and roads.

Laws providing for the public's right of access to information and participation in decision-making processes were almost non-existent in the early days of nuclear energy development and production.[64] But in the light of the widespread public concern about nuclear risks, it is realized that public participation in decision-making relating to nuclear energy projects needs to be integrated in nuclear law and policy to foster confidence in the nuclear industry.[65] For example, during construction of the Temelin nuclear power plant in the Czech Republic, public hearings were held due to pressure from civil society and protest against the project.[66]

Public participation in decision-making relating to nuclear energy projects requires access to relevant information relating to a broad range of issues including safety, security, nuclear wastes and the decommissioning of nuclear installations, so that they can put forward their informed opinion on nuclear projects. Access to information on nuclear safety issues held by regulatory authorities can enhance public knowledge of nuclear safety and radiation protection. Accurate and complete information about plant operations, radiation releases and waste management activities is a pre-requisite for effective stakeholder involvement in

62 The Rio Declaration on Environment and Development, U.N.Doc. A/CONF.151/5/Rev. 1(1992) 31 ILM 874.

63 The 1998 UN Economic Commission for Europe Convention on Access to Information, Public Participation in Decision-Making and Access to Justice in Environmental Matters. June 25, 1998, UN Doc. ECE ICE P/43(1998). The Convention entered into force in 2001.

64 Emmerechts, 'Environmental Protection under Nuclear Law: Still a Long Way to Go' (n 3) 129.

65 'Nuclear Energy in a Sustainable Development Perspective', (NEA, OECD, 2000) 10; see also Harold P. Green, 'Participation in Nuclear Power Plant Licensing: The Great Delusion' (1974) 15 *William and Mary Law Review* 503.

66 Regina S. Axelrod, 'Democracy and the Global Nuclear Renaissance' in Regina S. Axelrod and Stacy D. VanDeveer (eds), *The Global Environment: Institutions, Law and Policy* (4th edn, Sage 2015) 313.

nuclear energy decision-making. With the exception of information relating to sensitive nuclear security, restrictions on information should be limited. Stakeholders' involvement in the important process of nuclear energy, such as the siting and construction of a nuclear power plant, is necessary. A range of stakeholders in the nuclear industry – national regulatory authorities, nuclear power plant designers and operators, public interest organizations and individuals, the media and local people – are entitled to easy access to objective, unbiased information so that they can reach an informed opinion on nuclear issues in general and can participate meaningfully in matters relating to the development of nuclear projects.[67] Stakeholder involvement may enhance safety through more socially responsible decisions, dispel misconception of various nuclear safety matters, encourage public confidence and trust, and can ensure transparency by making regulatory organizations and other authorities aware that their actions are under public scrutiny.[68] Public participation in decisions can promote a greater degree of understanding and ensure more reasonable appreciation of risks and benefits, and can enhance the general acceptability of the ultimate decisions made.[69] Public participation can provide valuable health and safety oversight of both regulators and plant operators, ensuring that secrecy, lax safety enforcement and failed compliance do not go unnoticed.[70]

Public participation in the nuclear industry is now integrated in environmental and planning law.[71] In many developed countries with nuclear power plants, consultation with the public is undertaken whenever decisions are taken on nuclear energy projects requiring permits or licences, such as the construction of a radioactive waste management facility or the decommissioning of a nuclear reactor.[72] For example, the US Department of Energy (DOE) of has a strong Public Participation Policy which is also applied in the field of nuclear energy to promote improvements in nuclear safety by ensuring that its decisions benefit from the perspective of those interested in and affected by DOE activities, such as workers and those who live in communities where DOE activities take place.[73] To implement this policy, the DOE has established 'citizens advisory boards' (CABs) at all its major sites to establish open communication with stakeholders in order to

67 'Stakeholder Involvement in Nuclear Issues', INSAG-20 A report by the International Nuclear Safety Group, (Vienna, IAEA 2006) <https://www-pub.iaea.org/MTCD/Publications/PDF/Pub1276_web.pdf, accessed 4 July 2018.

68 Ibid.

69 Ibid.

70 Jean-Rene Jubin, 'Transparency and Openness' 7 (2011) IAEA, available at https://ansn.iaea.org/Common/topics/OpenTopic.aspx?ID=9087 accessed 4 July 2018.

71 Peter D. Cameron, 'The Revival of Nuclear Power: An Analysis of the Legal Implications', (2007) 19(1) *Journal of Environmental Law* 71–87 at 87.

72 Emmerechts, 'Environmental Protection under Nuclear Law: Still a Long Way to Go' (n 3) 132.

73 Report to Congress on the Price-Anderson Act, US Department of Energy, available at https://www.energy.gov/sites/prod/files/gcprod/documents/paa-rep.pdf, accessed 4 July 2018.

gain diverse perspectives, and values about the projects.[74] The UK's nuclear industrial strategy titled 'The UK's Nuclear Future', published in 2013 recommended a series of actions including 'public engagement and awareness' about nuclear energy in order to adopt 'deliberative engagement approach' for developing public understanding of nuclear energy related matters; informing and enabling the public to make their own decision in regards to nuclear energy.[75]

However, effective public participation requires availability and adequacy of environmental information and nuclear data may be held by several departments, private operators and government agencies at different levels.[76] It is important to coordinate among such organizations and agencies and avoid overlapping responsibilities of agencies to avoid complexity of gaining access to information.

Conclusion

Operational safety and reliability of nuclear power plants has remained the main concern from an environmental perspective. An environmentally sound nuclear energy regime should address and alleviate concerns about safety, waste and weapons proliferation. International treaties on nuclear energy have increasingly integrated many environmental principles with the use of nuclear energy. In fact, the objective of environmental protection is becoming more important in recent nuclear treaties. It is evident that the relationship between environmental law and nuclear energy law is still evolving and environmental law has profoundly influenced the development of important norms and principles of nuclear energy law.

74 Ibid.

75 Public Engagement in the Nuclear Sector: A UK and EU Perspective, National Nuclear Laboratory, EU08051/06/10/01, Issue 3, 2016, available at http://s538600174.onlinehome.fr/nugenia/wp-content/uploads/2016/08/EU08051-06-10-01-Issue-3-Public-Engagement-in-the-Nuclear-Sector-A-UK-and-EU-Perspective.pdf, accessed 5 July 2018.

76 Emmerechts (n 3) 131.

3 Legal framework on non-proliferation of nuclear weapons and denuclearization

Introduction

The international regulation of nuclear risks consists of both hard law instruments and soft law standards designed to achieve denuclearization, prohibition of nuclear weapons testing, ensuring nuclear safety, peaceful use of nuclear energy and international cooperation in trans-boundary movement of nuclear wastes, and establishing a nuclear liability regime for environmental pollution or harm. In particular, multilateral treaties regulating nuclear energy also deal with denuclearization, non-proliferation, nuclear safety and security, third-party liability, management of radioactive waste, and emergency preparedness. The earlier nuclear treaties mainly focused on ensuring of use of nuclear energy for peaceful purposes, denuclearization and non-proliferation of nuclear weapons. A significant number of recent nuclear treaties aim at nuclear disarmament and denuclearization at regional level. While denuclearization aims at elimination of the military infrastructure and materials necessary for nuclear weapons production, non-proliferation refers to facilitating the peaceful use of nuclear technologies and abstention from nuclear weapons by non-nuclear weapon states. However, treaties on nuclear disarmament are not new phenomena as the USA and Russia had concluded many bilateral agreements on restrictions and reductions and deployment of nuclear weapons. While the risk of nuclear weapon proliferation should not be used as an argument in favour of stopping the use of nuclear energy for satisfying human needs, international agreement on regulations and safeguards needs to be in place to prevent such risks.[1]

Treaty on Non-Proliferation of Nuclear Weapons 1968

Its objectives are to prevent the spread of nuclear weapons and weapons technology, to foster the peaceful uses of nuclear energy, and to further the goal of achieving general and complete disarmament. The treaty establishes a safeguards system

1 Jacques Bouchard, 'The Future of Nuclear Power: Reducing risks', in Joseph F. Pilat, Nathan E. Busch (eds), *Routledge Handbook of Nuclear Proliferation and Policy* (Routledge 2018) 366.

under the responsibility of the International Atomic Energy Authority (IAEA), which also plays a central role under the NPT in areas of technology transfer for peaceful purposes. Considering the devastating consequence of nuclear war, the preamble of the NPT calls for the prevention of proliferation of nuclear weapons, while affirming the benefits of peaceful use of nuclear energy. Article 1 of the NPT obliges each nuclear-weapon State Party not to transfer any technology or assist any non-nuclear-weapon state to manufacture or acquire nuclear weapons. The Treaty on Non-Proliferation of Nuclear Weapons (NPT) asks each NNWS to ensure that nuclear materials, equipment, facilities and information are not used to advance military purposes.[2] The Treaty entered into force in 1970. On 11 May 1995, the Treaty was extended indefinitely. A total of 191 states have joined the Treaty, including the five nuclear-weapon states. It requires the Contracting States to accept international safeguards under the supervision of the IAEA and to increase 'the contribution of atomic energy to peace, health and prosperity throughout the world'. The NPT requires the nuclear weapons states to pursue in good faith negotiations relating to nuclear disarmament, but does not oblige them to reach agreement.[3]

The NPT remains a major instrument in the prevention of nuclear proliferation. The NPT created two types of states – 'nuclear weapon' and 'non-nuclear weapon' – each responsible for certain differentiated obligations. The Treaty requires nuclear weapon states to avoid the direct and indirect transfer of nuclear weapons or devices to a non-nuclear weapon state and also not to 'assist, encourage or induce' such a state in the manufacture or acquisition of nuclear weapons. Furthermore, transfer of material even for peaceful purposes is also restricted. Under Articles I and II of the treaty, nuclear weapon states agree not to transfer or assist in the development of nuclear weapons or other nuclear explosive devices, and non-nuclear weapon states agree not to receive or seek the same. In exchange, Article IV of the NPT provides that non-nuclear weapon states are granted the inalienable right to the development, research, production and use of nuclear energy for peaceful purposes without discrimination. The non-nuclear states agreed not to acquire nuclear weapons; and to allow verification of that pledge by placing all of their nuclear equipment and facilities under the safeguard system of the IAEA.

Thus, the right to peaceful nuclear energy as codified in the 1968 Nuclear Non-proliferation Treaty is recognized as a fundamental right of states.[4] Article IV(1) of the NPT recognizes the inalienable right of all States Parties to the treaty to the development, research, production and use of nuclear energy for peaceful purposes without discrimination. In the context of the NPT, Article IV(I) is an important part of the Grand Bargain which the NPT codifies as between the

2 Article II.

3 Article VI.

4 See Daniel H. Joyner, 'Fundamental Rights of States in International Law and the Right to Peaceful Nuclear Energy' (2015) 4(3) *Cambridge Journal of International and Comparative Law* 661.

nuclear weapon States Parties to the treaty and the non-nuclear weapon States Parties. Article IV(2) asks advanced nuclear states to assist and cooperate in contributing to the further development of the applications of peaceful nuclear energy programmes for non-nuclear weapon states and developing states.[5] The NPT is the only multilateral treaty whose objective is to prevent the spread of nuclear weapons and weapons technology, to promote cooperation in the peaceful uses of nuclear energy and to further the goal of achieving complete disarmament by the nuclear weapon states.[6]

In order to achieve the goal of non-proliferation, the NPT asks non-nuclear weapon States Parties to accept the safeguards system established by the IAEA with a view to preventing diversion of nuclear energy from peaceful uses to nuclear weapons.[7] Procedures for such safeguards shall be followed with respect to source or special fissile material whether it is being produced or used in any nuclear facility or is outside any such facility.[8] Safeguards are used to verify compliance with the Treaty obligations through inspections conducted by the IAEA. The treaty promotes cooperation in the field of peaceful nuclear technology and equal access to this technology for all States Parties, while safeguards prevent the diversion of fissile material for weapons use.[9]

The effectiveness of the NPT is, however, questioned in light of historical and recent events.[10] The main limitations and weaknesses of the present safeguard arrangements which give cause for environmental concern can be summarized as follows: the failure of many states to become parties to the NPT; the inability of safeguards to prevent the transfer of nuclear technology from nuclear power production to the acquisition of nuclear weapons competence; the practical problems of maintaining effective checks on nuclear inventories; the ease with which states can withdraw from the NPT and from most non-NPT safeguards agreements; deficiencies in accounting and warning procedures; and the absence of reliable sanctions to deter division of safeguarded material. Another weakness of the treaty is that Article X allows States Parties to withdraw from the NPT altogether.

Finally, the NPT's broad language allows a state to develop capacities for the production of fissile materials or the production and stockpiling of such materials or other components that might be used in nuclear weapons. The implications of this tension are that a state can legitimately stockpile nuclear material, withdraw from the NPT using the Article X exit provision, and declare itself a nuclear power.[11]

5 Ibid, 669.
6 See https://www.un.org/disarmament/wmd/nuclear/npt/, accessed 12 July 2018.
7 Article III(I).
8 Article III(I).
9 Ibid.
10 Richard Sieg, 'A Call to Minimize the Use of Nuclear Power in the Twenty-First Century' (2008) 9(2) *Vermont Journal of Environmental Law* 305–370.
11 Joseph G. Silver, 'The Global Partnership: The Final Blow to the Nuclear Non-Proliferation Regime?' (2008) 21(1) *New York International Law Review* 69.

Global treaties on denuclearization

The Antarctic Treaty 1959

One of the oldest treaties prohibiting nuclear activities is the Antarctic Treaty of 1959. Article V(1) of the Antarctic Treaty prohibits any nuclear explosion or the disposal of radioactive waste on the sixth continent. A Protocol on Environmental Protection to the Antarctic Treaty was adopted in 1991. Annex VI to this Protocol deals with liability arising from environmental emergencies, and imposes liability for damage to the environment caused by 'environmental emergencies'. The broad definition of 'environmental emergency' under the Protocol suggests that it may also include a nuclear accident that may be caused by nuclear explosion and the disposal of radioactive wastes.[12] A state will, therefore, incur liability for any nuclear explosion in the Antarctic that results in damage to that environment.

Agreement Governing the Activities of States on the Moon and Other Celestial Bodies of 1979

This treaty provides that the moon shall be used by all States Parties exclusively for peaceful purposes and shall be treated as a common heritage of mankind. Any threat or use of force on the moon is prohibited by this treaty. This treaty prohibits placing on the moon or in orbit around the moon objects carrying nuclear arms.[13] The establishment of military bases, installations and fortifications, the testing of any type of weapons including nuclear weapons on the moon is prohibited.[14]

Treaty Banning Nuclear Weapon Tests in the Atmosphere, in Outer Space and Under Water 1963

This is the first treaty that exclusively regulates nuclear activities in certain areas. This treaty has gained universal acceptance since most states of the world are party to it. It prohibits nuclear weapon test explosions in the atmosphere, outer space, at sea, in Antarctica, or in any circumstances where radioactive debris spreads beyond the territory of the testing state.[15] Thus, it means that tests must be conducted underground and must cause no pollution. However, some nuclear power states are outside the scope of the treaty and thus the effectiveness of the treaty

12 'Environmental emergency' means any accidental event that has occurred, having taken place after the entry into force of this Annex, and that results in, or imminently threatens to result in, any significant and harmful impact on the Antarctic environment: Article 2(b) of Annex VI to the Protocol.

13 Article 3(3).

14 Article 3(4).

15 1963 Treaty Banning Nuclear Weapons Tests in the Atmosphere, in Outer Space and Under Water.

is questionable. Although this treaty does not directly deal with environmental consequences of nuclear weapons testing, its preamble mentions that one of the objectives of the treaty is to put an end to the contamination of the environment by radioactive wastes.

Treaty on the Prohibition of the Emplacement of Nuclear Weapons and other Weapons of Mass Destructions on the Seabed and the Ocean Floor and in the Subsoil thereof (Seabed Arms Control Treaty) 1971

The Seabed Arms Control Treaty entered into force on 18 May 1972. Article I sets forth the principal obligation of the treaty. It prohibits parties from placing nuclear weapons or weapons of mass destruction on the seabed and the ocean floor beyond a 12-mile coastal zone. Article II provides that the 'seabed zone' is to be measured in accordance with the provisions of the 1958 Convention on the Territorial Sea and the Contiguous Zone. Article III provides that, in order to promote the objectives of this treaty, each State Party shall have the right to verify through observations the activities of other States Parties to the Treaty on the seabed zone. The States Parties are required to consult with one another in case of doubt about the compliance with the treaty provisions. If such consultation fails, the States Parties shall conduct enquiries and inspections of objects, structures, installations or other facilities and, if necessary, they can refer the matter to the UN Security Council.[16] Verification may be undertaken by any State Party using its own means, or with the full or partial assistance of any other State Party, or through appropriate international procedures. Article VII included provision for a review conference to be held five years after entry in force of the treaty.

Regional treaties on denuclearization

According to the UN General Assembly, a NWFZ is any treaty-based zone established by a group of states that provides for the total absence of nuclear weapons in the zone, and for an international system of verification and control to ensure compliance.[17] Legal validity of a NWFZ also derives from Article VII of the NPT, which allows any group of states to conclude regional treaties in order to assure the total absence of nuclear weapons in their respective territories. Currently, five regional treaties on denuclearization have been established. NWFZ treaties serve both non-proliferation and nuclear disarmament goals by limiting the areas where nuclear weapons can be produced, tested, deployed or used, and thus effectively complement the NPT. Regional treaties on denuclearization even predate the

16 Article III(4).

17 United Nations Agency for the Prohibition of Nuclear Weapons in Latin America and the Caribbean, 'Comprehensive Study of the Question of Nuclear-Weapon-Free Zones in all its Aspects', UN General Assembly Resolution 3472 (XXX), 11 December 1975, available at www.un.org/disarmament/WMD/Nuclear/NWFZ.shtml accessed 4 July 2018.

NPT. The first such regional arrangement for non-proliferation was the Treaty for the Prohibition of Nuclear Weapons in Latin America, signed in 1967, known as the Treaty of Tlatelolco, to insulate the region from the nuclear threat represented by the Cold War. The UN Disarmament Commission in its report of 30 April 1999 recommended a set of principles and guidelines for the establishment of a nuclear-weapon-free zone. Such Guidelines require that NWFZs should be established on the basis of arrangements freely arrived at among the states of the region concerned and such initiative should emanate exclusively from states within the region concerned.[18] The Guidelines also state that the nuclear-weapon states should be consulted during the negotiations of each treaty and its relevant protocol establishing a nuclear-weapon-free zone in order to facilitate their ratification of the relevant protocol to the treaty, through which they undertake legally binding commitments to the status of the zone and not to use or threaten to use nuclear weapons against States Parties to the treaty. A NWFZ should not prevent the use of nuclear science and technology for peaceful purposes.

Treaty for the Prohibition of Nuclear Weapons in Latin America 1967 (Treaty of Tlatelolco)

It entered into force in 1969. All 33 states of the region of Latin America and the Caribbean have signed and ratified the treaty.[19] Whilst the treaty allows the use of nuclear energy for peaceful purposes, it prohibits the testing, use, manufacture, production or acquisition of any nuclear weapons in the Latin America region by the States Parties.[20] A unique characteristic of this treaty is that, in addition to prohibiting any form of acquisition or use of nuclear weapons, it prohibits receipt, storage, installation, deployment and possession of any nuclear weapons by the States Parties in their territories.[21] The treaty is the first international instrument providing for the total prohibition of the use of nuclear weapons in a region.

The treaty contains both a verification procedure and a compliance mechanism. Verification is accomplished by concluding multilateral or bilateral agreements with the IAEA for the application of its safeguards to nuclear activities of States Parties to the treaty.[22] The treaty provides for an institutional framework, the Agency for the Prohibition of Nuclear Weapons in Latin America and the

18 Report of the Disarmament Commission General Assembly Official Records, Fifty-fourth session Supplement No. 42 (A/54/42), UN, 1999, available at http://www.undocs.org/A/54/42(SUPP), accessed 4 July 2018.

19 Antigua and Barbuda, Argentina, Bahamas, Barbados, Belize, Bolivia, Brazil, Chile, Colombia, Costa Rica, Cuba, Dominica, Dominican Republic, Ecuador, El Salvador, Grenada, Guatemala, Guyana, Haiti, Honduras, Jamaica, Mexico, Nicaragua, Panama, Paraguay, Peru, St. Kitts and Nevis, St. Lucia, St. Vincent and the Grenadines, Suriname, Trinidad and Tobago, Uruguay, Venezuela.

20 Article 1.

21 Ibid.

22 Article 13.

Caribbean, to supervise implementation of its purposes and procedures.[23] The General Conference remains the main compliance mechanism of the treaty. The General Conference will take note of all cases in which any State Party is not complying fully with its obligations under this treaty and shall draw the matter to the attention of the Party concerned. If such non-compliance constitutes a violation of this treaty which might endanger peace and security, the General Conference may report simultaneously to the United Nations Security Council and the General Assembly through the Secretary-General of the United Nations, and to the Council of the Organization of American States.[24]

The treaty also establishes a control system for verifying compliance with treaty obligations,[25] provides for reporting obligations for the States Parties[26] and allowing 'special inspections' by the IAEA and the council established under the treaty in case of any suspicion that prohibited activities are carried out by a State Party.[27] In particular, the control system is to verify that devices, services and facilities intended for peaceful uses of nuclear energy are not used in the testing or manufacture of nuclear weapons.[28] The treaty provides that the States Parties shall submit a report to the Agency and the IAEA regarding their compliance with it. Thus, the treaty has strongest compliance mechanisms on denuclearization. The provisions regarding verification of compliance are more detailed and more comprehensive than those provided for in the NPT. However, this treaty allows nuclear explosions for peaceful purposes, which is a source of controversy.

There are two Additional Protocols to the treaty. Additional Protocol I provides for the application of the status of denuclearization in territories for which France, the Netherlands, the United Kingdom, and the United States are internationally responsible, and which lie within the limits of the geographic zone established by the treaty. All four states have acceded to Protocol I. Additional Protocol II obliges all nuclear weapon states (NWS) to respect the status of denuclearization of the zone and commits them not to use or threaten to use nuclear weapons against Parties to the treaty. All five NWSs acceded to the protocol.

South Pacific Nuclear Free Zone Treaty 1985 (Rarotonga Treaty)

This treaty provides for the establishment of a nuclear free zone in the South Pacific region, given that the region had the bitter experience of becoming a testing ground for such weapons during 1960s and 1970s. The treaty came into force in 1986.[29] The preamble of the treaty affirms the status of the South Pacific

23 Article 7.
24 Article 20.
25 Article 12.
26 Article 14.
27 Article 16.
28 Article 12, Part 1.
29 24 ILM 142 (1988). The treaty has 13 full members: Australia, Cook Islands, Fiji, Kiribati, Nauru, New Zealand, Niue, Papua New Guinea, Samoa, Solomon Islands, Tonga, Tuvalu and Vanuatu.

region as 'free of environmental pollution by radioactive waste and other radioactive matter'. Under the treaty, the States Parties undertake to not to manufacture or have control over any nuclear explosive device anywhere inside or outside the treaty zone; or seek assistance in the manufacture of nuclear weapons.[30] It also obliges States Parties not to provide sources or special fissile materials or equipment to any non-nuclear weapon state (NNWS), or NWS unless it is subject to safeguard agreements with the IAEA. It also asks States Parties to prevent the stationing in their territories of any nuclear device or testing of nuclear weapons.[31]It also prohibits dumping of radioactive wastes at sea.[32] The treaty establishes a control system for verification of compliance with the treaty obligations. The control system comprises submission of reports and exchange of information, consultation and cooperation among the States Parties.[33] The treaty also provides for a compliance mechanism by the application of the IAEA safeguards by States Parties for the use of nuclear energy for peaceful purposes, and a complaints procedure in case of non-compliance with the treaty provisions by a State Party.[34] It envisages the establishment of a Consultative Committee for the purpose of consultation and cooperation on any matter arising out of the treaty.[35]

Unlike the treaty of Tlatelolco, this treaty contains provisions preventing the dumping of nuclear wastes and banning nuclear explosions even for peaceful purposes.

The treaty has three protocols. Of the five nuclear-weapon states, France and the United Kingdom have ratified all three protocols, while Russia and China have ratified only Protocols II and III. US ratification of all three protocols is pending. Protocol I calls on each State Party to apply the prohibitions of the treaty with respect to the territories situated within the SPNFZ for which it is internationally responsible. Protocol II calls on the NWS not to use or threaten to use nuclear explosive devices against any State Party to the treaty or against one another's territories located within the zone. Protocol III calls on the NWS not to test nuclear explosive devices within the zone established by the Treaty.

Treaty Declaring Africa a Nuclear Weapon-Free Zone 1995 (Treaty of Pelindaba)

The treaty came into force on 15 July 2009.[36] Under the treaty, the African states commit themselves to refraining from manufacturing developing nuclear

30 Article 3.
31 Articles 5 and 6.
32 Article 7.
33 See Articles 8, 9 and 10.
34 Annexes 2 and 4.
35 Article 10.
36 There are 39 States Parties to this treaty: Algeria, Angola, Benin, Botswana, Burkina Faso, Burundi, Cameroon, Chad, Comoros, Congo, Cote d'Ivoire, Equatorial Guinea, Ethiopia, Gabon, Gambia, Ghana, Guinea-Bissau, Guinea, Kenya, Lesotho, Libya, Madagascar, Malawi, Mali, Mauritania, Mauritius, Mozambique, Namibia, Nigeria, Rwanda, Sahrawi Arab Democratic Republic, Senegal, South Africa, Swaziland, Togo, Tunisia, Tanzania, Zambia, Zimbabwe.

weapons, conducting research on nuclear explosive devices, receiving or providing assistance in that aspect, and to preventing the testing of nuclear weapons and stationing nuclear weapons in their territories.[37] The States Parties undertake to declare any capability for the manufacture of nuclear explosive devices; dismantle and destroy any nuclear explosive device that they have manufactured prior to the coming into force of this treaty; destroy facilities for the manufacture of nuclear explosive devices or, where possible, to convert them to peaceful uses.[38] Unlike other regional instruments, it asks States Parties to maintain the highest standards of security and physical protection of nuclear materials for peaceful use and prohibit armed attack on nuclear installations.[39] As a mechanism of compliance, the treaty provides for exchange of information, consultations, and submission of annual reports to the African Commission.[40]

However, they are allowed to decide whether to allow visits by foreign ships and aircraft to their ports and airfields, transit of their airspace by foreign aircraft, and navigation by foreign ships in their territorial seas or archipelago waters. The treaty permits the IAEA to verify the processes of dismantling and destruction of nuclear explosive devices. The treaty allows the States Parties to engage in peaceful nuclear activities and obliges them to conclude full-scope safeguard agreements with the IAEA to verify the peaceful character of such activities.

The treaty provides for the establishment of the African Commission on Nuclear Energy (AFCONE) for the purpose of ensuring compliance with the obligations under the Treaty. AFCONE is responsible for collating reports and the exchange of information; arranging consultations; reviewing the application to peaceful nuclear activities of safeguards by the IAEA; handling complaints regarding non-compliance with the treaty by State Parties; and encouraging regional and sub-regional cooperation programmes for peaceful uses of nuclear science and technology.[41]

The treaty has three Protocols and the contents of these protocol are similar to those of other treaties. Protocol II calls on the NWS not to test or assist or encourage the testing of any nuclear explosive device anywhere within the Pelindaba NWFZ.

Treaty on the Southeast Asia Nuclear Weapon-Free Zone 1995 (Treaty of Bangkok)

This treaty entered into force on 28 March 1997.[42] While its provisions are substantially similar on non-nuclearization of the region and compliance mechanisms,

37 Articles 3, 4, and 5.
38 Articles 6 and 7.
39 Articles 9 and 10.
40 Articles 12 and 13.
41 Annex III.
42 The parties to the treaty are Brunei Darussalam, Cambodia, Indonesia, Laos, Malaysia, Myanmar, Philippines, Singapore, Thailand, and Vietnam. The text of the treaty is available at http://www.icnl.org/research/library/files/Transnational/1995Treaty.pdf, accessed 13 July 2018.

it contains additional provisions on early notification of a nuclear accident, and restrictions on innocent passage of foreign ships and aircraft containing nuclear materials.[43] The treaty provides that prior to embarking on a peaceful nuclear energy programme, States Parties shall undertake rigorous nuclear safety assessments conforming to guidelines and standards recommended by the IAEA for the protection of health and minimization of danger to life and property.[44] The treaty establishes a Commission to oversee its implementation.[45] The treaty zone covers the territories, continental shelves, and EEZ of the States Parties within the zone, which is much broader than the geographical areas covered by other denuclearization treaties. This Treaty is supplemented by only one Protocol. Under the Protocol, the NWS would undertake to respect the treaty and not to use or threaten to use nuclear weapons against any State Party to the treaty and not to use or threaten to use nuclear weapons within the Southeast Asian Nuclear Weapon-Free Zone (SEANWFZ). However, as of 30 June 2017 none of the nuclear weapon states has signed the protocols, largely due to the strict nature of negative security assurances, the restriction on the passage of nuclear-powered ships through the zone and over the definitions of territory, including continental shelves and exclusive economic zones (EEZ).[46]

Treaty on a Nuclear Weapon-Free Zone in Central Asia (CANWFZ) 2006

This treaty was adopted on 8 September 2006 and entered into force on 21 March 2009.[47] The provisions of the treaty are substantially similar in nature. It contains one protocol to which except USA, all other NWS states are parties.

From the above discussion, it can be gleaned that while the denuclearization treaties do not prevent use of nuclear energy for the peaceful purposes, they prohibit the stationing of any nuclear explosive device on the territory of a State Party. These treaties also contain a pledge that a State Party will not use nuclear weapons against another State Party and will assist a State Party which is the victim of an act of nuclear attack in what is known as positive assurance. The protocols to the treaties contain negative security arrangements which means the nuclear weapon states will not to use or threaten to use nuclear weapons against zonal states.

Comprehensive Nuclear Test-Ban Treaty (CTBT) 1996

The adoption of the Comprehensive Nuclear Test-Ban Treaty in 1996 provided an important step forward in nuclear disarmament and non-proliferation

43 Articles 6 and 7.

44 Article 4.

45 Article 8.

46 See Southeast Asia Nuclear Weapon-Free Zone (SEANWFZ) 1995 (Treaty of Bangkok), available at http://www.nti.org/learn/treaties-and-regimes/southeast-asian-nuclear-weapon-free-zone-seanwfz-treaty-bangkok-treaty/, accessed 4 July 2018.

47 The States Parties are Kazakhstan, Uzbekistan, Tajikistan, Turkmenistan and Kyrgyzstan.

by banning nuclear tests and limiting the technological development of nuclear weapons. The basic obligation it imposes upon the Contracting Parties is not to carry out any nuclear test explosion and to prohibit and prevent any such nuclear explosion under its jurisdiction or control.[48] Furthermore, Parties must refrain from causing, encouraging or ay participating in the carrying out of any nuclear weapon test explosion or any other nuclear explosion. The CTBT also imposes a ban on the production of fissile material for anything other than verified peaceful use. Such a ban would impose a quantitative limit on the amount of nuclear material available for weapons use.[49] Article 3 of the CTBT requires each State Party, in accordance with its constitutional process, to take any necessary measures to implement its treaty obligations.

This treaty established the Comprehensive Nuclear Test-Ban Treaty Organization (CTBTO) located in Vienna in order to ensure the implementation of its provisions.[50] The CTBTO consists of a plenary body composed of all the States Signatories (also known as the Preparatory Commission), an Executive Council with 51 Member States, and the Provisional Technical Secretariat (PTS). A State becomes a member of the CTBTO Preparatory Commission upon signing the treaty. The main task of the Preparatory Commission is to establish a global verification regime as foreseen in the CTBT so that it will be operational by the time the treaty enters into force.[51] The Executive Council shall act on requests for on-site inspection. A Technical Secretariat shall carry out verification functions, including operating an International Data Center (IDC), processing and reporting on data from an International Monitoring System, and receiving and processing requests for on-site inspections.

As of October 2016, 166 states had ratified the CTBT. The treaty is yet to enter into force as it is has not been ratified by all 44 designated 'nuclear-capable states' (as listed in Annex 2 of the treaty). It has been ratified by 36 out of 44 such countries. Eight such countries that have not ratified the treaty, include China, India, Pakistan, North Korea, Israel, Iran, Egypt, and the United States.

The CTBT contains a Protocol which deals mainly with verification mechanisms. The Protocol, which is also known as the verification protocol, provides details on the International Monitoring System (IMS) and on functions of the International Data Center (Part I); spells out on-site inspection procedures in great detail (Part II); and provides for certain confidence-building measures (Part III). Annex 1 to the Protocol lists IMS facilities: seismic stations, radionuclide stations and laboratories, hydroacoustic stations, and infrasound stations. Annex 2 to the Protocol provides a list of variables that may be used in analyzing data from these stations to screen for possible explosions. Article IV and the

48 Article 1.

49 Comprehensive Nuclear Test-Ban Treaty (CTBT), available at http://www.nti.org/learn/treaties-and-regimes/comprehensive-nuclear-test-ban-treaty-ctbt/, accessed 4 July 2018.

50 Article 2.

51 Preparatory Commission for the comprehensive nuclear-test-ban treaty organization (CTBTO): An Overview, http://www.nti.org/media/documents/ctbto.pdf, accessed 4 July 2018.

verification protocol establish the treaty's verification regime, which consists of four basic elements: the IMS, consultation and clarification, on-site inspections and confidence-building measures. The IMS will determine location and nature of a possible nuclear event by analysing, integrating and comparing data. There are 321 stations worldwide to monitor evidence that might indicate a nuclear explosion. The verification regime will not be completely operational until the treaty enters into force.

The CTBT provides for sanctions in case of non-compliance by States Parties and provisions for the settlement of disputes. Article V of the CTBT obliges the Conference to take the necessary measures, such as restriction or suspension of rights and privileges, and collective measures to ensure compliance with the treaty and to redress and remedy any situation that contravenes the provisions of the treaty. The term 'collective measures' is intended to include, but is not limited to, sanctions. But the Conference does not have the power to impose collective measures, only to recommend them in cases of a serious breach of the Treaty.

It is expected that entry into force of the CTBT will play an important role toward a world of diminished reliance on nuclear weapons, reduced nuclear competition, and eventual nuclear disarmament. But the treaty has two main weaknesses: first, it fails to define a 'nuclear test'; second, the treaty provides that a State Party has the right to withdraw from it 'if it decides that extraordinary events related to the subject matter of this Treaty have jeopardized its supreme interest.[52]

Judicial developments on regulation of nuclear activities

Nuclear test cases

In the backdrop of many atmospheric nuclear tests carried out by France in the Pacific Ocean, in 1974 Australia and New Zealand challenged the legality of such nuclear weapons testing in the ICJ. Both states argued that France's tests were illegal under international law because they would pollute air, atmosphere and territorial sea. In addition, New Zealand claimed that France's tests resulted in radioactive fall-out that violated the rights of all members of the international community. In these cases, both countries had raised a number of legal issues arising out of such nuclear tests including protection of environment and prevention of trans-boundary harm. In particular, Australia's application made implicit reference to the prohibition of trans-boundary harm. France did not participate in the case as it unilaterally declared that it was to cease atmospheric tests. The court therefore held that the dispute had been resolved and did not need any judicial determination of the dispute. The court's judgment confronted neither the evidence relating to environmental harm arising from France's tests nor the

52 Article 9.

violation of international law.[53] As such, in the *Nuclear Tests* case, the ICJ made no determination as to whether atmospheric tests carried out by France violated customary international law. The Court held, however, that France should stop nuclear tests that led to the fall-out of radioactive waste on Australian territory because the French Government had committed to conducting no more tests of this kind.[54]

However, the *Nuclear Tests* case was reactivated in 1995 following France's announcement that it would resume nuclear testing and that it would do so only underground. New Zealand sought to reactivate the earlier proceedings through the provisions of the court's judgment in 1974 which stated that, if France were to rescind its undertaking, then the applicants could request an examination of the situation. However, the court dismissed New Zealand's claim on the ground that the 1974 decision related exclusively to atmospheric testing and the current situation was wholly concerned with underground nuclear tests. As with the 1974 decision, the 1995 conclusion attracted considerable criticism. But it is noteworthy that, in the formulation of the New Zealand's argument, there was considerably more focus on the environmental law dimensions of the dispute. New Zealand expressly raised the trans-boundary harm principle, intergenerational justice and the precautionary principle in its argument. The court in its ruling reminded the parties that its decision was 'without prejudice to the obligations … to protect the natural environment'.[55]

1996 Advisory Opinion on the Legality of the Threat or Use of Nuclear Weapons

The cataclysmic nature and the environmental risks associated with the use of nuclear weapons had been recognized by the International Court of Justice in its 1996 Advisory Opinion on the Legality of the Threat or Use of Nuclear Weapons.

In 1995, the UN General Assembly asked the International Court of Justice for an advisory opinion on the legality of the threat of use of nuclear weapons. The ICJ held that there is neither customary nor conventional international law on any comprehensive and universal prohibition of the threat or use of nuclear weapons as such. But it placed severe limits on the use of nuclear weapons. The ICJ emphasized that the use of nuclear weapons during armed conflict, as well as the peaceful use of nuclear energy, poses potential catastrophic threats to all of humanity. The Court also recognizes that the 'unique characteristics' of nuclear weapons lie in the vastly destructive power of such arms (including the radiation phenomenon), thus rendering the nuclear weapon 'potentially catastrophic'. The

53 Tim Stephens, 'The Development of International Environmental Law by the International Court of Justice', in Douglas Fisher (ed.), *Research Handbook on Fundamental Concepts of Environmental Law* (Cheltenham, Edward Elgar 2016) 228.

54 *Nuclear Tests Case (Australia v France)* (1974) ICJ Rep 257 and *Nuclear Tests Case (New Zealand v France)* [1974] ICJ Rep 457.

55 Tim Stephens (n 53) 229.

ICJ noted that nuclear weapons have the potential to destroy all civilization and the entire ecosystem of the planet. The Court undertook a more detailed examination of the relationship between the use of nuclear weapons and environmental protection. It observed that although existing international law pertaining to the protection of the environment does not specifically prohibit the use of nuclear weapons, 'important environmental factors' must be taken into account in the implementation of international humanitarian law. The Court recognized that the environment is not an abstraction but represents the living space, the quality of life and the very health of human beings, including generations unborn. By their very nature, nuclear weapons release not only immense quantities of heat and energy, but also powerful and prolonged radiation. The radiation released by a nuclear explosion would affect health, agriculture, natural resources and the people over a very wide area. Further, the use of nuclear weapons would be a serious danger to future generations.[56] According to the Court, however, 'the threat or use of nuclear weapons should is generally contrary to the principles and rules of international humanitarian law, as well as with specific obligations under treaties and other undertakings which expressly deal with nuclear weapons'.

One of the important aspects of the Advisory Opinion is the Court's examination of the use or threat of nuclear weapons in the light of the principles and rules of international humanitarian law. The Court concluded that the threat or use of nuclear weapons is in general contrary to international law and in particular the principles and rules of humanitarian law. But the Court could not decide definitively whether the threat or use of nuclear weapons would be lawful or unlawful in an extreme circumstance of self-defence, in which the very survival of a state would be at stake. However, the Court declared that nations had a legal obligation to enter into agreement with a view to achieving nuclear non-proliferation and disarmament in accordance with the NPT.

Marshall Islands' legal battle for non-proliferation of nuclear weapons and compensation for nuclear test

The United States detonated 67 nuclear bombs on the Marshall Islands during the period between 1946 and 1962, when they were still a territory of the US, causing lasting cultural, environmental and biological damage to the people of the Islands and their traditional way of life. In the 1980s, the US faced lawsuits by the peoples of Marshall Islands in US courts for property and other damages for more than US$5 billion for nuclear tests in the Pacific Ocean. Pending the litigation, the Government of the Republic of Marshall Islands signed the Compact of Free Association with the United States. As part of the Compact of Free Association, an agreement between the Marshall Islands and the United States that came into effect in 1986, a $150 million compensation trust fund was agreed upon

56 *Legality of the Threat or Use of Nuclear Weapons*, Advisory Opinion, (1996) ICJ 226, 241–244 (8 July).

as the 'full and final settlement' of legal claims against the U.S. government'. Income from the $150 million Nuclear Fund was earmarked for those who had brought the suit 'as a means to address past present and future consequences of the Nuclear Testing Program'. As a result, it prohibited Marshall Islanders from seeking future redress in US courts.[57]

However, the Marshall Islands filed a suit on 24 April 2014 in the US Federal District Court in San Francisco, claiming that the US had failed its duties under Article VI of the Treaty on Non-Proliferation of Nuclear Weapons 1968 as it continued to modernize its weapons with no prospect of disarmament and was failing to pursue good faith negotiations, as set out in the treaty. In the same time, Marshall Islands also lodged a suit before the ICJ against nine nuclear weapon states, including the USA. In both suits, the Republic of the Marshall Islands did not seek financial compensation, rather it sought declaratory judgment on breach of nuclear disarmament obligations and an order that the nuclear weapon states start negotiations in good faith for nuclear disarmament. The NPT commits all nuclear weapon states 'to pursue negotiations in good faith on effective measures relating to cessation of the nuclear arms race at an early date'. In 1995, the Marshall Islands acceded to the Treaty.

The case filed in ICJ focused on the failure of the nine nuclear weapon States – the US, UK, Russia, China, France, Israel, India, Pakistan and North Korea – to dismantle their arsenals and eliminate nuclear weapons and failure to comply with the treaty obligations. The cases in the ICJ are founded on the 1996 ICJ Advisory Opinion on Nuclear Weapon Tests that there 'exists an obligation to pursue in good faith and bring to a conclusion negotiations leading to nuclear disarmament in all its aspects under strict and effective international control'.

In majority decisions on 5 October 2016, the ICJ decided against proceeding with the Marshall Island's nuclear disarmament case, which was lodged earlier against India, Pakistan and the United Kingdom. The ICJ held that there was a lack of evidence that a dispute even existed. The ICJ refused to take up cases against the other countries – China, France, Israel, North Korea, Russia and the United States – as they had not recognised the Court's jurisdiction. It explained that the existence of a dispute between the Parties was a condition of its jurisdiction.

In April 2014, the Marshall Islands sued the United States in the Federal District Court claiming that the United States had failed to pursue good-faith negotiations, and therefore breached Article VI of the Treaty. According to the Marshall Islands, the United States had a 'grim legacy' of a 'nuclear weapons program' and this included the detonation of 67 nuclear weapons in the Marshall Islands, resulting in 'horrific and multi-generational consequences'. The Marshall Islands sought a declaration stating that Article VI imposes obligations on the United States to

57 Lucy Westcott, 'Marshall Islands nuclear lawsuit reopens old wounds', available at http://www.newsweek.com/marshall-islands-nuclear-lawsuit-reopens-old-wounds-262491, accessed 4 July 2018.

pursue negotiations in good faith to cease the nuclear arms race at an early date. The District court concluded that the Marshall Islands lacked standing because the court had no power to bind other States Parties not before the court and the asserted injury 'cannot be redressed by compelling the specific performance by only one nation to the Treaty'.[58] In the proceedings of the Federal District Court, the issue was whether Article VI of the Treaty on the Non-Proliferation of Nuclear Weapons was a self-executing treaty, thus requiring the US to engage in good-faith negotiations under that Article. The US argued that their breach of obligations under a multilateral treaty was not subject to the court's jurisdiction. The Marshall Islands appealed against the decision of the Federal District Court. The Ninth Circuit panel concluded that Article VI of the Treaty on the Non-Proliferation of Nuclear Weapons was non-self-executing and, therefore, unenforceable by the US judicial branch. The Ninth Circuit affirmed the decision of the District Court to dismiss a suit filed by the Marshall Islands against the US claiming that the US had breached Article VI of the Treaty on the Non-Proliferation of Nuclear Weapons by failing to pursue good-faith negotiations. The panel held that Article VI of the Treaty is non-self-executing, and plaintiff's claims were not redressable because the claims presented inextricable political questions. The Ninth Circuit panel, therefore, held that Article VI was not judicially enforceable in the domestic court, and dismissed the claim.[59]

Conclusion

Despite some weaknesses of the NPT, it has helped to curtail the nuclear proliferation as NPT ratification significantly reduces the probability that states will seek nuclear weapons.[60] Effectiveness of the NPT in non-proliferation can be explained by greater transparency resulting from application of the IAEA safeguard, superpower enforcement, facilitating exchange of information by the IAEA and reducing uncertainty about a state's behaviour.[61] The treaties on denuclearization complement the global non-proliferation regime as the geographical scope of nuclear free zones has expanded considerably in the last decades. While NWFZs supplement and reinforce the global NPT regime, they have not the same problem as the NPT as its membership is divided between nuclear 'haves'

58 *Republic of the Marshall Islands v United States*, 79 F. Supp. 3d 1068, 1072 (N.D. Cal. 2015).

59 Marshall Islands Lawsuit against U.S. Over Nuclear Nonproliferation Dismissed, available at http://www.pireport.org/articles/2017/08/02/marshall-islands-lawsuit-against-us-over-nuclear-nonproliferation-dismissed, accessed 13 July 2018.

60 Matthew Fuhrmann and Yonatan Lufu, 'Do Arms Control Treaties Work? Assessing the Effectiveness of the Nuclear Nonproliferation Treaty' (2016) 60 *International Studies Quarterly* 530, 537.

61 Ibid. See also Andrew Coe and Jane Vaynman, 'Collusion and the Nuclear Nonproliferation Treaty' (2015) 77(4) *Journal of Politics* 983–97.

and 'have nots'.[62] The regional parties to each NWFZ Treaty all assume identical undertakings as non-nuclear weapon states and are subject to the same verification and enforcement provisions. Treaties on denuclearization and non-proliferation of nuclear weapons contain implementation mechanisms which are mainly based on compliance measures such as verification, exchange of information, consultations and submission of annual reports to the treaty bodies established at the regional level. These compliance measures ask for a non-confrontational, cooperative and problem-solving approach. Verification is generally accomplished by concluding multilateral or bilateral agreements with the IAEA for the application of its safeguards such as on-site inspection. The regional bodies, such as Commissions or Conferences of the Parties, established under these treaties also oversee or monitor the compliance of the treaties through the reporting mechanism. The success of nuclear disarmament through denuclearization treaties depends on exchange of information, cooperation and coordination between the zones. Formal secretarial linkages under the Zonal treaties for consultation, exchange of information and cooperation on verification and compliance can contribute to the effectiveness of these treaties. However, neither NPT nor denuclearization treaties make any reference to protection of the environment.

The ICJ's advisory opinion is a landmark development in the recognition of environmental consequences of nuclear weapon testing, and limiting methods of warfare which cause severe and long-term damage to the natural environment. However, it missed the opportunity to prohibit the use of nuclear weapons completely.

62 Susan Burk, 'Nuclear weapon-free zones', in Joseph F. Pilat, Nathan E. Busch (eds), *Routledge Handbook of Nuclear Proliferation and Policy* (Routledge 2018) 313.

4 Management of nuclear wastes

Introduction

Nuclear waste is a by-product of radioactive materials used in nuclear reactors, fuel processing plants, hospitals and research facilities. Safe and environmentally sound management of nuclear waste remains a great concern for the international community. Nuclear waste is generated as spent fuel, mainly from nuclear reactor operations. Given the risk factor involved, nuclear waste management is always a sensitive issue, regulated by special rules, which are different from the hazardous waste management regime. Proper nuclear waste disposal and management are essential for the protection of public health and safety and of the environment, and to keep the exposure well below the permissible limits. Radioactive waste is also generated while decommissioning and dismantling nuclear reactors and other nuclear facilities.

Waste from a nuclear plant can be a solid waste and spent fuel. Solid waste from a nuclear plant can be toxic and damaging to the environment. The management of spent nuclear fuel and nuclear wastes requires strategies and plans for the safe, secure and permanent disposal of radioactive material. The main strategies used for disposal of nuclear wastes include developing a geological repository, nuclear fuel reprocessing, and interim storage. Waste from nuclear power plants can remain active for hundreds or thousands of years. Currently, much of the radioactive waste from nuclear power plants has been stored at the power plant as no country has yet developed or implemented a long-term programme for the storage of nuclear waste. Geologically safe sites for waste storage and creation of multinational storage facility have sometimes been proposed but are yet to be implemented.[1]

Nuclear waste management is highly expensive, risky and the appropriate means of disposal is a matter of controversy. Although nuclear wastes can be recycled, such recycling has problems of its own as recycled waste can produce plutonium. Such plutonium and other transuranic materials could be used to

1 Mark Callis Sanders, Charlotta E. Sanders, 'A World's Dilemma "Upon Which the Sun Never Sets": The Nuclear Waste Management Strategy (part I): Western European Nation States and the United States of America'(2016) 90 *Progress in Nuclear Energy* 69–97.

develop nuclear weapons.[2] Even though some of this plutonium can be recycled in reactors as a fuel, the disposal of the growing amounts of separated plutonium and of transuranic waste in particular must be carefully planned to meet both environmental and non-proliferation objectives.[3] Reprocessing only marginally reduces radioactivity. One of the most interesting areas of debate over the management of nuclear waste in relation to crime and terrorist risks is the issue of transportation of the waste.[4] All forms of waste, from the most highly radioactive reactor contents to low-level waste, must be transported from their places of origin to their places of rest. Transportation of nuclear waste from the nuclear reactor to the repository itself, or to another country, often raises the risk of accidents, terrorist attack or criminal misappropriation, for example sale on the illicit market.[5] Appropriate regulation of the safety of such transportation should be in place to prevent such potential incident. Managing and disposing of nuclear waste represents a complex problem with technical, societal and political dimensions and implications.[6] Finding a socially acceptable solution for the disposal of nuclear wastes remains a daunting task for countries with nuclear power plants.

Sources and classification of nuclear wastes

Nuclear wastes can be produced from many nuclear activities ranging from uranium production (uranium mining and milling) to operation of nuclear reactors, fuel fabrication and reprocessing. Uranium mill tailings are the radioactive sand-like materials that remain after uranium is extracted by milling. A significant amount of high-level waste is generated from the reprocessing of nuclear fuel or spent fuel. After its use in a reactor, spent fuel is highly radioactive, emits significant radiation and heat and is transferred to a fuel pool for several years before being transferred to interim storage facilities.[7] Spent fuel can pose a significant risk to the environment. The manufacture and maintenance of nuclear weapons produces a particular type of waste known as transuranic (TRU) waste. The decommissioning of nuclear power plants is another source of nuclear waste. Since an increasing number of nuclear reactors are reaching the end of their

2 Tom Vander Beken, Nicholas Dornb, Stijn Van Daele, 'Security Risks in Nuclear Waste Management: Exceptionalism, Opaqueness, and Vulnerability' (2010) 91 *Journal of Environmental Management* 940–948

3 Environment Alert Bulletin, 'Nuclear Waste: Is Everything Under Control?' UNEP, available at http://www.grid.unep.ch/products/3_Reports/ew_nuclear.en.pdf, accessed 9 July 2018.

4 Ibid.

5 Tom Vander Beken, Nicholas Dornb, Stijn Van Daele (n 2).

6 Maria Rosaria Di Nucci, Achim Brunnengräber, Lutz Mez and Miranda Schreurs, 'Comparative Perspectives on Nuclear Waste Governance', in Achim Brunnengräber, Maria Rosaria Di Nucci, Ana María Isidoro Losada, Lutz Mez, Miranda A. Schreurs (eds), *Nuclear Waste Governance: An International Comparison* (Berlin, Springer 2015) 25.

7 'Status and Trends in Spent Fuel and Radioactive Waste Management', *IAEA Nuclear Energy Series No. NW-T-1.14*, 10.

life-span, a significant volume of waste is predicted to arise from the decommissioning and clearance of nuclear sites.[8]

There are six categories of radioactive waste: (1) high-level waste (HLW) results primarily from spent nuclear fuel used by power reactors to produce electricity. This is generated mainly from the civilian nuclear power programme. (2) transuranic waste (TRU) produced mainly from the defence programme or nuclear weapons. This kind of waste is also referred to as 'legacy waste' and it exists in several countries where nuclear power programmes were developed for a military purpose. (3) Uranium mill tailing waste results from commercial uranium ore processing activities following mining and uranium extraction research and development projects. (4) Low-level waste, which comes from reactor operations and from medical, academic, industrial, and other commercial uses of radioactive materials and generally contains relatively limited concentrations of radioactivity.[9] It consists of items such as paper, clothing and laboratory equipment that have been used in areas where radioactive substances are handled, as well as contaminated soil and building materials.[10] (5) Decommissioning waste results from the decontamination and removal of radioactive materials encountered during site closure and restoration activities. Usually high-level wastes are long-lived and their disposal requires deep, stable geological formations, usually several hundred metres or more below the surface.[11] (6) Exempt waste – a category of waste that meets the criteria for clearance and exemption from regulatory control for radiation protection purposes.

Radioactive waste is generally classified according to its level of radioactivity. Different categories of radioactive waste have different levels of hazard. requiring different health and safety precautions.[12] Classification of radioactive waste is useful in planning a disposal facility, in the following ways: at the conceptual level, in devising waste management strategies; in planning and designing waste management facilities; and in assigning radioactive waste to a particular conditioning technique or disposal facility. It is also useful at the legal and regulatory level as regulatory control can vary according to the type of radioactive waste. At the operational level, classification of radioactive waste helps to define operational activities and organize the work to be undertaken with the wastes.[13]

Disposal options

Responsibility for the management of nuclear waste rests mainly with each state that produces such waste. However, in the case of spent fuel being transferred

8 Environment Alert Bulletin, 'Nuclear Waste: Is Everything Under Control?' (n 3).
9 'Radioactive Waste', https://www.nrc.gov/reading-rm/doc-collections/fact-sheets/radwaste.pdf accessed 9 July 2018.
10 Ibid.
11 'Status and Trends in Spent Fuel and Radioactive Waste Management', (n 7), p. 6.
12 Ibid.
13 Ibid.

for processing in another country, the residual waste is generally returned to the originating country for its long-term management. Otherwise, most of the radioactive waste from nuclear power plants is currently stored at the nuclear power plant sites. Since the beginning of the world's first civil nuclear energy programme, very little radioactive waste produced has been permanently disposed of. Owing to space constraints in many nuclear power reactors, eventually the radioactive waste will need to be relocated. Moreover, following the decommissioning of many nuclear reactors over the next decades, the resulting waste will have to be disposed of even if no more nuclear reactors are built. While low-level waste can be commonly disposed of in near-surface facilities, high-level waste presents particular challenges.[14] Owing to its high radioactivity, HLW has to be well contained and isolated from the human environment. Although geological disposal of high-level radioactive waste in an underground repository is the option favoured by many countries, only Finland has begun the construction of a repository for the final disposal of its spent nuclear fuel. France and Sweden are also considering the construction of a deep geological repository. However, none of them has yet operated such a facility. The Nuclear Energy Act of Finland 1987 states that the nuclear waste generated in Finland shall be handled, stored and permanently disposed of in Finland. The Act further allocates responsibility between waste producers and government authorities, as well as incorporating waste management criteria into its licensing procedures.

A regional or multinational disposal facility has occasionally been proposed as a shared disposal facility for some states with limited amounts of radioactive waste or small quantities of spent fuel, for example, from a research reactor.[15] However, the implementation of such a facility may face many challenges, such as finding a willing host state and deciding on a funding arrangement.

International regulatory regime on nuclear wastes

Nuclear waste was dumped in sea during the 1960s and 1970s, leading to significant concentrations of radioactive materials in the adjacent seas and seabeds, which created a huge public outcry. For example, during 1960s significant amounts of nuclear waste had been dumped into the Artic seas by navy vessels belonging to the former Soviet Union (USSR).[16] Since then, the international regulation of nuclear waste has been made more stringent and the discharge of

14 Radioactive Waste, https://www.nrc.gov/reading-rm/doc-collections/fact-sheets/radwaste.pdf accessed 9 July 2018.

15 Final Summary Report, Fifth Review Meeting of the Contracting Parties of the Joint Convention, 11–22 May 2015, Vienna, Austria, http://www-ns.iaea.org/downloads/rw/conventions/fifth-review-meeting/summary-report-fifth%20review%20meeting-e.pdf accessed 9 July 2018.

16 See Olav Schram Stokke, 'Nuclear Dumping in Artic Seas: Russian Implementation of the London Convention' in David G. Victor, Kal Raustiala and Eugene B. Skolnikoff, *The Implementation and Effectiveness of International Environmental Commitments: Theory and Practice* (MIT Press 1998) 475–518.

nuclear waste by dumping at sea has dramatically reduced. The Stockholm Conference in 1972 had called for a register of radioactive emissions and international cooperation on radioactive waste disposal.[17] Several international Conventions contain provisions aimed at prohibiting the dumping of radioactive wastes. For example, Article IV of the London Convention on the Prevention of Pollution by Dumping of Wastes and Other Matter of 1972 prohibits the dumping of both high-level and low-level radioactive waste at sea. The main objective of the London Convention is to prevent the indiscriminate disposal at sea of waste liable to: create a hazard to human health; harm living resources and marine life; damage amenities; or interfere with other legitimate uses of the sea. Its objective is to promote the effective control of all sources of marine pollution and to take all practicable steps to prevent pollution of the sea by the dumping of wastes and other matter. The Convention contains a system in which dumping of items on the 'black list' is forbidden and dumping of items on the 'gray list' requires special permits from a designated national authority and such permits must be reported to the secretariat of the Convention.[18] However, the Convention has a 'opting out' provision that allows states to avoid being legally bound by provisions they do not wish to adhere to.[19]

Another weakness of the London Convention is that its' Article VII exempted military vessels and aircraft which are entitled to sovereign immunity under international law.

The 1996 Protocol to the London Convention, which replaced the 1972 Convention, contains both precautionary and polluter-pays principles. Although the purpose of the Protocol is similar to that of the Convention, the Protocol is more restrictive in its application. The Protocol adopts a 'reverse list approach', which implies that all dumping of wastes including nuclear wastes is prohibited unless explicitly permitted.[20] Thus it permits dumping only if the wastes fall into categories listed in an annex and a permit has been obtained. It prohibits the incineration of wastes at sea, bans the export of wastes to other countries for dumping or incineration at sea, and provides for a mechanism to settle complaints.

Chapter 22 of Agenda 21 adopted at the 1992 Rio Conference[21] addresses the management of radioactive wastes, and takes as its basis for action the radiological and safety risk resulting from radioactive waste. It focuses on four specific activities: promoting policies and practical measures to minimize and limit the generation of radioactive wastes and to provide for their safe processing, conditioning, transportation and disposal; supporting efforts within the IAEA to develop and

17 A/CONF.48/14/Rev. 1, Rec. 75, Action Plan for the Human Environment.

18 Article IV of the Convention.

19 Article XV of the Convention.

20 Convention on the Prevention of Marine Pollution by Dumping of Wastes and Other Matter, available at http://www.imo.org/en/OurWork/Environment/LCLP/Pages/default.aspx accessed 9 July 2018.

21 Conference on Environment and Development, 3–14 June 1992, Rio Declaration on Environment and Development, Principle 16, U.N. Doc A/Conf.151/26 (12 August 1992).

apply radioactive waste safety standards or guidelines and codes of practice; promoting safe storage, transportation and disposal; and prompting proper planning of safe and environmentally sound management, including environmental impact assessment where appropriate.[22] It also calls for international cooperation to implement the 1990 IAEA Code and keep under review a possible legally binding instrument.[23] It also calls upon the States not to promote or allow the storage or disposal of radioactive wastes near the marine environment and not to export radioactive wastes to countries that prohibit the import of such wastes.[24] The Convention for the Protection of Natural Resources and the Environment of the South Pacific Region 1986 addresses cooperation in combating pollution emergencies and prevention of pollution by dumping in the region. It also prohibits the dumping or storage of radioactive materials and waste in that area as well as the disposal of waste onto the sea-bed. The Convention for the Protection of the Marine Environment of the North East Atlantic 1992 addresses all sources of pollution of the marine environment and requires States Parties to adopt scientific programmes, to harmonize their environmental policies, to adopt the best available techniques and practices, and to apply the precautionary and the polluter pays principles. It prohibits the pollution of the marine environment by the dumping of radioactive materials and wastes at sea.

IAEA's 1990 Code of Practice on the Transboundary Movement of Radioactive Waste

As to the transportation of nuclear material, the IAEA adopted a Code of Practice on the International Transboundary Movement of Radioactive Waste in 1990. This Code fills a gap in the Basel Convention on Controlling Transboundary Movement of Hazardous Wastes 1989 which does not include radioactive wastes. The Code relies on international standards for the safe transport of radioactive material and the physical protection of nuclear material, as well as standards for basic nuclear safety and radiation protection and radioactive waste management.[25] The two basic principles of the Code are: first, States should take the appropriate steps necessary to ensure that radioactive waste within its territory, or under its jurisdiction or control, is safely managed and disposed of, to ensure the protection of human health and the environment. Second, State should take the appropriate steps necessary to minimize the amount of radioactive waste.[26]

While the Code recognizes that it is the sovereign right of every state to prohibit the movement of radioactive waste into its territory, every state involved in the international trans-boundary movement of radioactive waste should take the

22 Para. 22.4.

23 Para. 22.5.

24 Para. 22.5(d) and (e).

25 The Code is available at https://www.iaea.org/sites/default/files/infcirc386.pdf, accessed 9 July 2018.

26 Ibid.

appropriate steps necessary to ensure that such movement is undertaken in a manner consistent with international safety standards.[27] It states that transboundary movement of radioactive waste should take place only with the prior notification and consent of the sending, receiving and transit states in accordance with their respective laws and regulations.[28] Third, every state involved in the transboundary movement of radioactive waste should have a relevant regulatory authority and adopt appropriate procedures as necessary for the regulation of such movement. Fourth, no receiving state should permit the receipt of radioactive waste for management or disposal unless it has the administrative and technical capacity and regulatory structure to manage and dispose of such waste in accordance with international safety standards. Fifth, every state should introduce into its national laws and regulations relevant provisions as necessary for liability, compensation or other remedies for damage that could arise from the transboundary movement of radioactive waste. Finally, the IAEA should continue to collect and disseminate information on the laws, regulations and technical standards pertaining to radioactive waste management and disposal, and develop relevant technical standards.[29]

Although this Code is non-binding, it has been adopted by the UN and many other international organizations concerned with the transport of hazardous materials as well as by a large number of states.

Joint Convention on the Safety of Spent Fuel and Radioactive Waste Management 1997

This Convention, which came into force in 2001,[30] applies both to radioactive waste disposal and to spent fuel management. The Joint Convention is open for accession, not only to those states with nuclear power programmes, but also to those using radiation sources in medicine and industry. The aim of the Convention is to ensure the safety of spent fuel and radioactive waste. The scope of application of the Joint Convention is wide. It applies to the full range of radioactive wastes in liquid, gaseous and in solid form. It sets out general safety requirements for the management of spent fuel and radioactive waste, the design, siting and operation of related facilities, and the establishment of a regulatory framework and independent regulatory body. The Joint Convention 1997 reaffirms in its preamble that the ultimate responsibility for ensuring the safety of spent fuel and radioactive waste management rests with the state, aims to promote an effective nuclear safety culture, and stresses the importance of international cooperation in enhancing the safety of spent fuel and radioactive waste management. Article 1 of the Convention sets forth its objectives: to achieve and maintain a high

27 Para 4.
28 Para 5.
29 Ibid.
30 Joint Convention on the Safety of Spent Fuel and Radioactive Waste Management, 36 ILM (1997) 1436.

level of safety worldwide in spent fuel and radioactive waste management; to ensure effective defences during all stages of spent fuel and radioactive waste management for protecting individuals, society and the environment from harmful effects of ionizing radiation to preserve the interest of future generations; and to prevent accidents with radiological consequences.[31] Article 1 also recognizes the intergenerational implications of nuclear waste. The Convention defines 'radioactive waste' as radioactive material in gaseous, liquid or solid form, while 'radioactive waste management' means all activities, including decommissioning activities, that relate to the handling, pre-treatment, treatment, conditioning, storage or disposal of radioactive waste.[32]

Article 3 defines the scope of application of the Convention. This Convention shall apply to the safety of spent fuel and radioactive waste management when the spent fuel and radioactive waste result from the operation of civilian nuclear reactors or civilian applications.[33] However, application of the Convention has been excluded in three situations: first, it shall not apply to spent fuel held at reprocessing facilities as part of a reprocessing activity. Second, it shall also not apply to waste that contains only naturally occurring radioactive materials and that does not originate from the nuclear fuel cycle. Third, it shall not apply to the safety of management of spent fuel or radioactive waste within military or defence programmes except when such materials are transferred permanently to and managed within exclusively civilian programmes.[34] National law must provide effective protection for individuals, society and the environment and give due regard to internationally endorsed criteria and standards.[35]

Safety of spent fuel and radioactive waste management

State obligations relating to safety requirements with regard to spent fuel management is contained in Article 4, while safety requirements on radioactive waste management are dealt with by Article 11. These are based on the IAEA Safety Fundamentals and Safety Standards and other standards agreed upon by internationally recognized experts. These two articles use identical language on formulating obligations of Contracting Parties for the safety of spent fuel and radioactive waste management. Articles 4 and 11 of the Convention require each Contracting Party to take the appropriate steps to ensure that at all stages of spent fuel and radioactive management, individuals, society and the environment are adequately protected against radiological hazards. They provide that in order to ensure the protection of individuals and environment against radiological hazards, the Contracting Party shall take the following steps: (i) ensure that criticality and removal of residual heat generated during spent fuel and radioactive waste

31 Ibid.
32 Article 2 of the Convention.
33 Article 3 of the Convention.
34 Ibid.
35 Articles 4(iv) and 11(iv) of the Convention.

management are adequately addressed; (ii) ensure that generation of radioactive waste is kept to the minimum practicable; (iii) take into account interdependencies among the different steps in spent fuel management; (iv) provide for effective protection against radiological hazards in the framework of its national legislation which has due regard to internationally endorsed criteria and standards; (v) take into account the biological, chemical and other hazards that may be associated with spent fuel management; (vi) strive to avoid actions that impose reasonably predictable impacts on future generations greater than those permitted for the current generation; and (vii) aim to avoid imposing undue burdens on future generations.

Siting of proposed nuclear facilities[36]

Articles 6 and 13 of the Convention lay down the following procedures for the siting of proposed facilities for spent fuel management and radioactive waste management. Contracting Parties are required: to evaluate all relevant site-related factors likely to affect the safety of such a facility during its operating lifetime; to make information on the safety of a facility available to members of the public and to consult neighbouring Contracting Parties which are likely to be affected by that facility and provide them with general data relating to the facility.

Design and construction of facilities

Regarding the design and construction of facilities of spent fuel management and radioactive management, Contracting Parties shall take appropriate measures to limit possible radiological impacts on individuals, society and the environment. At the design stage, conceptual plans and technical provisions for the decommissioning of a spent fuel management facility are to be taken into account. The technologies incorporated in the design and construction of a spent fuel management facility must be supported by experience, testing or analysis.[37] Preparation of technical provisions for the closure of a disposal facility is also required.

Assessment of safety of facilities

Articles 8 and 15 are concerned with safety assessment of facilities of spent fuel management and radioactive management respectively. These provisions provide that a systematic safety assessment and an environmental assessment covering its operating lifetime shall be carried out before construction and operation of a spent fuel management and radioactive waste management facility. Updated and detailed versions of the safety assessment and of the

36 'Nuclear facility' means a civilian facility and its associated land, buildings and equipment in which radioactive materials are produced, processed, used, handled, stored or disposed of on such a scale that consideration of safety is required. Art. 2(f) of the Convention.

37 Articles 7 and 14 of the Convention.

environmental assessment are also required to be prepared by Contracting Parties before the operation of such a facility. In addition, in the case of radioactive waste management, before construction of a disposal facility, a systematic safety assessment and an environmental assessment for the period following closure shall also be carried out.[38]

Operation of facilities

Articles 9 and 16 of the Convention deal with operation of facilities of spent fuel management and radioactive waste management. Both Articles state that each Contracting Party shall take the appropriate steps to ensure that: (i) the licence to operate a spent fuel management facility or radioactive waste management facility is based upon appropriate assessments and is conditional upon the completion of a commissioning programme demonstrating that the facility is consistent with the design and safety requirements; (ii) operational limits and conditions derived from tests, operational experience and the assessments are defined and revised as necessary; (iii) operation, maintenance, monitoring, inspection and testing of a spent fuel management facility or radioactive waste management facility are conducted in accordance with established procedures; (iv) engineering and technical support in all safety-related fields are available throughout the operating lifetime of a spent fuel management facility and radioactive waste management facility; (v) incidents significant to safety are reported in a timely manner by the holder of the licence to the regulatory body; (vi) programmes to collect and analyse relevant operating experience are established; (vii) decommissioning plans for a spent fuel management facility and radioactive waste management facility are prepared and updated using information obtained during the operating lifetime of that facility, and are reviewed by the regulatory body. In addition to these requirements, the following procedures are prescribed: characterization and segregation of radioactive waste are applied and plans for the closure of a disposal facility are prepared and updated.[39]

Institutional measures after closure of radioactive waste disposal facility

Article 17 is concerned with institutional measures after the closure of a radioactive waste disposal facility. According to Article 17, after closure of a disposal facility, State parties shall preserve records of the location, design and inventory of that facility required by the regulatory body; and carry out institutional controls such as monitoring or access restrictions. If during any period of active institutional control, an unplanned release of radioactive materials into the environment is detected, State shall take intervention measures.

38 Article 15(ii) of the Convention.
39 Article 16(v) and (ix) of the Convention.

Implementation of the Convention

Article 18 says that each Contracting Party shall take the legislative, regulatory and administrative measures for implementing its obligations under this Convention and Article 19 provides that each Contracting Party shall establish a legislative and regulatory framework to govern the safety of spent fuel and radioactive waste management. This legislative and regulatory framework shall provide for: (i) the establishment of applicable national safety requirements and regulations for radiation safety; (ii) a system of licensing of spent fuel and radioactive waste management activities; (iii) a system of prohibition of the operation of a spent fuel or radioactive waste management facility without a licence; (iv) a system of appropriate institutional control, regulatory inspection and documentation and reporting; (v) the enforcement of applicable regulations and of the terms of the licences; and (vi) a clear allocation of responsibilities of the bodies involved in the different steps of spent fuel and of radioactive waste management.

Independent regulatory body

Article 20 provides that each Contracting Party shall establish an effective and independent regulatory body entrusted with the implementation of the legislative and regulatory framework and that such regulatory body be provided with adequate authority, competence and financial and human resources to fulfil its assigned responsibilities and to ensure its independence.

Responsibility of licence-holder

Article 21 deals with responsibility of the licence holder. According to Article 21, prime responsibility for the safety of spent fuel or radioactive waste management rests with the holder of the relevant licence and the state party shall take the appropriate steps to ensure that each such licence holder meets its responsibility.[40]

Human and financial resources and quality control

Contracting Parties shall make available qualified staff and adequate financial resources for safety-related activities during the operating lifetime of a spent fuel and a radioactive waste management facility. Each Contracting Party shall also ensure financial provision for continuation of the appropriate institutional controls and monitoring arrangements for the period following the closure of a disposal facility.[41] Article 23 requires each Contracting Party to ensure that appropriate quality assurance programmes concerning the safety of spent fuel and radioactive waste management are established and implemented.

40 Alexandre Kiss, 'State Responsibility and Liability for Nuclear Damage' (2006–2007) 35 *Denver Journal of International Law and Policy* 67.

41 Article 22 of the Convention.

Radiation protection

Since operation of nuclear installations and radioactive waste can generate radiation, and radiation risks may transcend national borders, international cooperation serves to promote and enhance safety globally by exchanging experience and by improving capabilities to control hazards, to prevent accidents, to respond to emergencies and to mitigate any harmful consequences. Three principles form the framework for protection concerning practices that involve exposure: justification of the activity; dose limitation (i.e., keeping individual doses within regulatory limits); and optimisation (i.e., keeping doses 'as low as reasonably achievable').[42] The principle of optimisation (As Low as Reasonably Achievable –ALARA principle) requires that exposures from practices shall be kept as low as reasonably achievable below the prescribed limits, economic and social factors being taken into account. This principle has to be recognised as the means of finding the best compromise between the desire to protect populations as far as possible and that of using efficiently as possible the resources available for that purpose.[43]

The principle of operational radiation protection has been incorporated in Article 24 of the1997 Joint Convention, which requires parties to implement 'appropriate corrective measures' to control or mitigate accidental releases of radioactivity. It states that Contracting Parties shall take steps to ensure that during the operating lifetime of a spent fuel or radioactive waste management facility: (i) the radiation exposure of the workers and the public caused by the facility shall be kept as low as reasonably achievable; (ii) no individual shall be exposed to radiation doses which exceed national prescriptions for dose limitation. In the event that an unplanned or uncontrolled release of radioactive materials into the environment occurs, the Contracting Parties must implement appropriate corrective measures to control the release and mitigate its effects.[44]

Emergency preparedness

The Convention requires each Contracting Party to ensure that before and during operation of a spent fuel or radioactive waste management facility there are appropriate on-site and off-site emergency plans. Such emergency plans should be tested at an appropriate frequency.[45] Each Contracting Party shall also take the appropriate steps for the preparation and testing of emergency plans if it is affected in the event of a radiological emergency at a spent fuel or radioactive waste management facility.[46]

42 'Nuclear Energy in a Sustainable Development Perspective' (2000) NEA, OECD 36.
43 Jean-Michel Courades, 'The Importance of the Principle of Optimisation for the Radiation Safety Culture in CEEC' in Nathalie L.J.T. Horbach (ed.), *Contemporary Developments in Nuclear Energy Law: Harmonising Legislation in CEEC/NIS* (The Hague, Kluwer Law International 1999) 91.
44 Article 24(3) of the Convention.
45 Article 25.
46 Article 25.

Regulation of transboundary movement

It also contains provision of safety measures for transboundary movement of spent fuel or radioactive waste. Article 27 provides that the Contracting Parties must develop programmes to ensure that transboundary movement is properly authorized and is conducted with prior notification and consent of the receiving state. In case of transboundary movement of nuclear wastes, it provides that waste or spent fuel may only be exported if the state of destination has the requisite capacity to deal with such materials in a manner consistent with the Convention and if it has given its prior informed consent.[47]

In brief, the Convention sets out five procedural requirements for the transboundary shipment: first, there is a requirement for prior notification and consent. Second, international rules governing transit must be respected. Third, there must be an existing spent fuel or radioactive waste management capacity in the state of destination. Fourth, the state of origin may not authorise a transboundary movement unless it can satisfy itself that the latter requirements have been met prior to the shipment. Finally, preparation has to be made for a re-entry of the shipment if it cannot be completed.[48]

The Joint Convention also addresses the concern for protection of Antarctica from the dumping of nuclear waste. Article 27 of the Convention completely prohibits the licensing of shipments of spent fuel or radioactive waste in Antarctica for storage or disposal.

Reporting obligation

Article 32 provides that each Contracting Party shall submit a national report to each review meeting of Contracting Parties. This report shall address the measures taken to implement each of the obligations of the Convention. For each Contracting Party the report shall also address (i) its spent fuel management policy; (ii) spent fuel management practices; (iii) radioactive waste management policy; (iv) radioactive waste management practices; and (v) the criteria used to define and categorize radioactive waste. This report shall also include: (i) a list of the spent fuel management facilities subject to this Convention, their location, main purpose and essential features; (ii) an inventory of spent fuel which shall contain a description of the material and, if available, information on its mass and its total activity; (iii) a list of the radioactive waste management facilities; (iv) an inventory of radioactive waste that is being held in storage at radioactive waste management and nuclear fuel cycle facilities; and has been disposed of; and (v) a list of nuclear facilities in the process of being decommissioned and the status of decommissioning activities at those facilities.

47 Article 27(iii).

48 Article 27(v).

Confidentiality

The Joint Convention was the first international nuclear law instrument to require Contracting Parties to make available to the public information about the safety of spent nuclear fuel facilities and radioactive waste management facilities. However, this Convention contains a confidentiality provision. Article 36 provides that the rights and obligations of the Contracting Parties under their laws to protect information from disclosure shall not be affected. Such information includes information relating to national security, or to the physical protection of nuclear materials, information protected by intellectual property rights or by industrial or commercial confidentiality and personal data.

The Joint Convention is an important contribution to the nuclear safety culture as it sets benchmark in internationally agreed standard on radioactive waste and spent fuel management and imposes obligations on Contracting Parties to apply these standards at the national level.

Weaknesses of the Convention

The Convention has also many short comings: first, reprocessing of spent fuel and spent fuel held for reprocessing are included only if the relevant Contracting Party so declares. Second, spent fuel or wastes from civilian installations are included only if transported to permanent civilian control, or if the relevant party so declares.[49] Additionally, the safety requirements of the IAEA are not legally binding. However, most countries have incorporated these standards into their legislation on a voluntary basis. There is no supervisory body to implement the treaty. The decision to permit implementation and interpretation of the rights and obligations of Contracting Parties to be carried out by the states themselves is also a potential source of weakness of this Convention.[50]

Environmental dimensions of nuclear waste management

Siting and operation of waste management facilities may require states to comply with environmental standards and concerns. Nuclear waste may involve safety and environmental risks for future generation. Disposal of nuclear waste in a repository is a long-term process and the liability regime for nuclear waste would be gradual and continuous, with radioactivity migrating through the soil or ground water so that the resulting damage might not be noticeable for a long

49 Patricia Birnie and Alan Boyle, *International Law and the Environment* (2nd edn, New York, Oxford University Press 2002) 463.

50 Peter D. Cameron, 'Joint Convention on the Safety of Spent Fuel Management and the Safety of Radioactive Management', in Nathalie L.J.T. Horbach (ed.), *Contemporary Developments in Nuclear Energy Law: Harmonising Legislation in CEEC/NIS* (The Hague, Kluwer Law International 1999) 128.

period of time and would affect the environment rather than cause direct damage to human beings."[51] The liability issue highlights a central issue of the duty to safeguard the rights of future generations to a preserved environment.[52] While the Government has the responsibility to provide for the permanent disposal of HLW to protect public health and safety and the environment, the costs of such disposal should be the responsibility of the generators and owners of such waste. Both the precautionary principle and future generation principle are against the transfer to future generation of the kind of risk and charges that would be regarded as unacceptable today.[53]

The environmental concerns have been addressed in many provisions of the Joint Convention. Under the Convention, Contracting Parties are required to take measures for the protection of the environment against radiological hazards.[54] to evaluate the likely safety impact of proposed nuclear facility on the environment,[55] to consider the issue of the environment in design, construction and assessment of facilities, and the siting of proposed facilities of spent fuel and radioactive waste management.[56]

Social aspects of nuclear waste management

Risk, uncertainty, and interest of future generations are inherent aspect of nuclear waste management. Disposal of nuclear waste and search for suitable sites for disposal raise social, political and economic concerns and addressing these concerns is essential for the long-term solution of this problem. However, a clear distinction between the environmental, societal, political, economic and technological dimensions of nuclear waste is difficult, as these domains are entangled in complex ways. Waste management decisions also involve the allocation of uncertain risks and benefits to different regions of the country, to different generations, and to different social groups. Stakeholders' involvement in the decision-making process relating to nuclear waste management is considered an important means of obtaining broad public acceptance of the process of long-term disposal of such wastes. In particular, the time-scales involved in long-term disposal of nuclear wastes are unusually long as the process of site selection, demonstrating the suitability of site, obtaining the necessary planning and regulatory approvals and constructing the repository to the point at which it can accept waste may take as long as several decades.[57] Public participation in the decision-making process, particularly extensive engagement with the local community, is required for

51 Ibid 81.
52 Ibid.
53 Ibid.
54 Article 4.
55 Article 6.
56 Articles 7, 8 and 13.
57 'Managing Our Radioactive Waste Safely' CoRWM Report, 2006, 125 http://130.88.20.21/uknuclear/pdfs/CoRWMFullReport060731.pdf, accessed 10 July 2018.

creating a climate of mutual understanding and trust in long-term disposal of nuclear wastes.[58]

Decisions relating to the siting of a disposal facility are shaped by different actors and different political and cultural contexts. Regulatory structures, legal frameworks and societal acceptance are necessary in the siting processes. In many countries, where a non-transparent top-down decision-making process has been used in site selections, latent public discontent may develop gradually and may lead to conflict.[59] Therefore, nuclear waste governance requires sensitivity to the multiple dimensions and perspectives associated with nuclear waste challenges. In all countries and at all levels, nuclear waste is simultaneously a technical, political and institutional matter. Various actors and factors, such as the nature of the political and legal systems, geographical and hydrological conditions, technical skills, the stock of available knowledge, formal and informal rules and procedures, political constraints, the degree of public rejection and acceptance, and a country's nuclear history can shape the siting processes.[60]

In particular, public participation in the planning and development of repositories is essential in order to promote public confidence in the safety of disposal of HLW. For example, Finland involved stakeholders in its ONKALO project, relating to the construction of its deep geological repository, and their involvement in the site selection for this geological repository in Olkiluoto (Finland's west coast) helped gain public acceptance of the project and was crucial in building the trust necessary for the success of the project.[61]

EU Directives

At EU level, spent fuel and radioactive waste management is largely governed by the treaty which established the European Atomic Energy Community (EURATOM Treaty). Under the Council Directive 2011/70/EURATOM, Member States are required to establish, implement and keep updated 'national programmes' for the management of nuclear waste. The preamble of the Directive on radioactive waste, including spent fuel, requires containment and isolation from humans and the living environment over the long term. It also acknowledges that deep geological disposal represents the safest and most sustainable option as the end point of the management of high-level waste and spent fuel. Since the implementation and development of a disposal facility will take place over many decades, national programmes should be adaptable, in order to incorporate new knowledge about

58 Environment Alert Bulletin, 'Nuclear Waste: Is Everything Under Control?' (n 3).

59 Maria Rosaria Di Nucci, Achim Brunnengräber, Lutz Mez and Miranda Schreurs, *Comparative Perspectives on Nuclear Waste Governance: An International Comparison* (Springer 2015) 29.

60 Ibid, 26.

61 Irena Chatzis, 'Solving the Back End: Finland's Key to the Final Disposal of Spent Nuclear Fuel', available at https://www.iaea.org/newscenter/news/solving-the-back-end-finlands-key-to-the-final-disposal-of-spent-nuclear-fuel, accessed 10 July 2018.

site conditions or the possible evolution of the disposal system.[62] Article 4 of the Directive provides that Member States shall adopt national policies on spent fuel and radioactive waste management. Such national policies shall be based on principles incorporated in the Joint Convention. States Parties shall establish and maintain a national legislative, regulatory and organizational framework for spent fuel and radioactive waste management that allocates responsibility and provides for coordination between relevant competent bodies.[63] The national framework shall provide for all of the following: (a) a national programme for the implementation of spent fuel and radioactive waste management; (b) arrangements for the safety of spent fuel and radioactive waste management; (c) a system of licensing of spent fuel and radioactive waste management activities; (d) a system of appropriate control, management system, regulatory inspections, documentation and reporting obligations for radioactive waste and spent fuel management activities, facilities or both, including appropriate measures for the post-closure periods of disposal facilities; (e) enforcement actions, including the suspension of activities and the modification, expiration or revocation of a licence; (f) the allocation of responsibility to the bodies involved in the different steps of spent fuel and radioactive waste management; (g) national requirements for public information and participation; (h) the financing scheme. Each Member State is also required to establish and maintain a competent regulatory authority in the field of safety of spent fuel and radioactive waste management.[64] Article 7 states that Member States shall ensure that the prime responsibility for the safety of spent fuel and radioactive waste management facilities rests with the licence holder to regularly assess, verify and continuously improve the safety of the radioactive waste and spent fuel management facility. More importantly, the Directive spells out in detail measures relating to transparency. Under Article 10, Member States shall ensure that necessary information on the management of spent fuel and radioactive waste be made available to workers and the general public. This obligation includes ensuring that the competent regulatory authority informs the public in the fields of its competence. Information shall be made available to the public in accordance with national legislation and international obligations. The public shall be given the necessary opportunities to participate effectively in the decision-making process regarding spent fuel and radioactive waste management in accordance with national legislation and international obligation. The Directive also contains notification and reporting obligations as a means of implementing the provisions. The EU Directive plays an important role in the mandatory implementation of national nuclear waste disposal plans in the Member States.

Conclusion

Currently many countries have adopted laws and strategies for the safe management of nuclear or radioactive wastes, but these national arrangements vary

62 Principle 23.
63 Article 5 of the Directive.
64 Article 6 of the Directive.

considerably and in many cases are not fully consistent with international standards. The Joint Convention deals with the safety of spent fuel and radioactive waste management, and the implementation mechanism. Although the principles and safety requirements of the Joint Convention are recognized internationally, there exist no sanctions in the case of non-compliance. The Joint Convention also has so-called incentive character. However, most countries have incorporated these standards in their legislation on a voluntary basis. No new international body is established to make it work and for its secretariat it relies on the services of an existing body, the IAEA. Although the use of nuclear material for military and defence purposes create significant waste, neither the Joint Convention nor the EU Directive requires states to report this kind of waste. At the domestic level, nuclear law must establish a legislative framework for the safe management of all sources and types of ionizing radiation and radioactive wastes. Such legislative framework should ensure that individuals, society and the environment are adequately protected against radiological hazards.

The third-party liability treaties are silent about liability that may arise from damage caused by the underground repositories for spent nuclear fuel and high-level radioactive waste which may remain hazardous for thousands of years. Although the chance of a release of radioactivity caused by our ordinary idea of an accident is very remote, these underground repositories may still release radiation following an unforeseen natural phenomenon, human intervention on the site or a progressive deterioration of the conditions.[65] Therefore, existing international and national legal and regulatory frameworks for the management of radioactive wastes should be modified to include the provision of liability in case of damage caused by underground repositories.

65 Patrick Reyners, 'Underground Nuclear Repositories and International Civil Liability: the Time Factor' (2014) 17(1) *Journal of Risk Research* 133–143, 135.

5 Legal regime on safety and security of nuclear installations

Introduction

Nuclear energy must be used in conformity with basic safety and security standards. In recent years there has been much concern about the safety and security of nuclear installations. Nuclear safety systems and operating techniques may vary with the use of different types of reactor. The global regime of nuclear safety includes the safety of nuclear installations, incorporating safe design, construction, operation and siting of nuclear facilities; radiation safety, the safety of radioactive waste management and safety in the transport of radioactive material. While nuclear safety and nuclear security aim to achieve the same objective – protection of public and environment from radiation – there are some differences between two concepts. According to the IAEA, nuclear safety is 'the achievement of proper operating conditions, prevention of accidents or mitigation of accident consequences, resulting in protection of workers, the public and the environment from undue radiation hazards'.[1] On the other hand, nuclear security is defined as 'prevention and detection of and response to theft, sabotage, unauthorized access, illegal transfer or other malicious acts involving nuclear materials, other radioactive substances, or their associated facilities'.[2] Nuclear safety is concerned with measures against radiological risks caused by human error, equipment failures, internal events (fire, pipe break) or external events (earthquakes, flooding or other natural calamities), while nuclear security focuses on measures against intentional acts such as theft or illegal transfer of radioactive material or terrorism.[3] Nuclear security is promoted through measures designed for the physical protection of nuclear material and nuclear facilities. A physical protection system of nuclear material and nuclear facility integrates people, procedures and equipment for the protection of assets or facilities against theft, sabotage and terrorist attacks.

1 'Nuclear Safety & Security, Concepts and Terms', IAEA 2007, available at http://www-ns.iaea.org/standards/concepts-terms.asp#3, accessed 10 July 2018.

2 Ibid.

3 Sonal Gandhi and Jungmin Kang, 'Nuclear Safety and Nuclear Security Synergy' (2013) 60 *Annals of Nuclear Energy* 357–361.

Convention on Nuclear Safety 1994

The Convention on Nuclear Safety 1994 (CNS) entered into force on 24 October 1996 and remains the main treaty on nuclear safety. The Convention defines state obligations in general terms regarding safety of operation of nuclear installations. The main objectives of the CNS include: to achieve and maintain a high level of safety of civil nuclear power plants and related facilities worldwide through the enhancement of national measures and international cooperation; to establish and maintain effective defences in nuclear installations against potential radiological hazards in order to protect individuals and society and the environment from the harmful effects of ionizing radiation from such installations; to prevent accidents with radiological consequences and mitigating such consequences should they occur.[4] This Convention entails a commitment of the Contracting Parties to the application of fundamental safety principles for nuclear installations but it does not contain detailed safety standards. It provides benchmark standards for the siting, design, construction and operation of nuclear installations, as well as the adequacy of human and financial resources, the assessment and verification of safety, quality assurance and emergency preparedness.

The Convention requires the Contracting Parties to take legislative, regulatory and administrative measures to implement its obligations.[5] The legislative and regulatory framework governing the safety of nuclear installations shall provide for the establishment of applicable national safety requirements and regulations; a system of licensing, a system of regulatory inspection and assessment of nuclear installations which covers the plant, equipment, materials, and personnel to ascertain compliance with applicable regulations; and the enforcement of applicable regulations and of the terms of licences.[6] Contracting Parties are also required to establish an independent regulatory body for implementing the legislative and regulatory framework and such regulatory body shall be provided with adequate authority, competence and human resources to fulfil its responsibilities.[7] The requirement to ensure adequate human resources involves the 'provision of sufficient numbers of qualified staff with appropriate education, training and retraining for all safety-related activities in or for each nuclear installation, throughout its life'. The CNS is the first treaty to commit states to control the risks of nuclear energy for environmental protection. Contracting Parties shall ensure that the prime responsibility for the safety of a nuclear installation rests with the licence holder.[8]

For ensuring safety of nuclear installation, the Convention requires each Contracting Party to ensure that all relevant organizations directly related to nuclear installations shall establish policies that give due priority to nuclear safety[9] and

4 Article 1 CNS.
5 Article 4 CNS.
6 Article 7 CNS.
7 Article 8 CNS.
8 Article 9 CNS.
9 Article 10 CNS.

adequate financial resources and that qualified staff are available to support the safety of each nuclear installations throughout its life.[10] The requirement to ensure adequate human resources involves the 'provision of sufficient numbers of qualified staff with appropriate education, training and retraining for all safety-related activities in or for each nuclear installation, throughout its life'.[11] However, the capabilities and limitations of human performance should be assessed throughout the life of a nuclear installation.[12]

Quality assurance, assessment and verification of safety

Contracting Parties are required to establish quality assurance programmes and implement these to build public confidence that the specified requirements are satisfied throughout the life of a nuclear installation.[13] Contracting Parties are also required to carry out comprehensive and systematic safety assessments before the construction and commissioning of a nuclear installation and such assessments shall be well documented, updated and reviewed in the light of operating experience and significant new information.[14] On the other hand, verification is to be carried out by analysis, surveillance, testing and inspection to ensure that the physical state and the operation of a nuclear installation continue to be in accordance with its design, applicable safety requirements, and operational limits and conditions.[15]

Radiation protection

The CNS also deals with radiation protection. Contracting Parties are required to take appropriate steps to ensure that the radiation exposure to workers and the public caused by a nuclear installation is kept as low as reasonably achievable and that no individual shall be exposed to radiation doses which exceed prescribed national dose limits.[16] This provision sets forth the well-established ALARA (as low as reasonably achievable) principle of radiation protection. This Convention does not include any further regulation of radiation protection.

Emergency preparedness

According to the Convention, Contracting Parties should ensure that both on-site and off-site emergency plans are available for both existing and future nuclear installations and that these are routinely tested.[17] In circumstances of

10 Article 11 CNS.
11 Ibid.
12 Article 12 CNS.
13 Article 13 CNS.
14 Article 14(i) CNS.
15 Article 14(ii) CNS.
16 Article 15 CNS.
17 Article 16(i) CNS.

potential radiological emergency, the Contracting Parties should provide appropriate information for emergency planning and response to their own population and the competent authorities.[18] Even those Contracting Parties that have no nuclear installation but are likely to be affected in the event of a radiological emergency shall take appropriate steps for the preparation and testing of emergency plans.[19]

Safety of installations

The Convention also provides for specific safety requirements and regulations that concern the siting, design, construction and operation of nuclear installations.

Siting

The Convention elaborates as to the siting of nuclear installations that states should evaluate all relevant site-related factors likely to affect the safety of a nuclear installation; the likely safety impact of a proposed nuclear installation on individuals, society and the environment; and re-evaluate all relevant factors for the continued safety acceptability of the nuclear installation.[20] In order to prevent transboundary harm, the Convention requires that states should consult with neighbouring Contracting Parties in the vicinity of a proposed nuclear installation and, upon request, provide the necessary information to such states in order to enable them to evaluate and make their own assessment of the likely safety impact on their own territory of the nuclear installation.[21] The Convention, however, fails to specify what happens if the neighbouring state does not agree to the siting of a nuclear installation in the vicinity of its border and if the consultations held with that state bring no solution to the situation.

Design and construction

Regarding the design and construction of nuclear installations, the Convention requires that Contracting Parties should ensure that design and construction provide for reliable levels and methods of protection against the release of radioactive materials with a view to preventing the occurrence of accidents and to mitigating their radiological consequences should they occur.[22] The technologies applied in the design and construction of a nuclear installation must be proven by experience or qualified by testing or analysis.[23]

18 Article 16(ii) CNS.
19 Article 16(iii) CNS.
20 Article 17 CNS.
21 Article 17(iv) CNS.
22 Article 18(i) CNS.
23 Article 18(ii) CNS.

Operation

The Convention provides detailed safety standards for the operation of a nuclear installation. According to Article 19, each Contracting Party shall ensure that: (i) the initial authorization to operate a nuclear installation is based upon an appropriate safety analysis and a commissioning programme demonstrating that the installation is consistent with design and safety requirements; (ii) operational limits and conditions derived from the safety analysis, tests and operational experience are defined and revised for identifying safe boundaries for operation; (iii) operation, maintenance, inspection and testing of a nuclear installation are conducted in accordance with approved procedures; (iv) procedures are established for responding to anticipated operational occurrences and to accidents; (v) necessary engineering and technical support in all safety-related fields is available throughout the lifetime of a nuclear installation; (vi) incidents significant to safety are reported in a timely manner by the licence holder to the regulatory body; (vii) programmes are established to collect and analyze operating experience; (viii) the generation of radioactive waste resulting from the operation of a nuclear installation is kept to the minimum practicable for the process concerned, both in activity and in volume.

The Convention provides that, to ensure the safe siting, design, construction and operation of nuclear installations, Contracting Parties should 'take the appropriate measures'. If existing nuclear reactors cannot be operated safely, they should be shut down on a timetable taking into account the social, economic and environmental impacts. The CNS relies on national actions that are established to fulfil their obligations under the Convention. The CNS does not set out any international standards for the siting, design, construction and operation of nuclear installations in addition to the established national procedures.

Environmental concerns in the Nuclear Safety Convention

Environmental concerns have been addressed in the 1994 Convention on Nuclear Safety in both its Preamble and operative text. In the Preamble, Contracting Parties declare their awareness of the 'importance to the international community of ensuring that the use of nuclear energy is safe, well regulated and environmentally sound'. Accordingly, Article 1(ii) of the CNS states that one of its objectives is 'to establish and maintain effective defences in nuclear installations against potential radiological hazards in order to protect individuals, society and the environment from harmful effects of ionizing radiation from such installations'. The Convention obliges states to take appropriate steps to ensure that procedures are established and implemented 'for evaluating the likely safety impact of a proposed nuclear installation on individuals, society and the environment'.[24] However, the CNS does not provide detailed provisions on the environmental impact assessment

24 Article 17(ii) CNS.

of the proposed installation and is also silent about the potential environmental impact during operation of such installations.

Compliance mechanism

The Convention provides that each Contracting Party must submit a report on the measures it has taken to implement each of the obligations of the Convention.[25] These reports are to be reviewed at the review meetings[26] that should finish with the adoption of summary reports. Summary reports should be made available to the public. Such reports should address issues discussed and conclusions reached during a meeting.[27] The CNS peer review process comprises three main elements. First, Contracting Parties must prepare national reports on compliance with the Convention's obligations (Article 4 and Rules 39 and 40). Second, Contracting Parties must review the reports of other Parties and decide whether to submit questions or comments to them in advance of the peer review meeting (Rule 43.1(b)). Third, Contracting Parties must attend a meeting of the Contracting Parties at least every three years to participate in a review of national reports (Article 24).

The most important and innovative part of the Convention is the 'peer review process', which aims to increase the transparency, cooperation, effectiveness and efficiency and the incentive to comply with the Convention.[28]

The peer review process is the main implementation process of the Convention at the international level. By means of the peer review system, the CNS regime is intended to provide 'incentives' for nations to improve nuclear safety, rather than to impose 'regulatory' or 'penal' measures to this end.[29] This preference for 'incentive' rather than regulatory or penal measures is adopted for the following reasons. First, ultimate legal responsibility for nuclear safety rests with the state having jurisdiction over a nuclear installation. Second, states did not want to subject themselves to intrusive inspections and accompanying costs that an international regulatory bureaucracy would entail. Third, they were not prepared to undertake the rather difficult and protracted task of codifying an extensive list of safety-related regulatory standards which would be difficult to apply to the different types of nuclear technologies being used for power production and which could rapidly become outdated. Finally, the drafters did not want to establish a

25 Article 5 CNS.

26 Article 20 CNS.

27 Article 25 CNS.

28 Dr Nathalie L.J.T. Horbach, 'Nuclear Safety and Liability Conventions', in Nathalie L.J.T. Horbach (ed.), *Contemporary Developments in Nuclear Energy Law: Harmonising Legislation in CEEC/NIS* (The Hague, Kluwer Law International 1999) 8.

29 Carlton Stoiber, 'International Convention on Nuclear Safety: National Reporting as the Key to Effective Implementation', in Nathalie L.J.T. Horbach (ed.), *Contemporary Developments in Nuclear Energy Law: Harmonising Legislation in CEEC/NIS* (The Hague, Kluwer Law International 1999) 100.

set of externally imposed sanctions that could impede the development of civilian nuclear power.[30]

According to some commentators, preparation of a national report is a substantive obligation for Contracting Parties and failure to fulfil these procedural requirements would represent a serious breach of treaty obligations, given that the review process represents the sole 'enforcement' feature of the CNS regime.[31] A fundamental dilemma concerning national reports stems from the sometimes significant disparities in the nuclear power programmes of Contracting Parties. Variations in the size of civilian nuclear industries, and ways of managing and regulating them, reactor designs and differing legal, political and institutional arrangements make assessing compliance among the various Contracting Parties a complicated endeavour.[32]

Confidentiality of information

There are three aspects of confidentiality under the CNS. Firstly, the provisions of this Convention shall not affect the rights and obligations of the Contracting Parties under their law to protect information from disclosure. Such 'information' includes, *inter alia*, (i) personal data; (ii) information protected by intellectual property rights or by industrial or commercial confidentiality; and (iii) information relating to national security or to the physical protection of nuclear materials or nuclear installations. Secondly, when a Contracting Party provides information identified by it as protected under paragraph 1, such information shall be used only for the purposes for which it has been provided and its confidentiality shall be respected. Thirdly, the content of the debates during the reviewing of the reports at each meeting shall be confidential.[33] This confidentiality provision has been criticized as a hindrance to achieving transparency and openness in the safety process. According to one commentator:

> The primary objective of the CNS is to contribute to the further enhancement of nuclear safety world-wide and to reduce further the risks of a catastrophic nuclear reactor accident. The Convention can only help to advance this objective if contracting parties produce a candid, objective and transparent record of issues affecting nuclear safety and how they are being process.[34]

Weaknesses of the Convention on Nuclear Safety

Notwithstanding this, the Convention has numerous shortcomings. First, it does not require internationally uniform minimum safety standards. Instead of standards, the Convention requires adherence to a broader set of 'safety

30 Ibid.
31 Ibid.
32 Ibid, 101.
33 Article 27 CNS.
34 Carlton Stoiber (n 29) 113.

principles' that cannot be interpreted as standards. Second, the Convention cannot enforce its mandates through sanctions; it contains no provisions for enforcement or dispute resolution. The Convention is an 'incentive' instrument only in the sense that its implementation depends on undertaking national measures, exchange of information and reporting obligations. It depends for its effectiveness on a process of peer review. The lack of enforcement power harms the Convention's usefulness because Contracting Parties have less incentive to adopt safe measures. Third, the vague language gives states wide latitude in implementation possibilities, and therefore undercuts the assurance of safety. The Contention is also silent about environmental protection and environmental requirements such as environmental impact assessment. A final problem with the Convention's efficacy is that it was not signed by all states operating nuclear power plants.[35]

The current international legal framework for regulating nuclear safety is inadequate. This inadequacy is evidenced by the fact that, despite the Convention on Nuclear Safety, unsafe plants continue to operate, some safely designed plants lack adequate technology and management, and avoidable accidents continue to happen.[36] The international legal framework for nuclear safety should be stronger and more developed.

Convention on the Physical Protection of Nuclear Material 1980

This Convention deals with security of nuclear material. Transportation of nuclear fuel to and from nuclear power plants requires adequate packaging and regulatory measures to protect humans and the environment from exposed to hazards from radiation. Physical security of sensitive materials should also be ensured. This Convention is the only international legally binding undertaking in the area of physical protection of nuclear material. The Convention on the Physical Protection of Nuclear Material was adopted in 1980 and entered into force on 8 February 1987.

This Convention applies to nuclear material used for peaceful purposes while in international nuclear transport and in domestic use, storage and transport.[37] The Convention requires States Parties to take steps to ensure that during international or domestic nuclear transport, nuclear material within its territory or on board a ship or aircraft under its jurisdiction is protected at the levels described in Annex I.[38] The Convention imposes certain restrictions on the export of nuclear materials. Article 4 states that a State Party shall not export or import nuclear material unless the State Party has received assurances that such material will be protected during the international nuclear transport. Similarly, a State Party shall not allow

35 Karen McMillan, 'Strengthening the International Legal Framework for Nuclear Energy' (2000–2001) 13 *Georgetown International Environmental Law Review* 983–1031.

36 Ibid.

37 Article 2 of the Convention.

38 Article 3.

the transit of its territory by land or internal waterways or through its airports or seaports of nuclear material between states that are not parties to this Convention unless the State Party has received assurances that this nuclear material will be protected during international nuclear transport. Similar physical protection should be given to nuclear material being transported from a part of that state to another part of the same state through international waters or airspace. States Parties shall identify and make known to one another directly or through the International Atomic Energy Agency (IAEA) their central authority and point of contact having responsibility for physical protection of nuclear material and for the coordinating of recovery and response operations in the event of any unauthorized removal, use or alteration of nuclear material or in the event of credible threat thereof.[39] In the case of theft, robbery or any other unlawful taking of nuclear material, States Parties shall provide cooperation and assistance to the maximum feasible extent in the recovery and protection of such material to upon request of any state.[40] States Parties shall also inform other states, shall exchange information with one another, and coordinate their efforts through diplomatic channels to render assistance for recovery of nuclear material.[41] States shall make intentional commission of transfer, alteration, theft or robbery of nuclear material a criminal offence and establish jurisdiction over such crimes.[42] States Parties shall afford one another assistance in connection with criminal proceedings brought in respect of such offences.[43]

It establishes measures related to the prevention, detection and punishment of offences relating to theft or robbery of nuclear material. The Convention was amended in 2005 to strengthen its provisions. The amended Convention makes it legally binding for States Parties to protect nuclear facilities and material in peaceful domestic use, storage as well as transport. It also provides for expanded cooperation between and among States Parties regarding rapid measures to locate and recover stolen or smuggled nuclear material, mitigate any radiological consequences of sabotage, and prevent and combat related offences.[44]

UN Security Council Resolution 1540 on Nuclear Terrorism 2004

Given the potential involvement of non-state actors such as terrorist groups in obtaining nuclear material, in Resolution 1540 (2004) the Security Council decided that all states shall refrain from providing any form of support to non-state actors who attempt to develop, acquire, manufacture, possess, transport, transfer or use nuclear, chemical or biological weapons and their means of

39 Article 5(i).
40 Article 5(ii).
41 Article 5(iii)
42 Articles 7 & 8.
43 Article 13.
44 See https://www.iaea.org/publications/documents/conventions/convention-physical-protection-nuclear-material, accessed 10 July 2018.

delivery, in particular for terrorist purposes.[45] The Resolution requires all states to adopt and enforce appropriate laws to this effect to prevent the proliferation of these weapons and their means of delivery to non-state actors, in particular for terrorist purposes.[46] This Resolution is an important step in including non-state actors in the legal framework of nuclear security.

Convention for the Suppression of Acts of Nuclear Terrorism 2005

The Nuclear Terrorism Convention elaborates on acts of nuclear terrorism and prescribes that unlawful and intentional possession of radioactive material or making a nuclear device, or using radioactive material in a way which releases or risks the release of radioactive material is a criminal offence. The Convention applies exclusively to acts by individuals and not to acts by states or international organizations. Article 3 of the Convention specifies the scope of the Convention and makes it applicable only in a transboundary context, for example where the offence involves more than one state. Article 3 states that this Convention shall not apply where the offence is committed within a single state, the alleged offender and the victims are nationals of that state, the alleged offender is found in the territory of that state and no other state has a basis to exercise jurisdiction.

Under the Convention, States Parties shall adopt measures necessary to establish as criminal those offences under its national law those described in Article 2 of the Convention. and make those offences punishable by appropriate penalties.[47] The Convention intends to facilitate international cooperation through the sharing of information and the provision of assistance in the prevention, investigation, prosecution and extradition of persons who commit an offence involving the use of nuclear material and other radioactive substances or devices.[48] States Parties shall make every effort to adopt appropriate measures to ensure the protection of radioactive material[49] and to establish its jurisdiction over the offences.[50] This Convention fills a gap in the existing international legal framework on nuclear safety by provisions against nuclear terrorist acts using nuclear weapons, facilities and radioactive material. The Convention entered into force in July 2007.

ILO Convention (No. 115) Concerning the Protection of Workers against Ionizing Radiations 1960

This Convention aims to ensure effective protection of workers against ionizing radiations by prescribing that their exposure to it must be restricted to the lowest

45 UN Office for Disarmament Affairs, https://www.un.org/disarmament/wmd/sc1540/ accessed 10 July 2018.

46 Ibid.

47 Articles 5 and 6 of the Convention for the Suppression of Acts of Nuclear Terrorism 2005.

48 Ibid, Arts 7, 10, 11, 12.

49 Ibid, Art. 8.

50 Ibid, Art.9.

practicable level. For this purpose the States Parties must fix maximum permissible doses of radiation that the workers may receive and maximum permissible amounts that can be taken into the body of workers directly engaged in radiation work, as well as others who may be exposed.[51] The Convention contains provisions on warnings to be used to indicate radiation hazards, the instructions of workers on precautions and the monitoring of workers and workplaces.[52]

Additional Protocols to the Geneva Conventions of 1949 on Armed Conflict

The Geneva Conventions of 1949 and their Additional Protocols contain the most important rules that regulate the conduct of armed conflict and seek to limit its effects. Article 56 of Additional Protocol 1 and Article 15 of Additional Protocol II of the Geneva Conventions of 1949 relate to the protection of, among other things, nuclear electrical generating stations during armed conflicts. The protection accorded by the Protocol applies only to a limited category of nuclear installation. However, the phrase 'nuclear electrical generating stations' obviously includes nuclear power reactors. But it would not include nuclear research reactors, enrichment facilities, fuel fabrication facilities, reprocessing facilities, and spent fuel storage facilities.[53]

IAEA Safety Guide

The IAEA's function of setting safety standards derives from Article III.A.6 of its Statute which authorizes the IAEA to establish or adopt standards of safety for the protection of health and minimization of danger to life and property, and to provide for their application. It also requires that those standards be applied in three distinct fields: the IAEA's own operations and operations making use of materials, services, equipment, facilities and information made available by the Agency or at its request or under its control or supervision; secondly, to national operations carried out with Agency assistance or association; and finally the standards may serve as examples or guidelines for national regulatory authority.

With a view to ensuring the protection of people and the environment from the harmful effects of ionizing radiation, the IAEA safety standards establish fundamental safety principles, requirements and measures to control the radiation exposure of people and the release of radioactive material into the environment, to restrict the likelihood of events that might lead to a loss of control over a nuclear reactor core, nuclear chain reaction, radioactive source or any other source of radiation, and to mitigate the consequences of such events if they were

51 431 UNTS 41, Arts 3, 5, 6, 7 and 8.

52 Articles 9–11 ILO Convention.

53 Mohamed El Baradi, Edwin Nwogugu and John Rames, 'International Law and Nuclear Energy: Overview of the Legal Framework' (1995) 3 *IAEA Bulletin* 20–21.

to occur.[54] The standards apply to facilities and activities that give rise to radiation risks, including nuclear installations, the use of radiation and radioactive sources, the transport of radioactive material and the management of radioactive waste.

The IAEA Safety Guide on the Governmental, Legal and Regulatory Framework for Safety provides a comprehensive checklist of issues to be prescribed by national legislation and a list of competences and functions to be entrusted to the regulatory body. The IAEA Safety Guide covers the variety of issues to be regulated in the domain of civilian nuclear energy and encourages national regulatory bodies to cooperate with other relevant authorities. Depending on the safety matter, the IAEA differentiates between three categories of 'Safety Standards' covering different issues in relation to this radiation risk: Safety Fundamentals – which present the fundamental safety objective and principles of protection and safety, and provide the basis for the safety requirements; Safety Requirements – an integrated and consistent set of the requirements that must be fulfilled by countries to ensure the protection of people and the environment;[55] and Safety Guides – these provide 'recommendations and guidance on how to comply with the safety requirements'.[56] Although these standards are not considered binding, they have been widely accepted by the states in their laws regulating nuclear risks and nuclear facilities. The IAEA safety standards are a cornerstone of the global safety regime and constitute a useful tool for states to assess their performance under these international instruments.

Conclusion

The current international legal framework for regulating nuclear safety is inadequate. The Convention on Nuclear Safety is considered an 'incentive Convention', prescribing general safety rules without directly interfering in the competence of the national regulatory bodies. Responsibility for nuclear safety and nuclear security rests on each State Party. States should develop and establish effective national systems for nuclear safety and nuclear security. The legal framework should be further improved so that states are responsible under international law for any failure to exercise due diligence over the siting and operation of nuclear facilities and the transport and disposal of nuclear wastes.[57] Although the current nuclear safety regime has led to a significant improvement in nuclear safety, there remain serious environmental risks, which mandate an improved international nuclear safety regime. The safety regime should be further improved by drawing lessons

54 IAEA Safety Standards, Classification of Radioactive Waste, General Safety Guide IAEA Safety Standards Series No. GSG-1, IAEA, Vienna, 2009.

55 IAEA Safety Standards: The Global Reference for Protecting People and the Environment from Harmful Effects of Ionizing Radiation (June 2009), http://www-ns.iaea.org/downloads/standards/iaea-safety-standards-brochure.pdf, accessed 10 July 2018.

56 Ibid.

57 Ved P. Nanda, Jon M. Van Dyke, 'International Nuclear Law: An Introduction' (2006) 35(1) *Denver Journal of International Law and Policy* 47–65.

from the Fukushima accident, so that any nuclear power plant can withstand any natural calamity of catastrophic scale. At the national level, nuclear energy regulatory regimes should be strengthened to reflect the post-Fukushima safety requirement so that the operation of a nuclear power plant does not pose an unacceptable level of risk to the environment and humanity. Nuclear safety issues cannot be fully separated from the issue of nuclear security. Both nuclear safety and nuclear security should be treated as interrelated and mutually reinforcing, and the synergy between nuclear safety and nuclear security must be maximized and harmonized through a regulatory framework, monitoring and appropriate designing concepts.[58] National legal frameworks and measures on nuclear security should adopt strategies including ensuring safe and secure custody of sensitive nuclear materials, technologies and equipment; strengthen national export controls and border security; and apply the criminal law to non-state actors who are likely to be involved in illegal weapons programmes. However, both safety and security measures have in common the aim of protecting human life and health and the environment and these measures must be designed and implemented in an integrated manner so that each complements the other.

58 Sonal Gandhi and Jungmin Kang, 'Nuclear Safety and Nuclear Security Synergy' (n 3) 360.

6 Decommissioning of nuclear installations

Introduction

As commercial production of nuclear energy power is running into its sixth decade, a growing number of nuclear installations are at or reaching the decommissioning phase. Since the beginning of the commercial nuclear industry, as of July 2016, 157 civilian nuclear power reactors worldwide have been permanently shut down or are undergoing decommissioning.[1] They were either shut down at the end of their life as originally envisaged in the design, or prematurely closed as a result of financial, political or technical reasons. More than 56 per cent of all the operating reactors are more than 30 years old and about 15 per cent are more than 40 years old.[2] In addition, more than 480 research reactors and several hundred other fuel cycle facilities have been decommissioned or are undergoing decommissioning.[3] Decommissioning of the nuclear facilities poses a huge management, technological and environmental challenge for the international community as nearly 75 per cent of the total waste volume predicted to arise from the whole nuclear programme is from decommissioning and clearance of nuclear sites.[4] Decommissioning of nuclear installations may include the decommissioning of power plants, nuclear research reactors and nuclear fuel cycle facilities. Decommissioning is also a complex and multi-dimensional problem that involves both technical and non-technical aspects. In its broadest sense decommissioning covers all of the administrative and technical actions relating to early planning for cessation of operations and release of the site from nuclear regulatory control.[5] These actions may include early strategic and financial planning, removal of spent or unused fuel to a reprocessing or storage site, decontamination of

1 Nuclear Technology Review 2016, IAEA, available at https://www.iaea.org/About/Policy/GC/GC60/GC60InfDocuments/English/gc60inf-2_en.pdf, accessed 10 July 2018.

2 Ibid.

3 Ibid.

4 Environment Alert Bulletin, 'Nuclear Waste: Is Everything Under Control?,' UNEP, available at http://www.grid.unep.ch/products/3_Reports/ew_nuclear.en.pdf, accessed 10 July 2018.

5 'The Regulatory Challenges of Decommissioning Nuclear Reactors', Nuclear Energy Agency, OECD, 2003, 7.

structures and equipment, dismantling of plant and equipment, shipping radioactive and other waste to offsite disposal sites, remediation of contaminated land and remaining structures, and other related activities leading to an acceptable end state for the site.[6] Decommissioning requires activities such as planning, physical and radiological characterization, facility and site decontamination, and dismantling of materials.

The main regulatory objectives in the decommissioning process include: (a) the decommissioning activities must be conducted safely; (b) good waste management principles must be followed; and (c) the site is left in an acceptable end state.[7] The fundamental requirements of decommissioning safety are the protection of workers and the public against radiation, the management of industrial and non-radiological hazards and protection of the environment during project implementation and the post-implementation stage.[8]

Typically, the decommissioning of a nuclear facility is a long-term process and may involve a few years or even decades. As a consequence, decommissioning may be carried out in one continuous operation following shutdown or in a series of operations over time (phased decommissioning).[9] The relatively long time involved in the process demands that the health and environmental hazards and physical protection measures at the facility must be managed properly during this shutting-down process to protect the health and safety of the public and workers and to safeguard any nuclear materials.[10] However, the decommissioning plan should be prepared during operation. This is especially important in cases where a facility is unexpectedly shut down before the end of its lifetime, perhaps for economic reasons or because of political decisions or even an abnormal event that may result in serious damage to nuclear facility.[11] Decommissioning activities may involve many different organizations such as the regulatory body, operating organization or licence holder. However, the licence holder or operating organization of the installation undergoing decommissioning is ultimately responsible for the safety of the installation during the decommissioning operations.[12] In some countries the decommissioning of nuclear facilities requires a licensing process which includes an environmental impact assessment as well as aspects of radiological protection. The regulatory control of decommissioning can be done by a single overall licence, by separate licence, or by direct control by a regulatory body, whichever is considered to be most appropriate in the circumstances. However, the regulatory body should review and approve the selected decommissioning

6 Ibid.

7 Ibid, 8.

8 'Decommissioning of Nuclear Installations', IAEA, https://www.iaea.org/topics/decommissioning, accessed 11 July 2018.

9 Decommissioning of Nuclear Power Plants and Research Reactors Safety Guide, Safety Standard Series No. WS-G-2.1 IAEA, Vienna 1999, 3.

10 'The Regulatory Challenges of Decommissioning Nuclear Reactors' (n 5) 7.

11 Ibid, 10.

12 Decommissioning of Nuclear Power Plants and Research Reactors Safety Guide (n 9) 4.

option, decommissioning plans, and quality assurance programmes. The regulatory body has also the responsibility for assuring that decommissioning activities are conducted safely, radioactive materials and spent nuclear fuel are disposed of properly and the site is in an acceptable end state.

Regulatory issues in decommissioning

Generally, there should be a clear regulatory framework on the decommissioning of nuclear power plants. Regulatory tasks in the decommissioning of a reactor vary with reactor type, size and age and with the decommissioning option chosen.[13] The main regulatory challenges at different stages of decommissioning include the following issues:

Decommissioning plans

Decommissioning plans are needed during the operation of nuclear plants for the reasons explained above. At present, preliminary decommissioning plans are generally prepared before reactor operation but more detailed plans are required before decommissioning can start. Successful decommissioning depends on careful and organized planning. These plans must consider all aspects of the work, including radiation protection precautions for the decommissioning workers as well as for the public. Generally, final shutdown of a nuclear facility will be followed by a formal notification to the regulatory body and a public announcement of the shutdown. However, the operator can start decommissioning activities with regulatory approval. A decommissioning plan should be prepared for each reactor. The extent of such plans, their content and the degree of detail required may differ, depending on the complexity and hazard potential of the nuclear installation.[14] A survey of both radiological and non-radiological hazards should be carried out for the safety assessment of decommissioning activities.[15]

Facility shutdown activities

This group of activities includes permanent shutdown of the facility; removal of spent fuel and nuclear material; and decontamination. Decontamination aims at reduction of exposure during decommissioning activities; and minimization of the volume of the categories of materials to be classified. Spent fuel and nuclear material are transferred to the spent fuel pool or site storage facility. Radioactive and clean material removed from the facility is prepared for temporary storage, or for packaging, transport and final disposition. Immediate post-shutdown activities also include placing the facility in a safe and secure condition; removal of fuel and other

13 L. Lanni, 'Some Realities of Nuclear Power Plant Decommissioning' 20(6) *IAEA Bulletin* 25.
14 Decommissioning of Nuclear Power Plants and Research Reactors Safety Guide (n 9) 12.
15 Ibid, 19.

materials to a safe interim storage location; and documentation of the radioactive inventory. The regulatory framework of many countries on decommissioning requires environmental impact assessment, the dismantling of systems, structures, components and buildings, and shipping materials to a waste disposal facility.

Radiation protection, safety and security

The radiological protection and physical safety of workers is a key concern during the decommissioning process. At all phases of decommissioning, workers, the public and the environment should be properly protected from hazards from the decommissioning process. A thorough safety assessment of the hazards involved during decommissioning should be conducted to define protective measures.[16] The decommissioning plan must include radiation protection of both workers and members of the public, not only during the course of decommissioning but also as a result of any subsequent occupancy of the decommissioned site.[17] Radiation protection in a decommissioning operation calls for: (1) a detailed knowledge of the radioactivity at various locations in the plant; (2) a physical description of each area of the facility; (3) an assessment of decommissioning procedures before and during the operation to ensure that worker and public radiological safety is adequate; and (4) continued environmental monitoring while decommissioning is in progress.[18] The radiation protection programme should ensure that radiation protection is optimized and that doses are kept within appropriate limits. Although the principles and aims of radiation protection during operations and during decommissioning are fundamentally the same, the methods and procedures of implementation of radiation protection may be different.[19] Article 26 of the Joint Convention on Spent Fuel Management is concerned with radiation protection and safety during decommissioning of a nuclear facility. It provides that each Contracting Party shall take appropriate steps to ensure the safety of decommissioning of a nuclear facility. Such steps include ensuring qualified staff and adequate financial resources; measures of operational radiation protection, discharges and unplanned and uncontrolled releases; emergency preparedness; and keeping records of information important to decommissioning.

A key safety and security question concerns the transportation of the spent fuel after a cooling period to a storage site or a reprocessing facility. Ensuring safety and security requires the training of workers, emergency planning, programmes such as fire protection, quality assurance and oversight, protection against diversion of nuclear materials to unauthorized uses or sabotage during decommissioning.[20] Site security, surveillance and maintenance are needed for the safety of the facility during the decommissioning process.

16 Decommissioning of Nuclear Power Plants and Research Reactors Safety Guide (n 9) 5.
17 Ibid, 6.
18 Lanni (n 13) 25.
19 Decommissioning of Nuclear Power Plants and Research Reactors Safety Guide (n 9) 26.
20 'The Regulatory Challenges of Decommissioning Nuclear Reactors' (n 5) 21.

Radioactive waste management

Radioactive waste is an inevitable outcome of any decommissioning operation. Usually, wastes generated in the course of decommissioning are different from wastes routinely handled during the operational phase of a nuclear power plant. A significant amount of waste is generated from the decommissioning of a nuclear facility. A waste management plan should be part of the overall decommissioning plan, to consider the different categories of waste produced during decommissioning and aim at the safe management of such wastes.[21] In order to conduct decommissioning of a nuclear facility successfully, a repository for disposing of low-level and intermediate-level radioactive waste is needed for storing such wastes. When no repository is available, new interim waste storage capacity will have to be constructed. The availability of disposal facilities greatly affects the degree of decontamination and dismantlement of radioactive wastes.[22] According to IAEA Safety Guide on Decommissioning, a significant reduction in volumes of radioactive waste can be achieved through decontamination programmes, controlled dismantling techniques, contamination control, sorting of waste materials, effective processing and administrative controls and thereby reducing radiation exposure to workers and the public.[23]

Decommissioning costs

A major concern of the public and operators of nuclear facilities is the cost of decommissioning.

Successful completion of decommissioning activities is dependent on adequate funds to complete the work without risk to public and worker health and safety or to the environment. The decommissioning plans should include cost estimation and a clearly defined and reliable source of funding for these activities.[24] The funding for decommissioning must be sufficient, available and transparently managed.[25] The cost of decommissioning should reflect all activities described in the decommissioning plan, including management of waste, remediation and environmental protection, maintenance, dismantling and decontamination. The regulatory framework should clearly identify funds for decommissioning.

The health and safety of current and future generations is the primary concern of decommissioning and decommissioning funding. Ultimately, the availability of adequate funds for decommissioning is linked to the safety and protection of current and future generations. Thus, funding for the costs of decommissioning nuclear power facilities should be guided by the principle of avoiding imposition of undue burdens on future generations.[26] Sound financial provisions should be

21 Decommissioning of Nuclear Power Plants and Research Reactors Safety Guide (n 9) 28.
22 'The Regulatory Challenges of Decommissioning Nuclear Reactors' (n 5) 22.
23 Decommissioning of Nuclear Power Plants and Research Reactors Safety Guide (n 9) 29.
24 'The Regulatory Challenges of Decommissioning Nuclear Reactors' (n 5) 10.
25 'Financial Aspects of Decommissioning', IAEA-TECDOC-1476, 2005.
26 Financing the Decommissioning of Nuclear Facilities, OECD 2016 NEA No. 7326, 7.

arranged to ensure that all decommissioning costs are covered to reduce the potential risks of residual unfunded liabilities and burden on future generations, while ensuring environmental protection.[27] The amount of funding needed is based on the establishment of a decommissioning plan estimating the decommissioning costs, and a waste management plan estimating the associated waste management costs. In addition, these cost estimates should take into account the analysis of associated risks and uncertainties. The cost can include facility shutdown activities, procurement of general equipment and material, dismantling activities, decontamination, storage, fuel and nuclear material transportation, disposal, site security, site restoration, and clean-up.

Remediation

The term 'remediation' refers to actions taken to reduce the impact from contamination in land areas and in the associated groundwater in order to leave the site in a state that is suitable for re-use.[28] In the decommissioning of nuclear facilities in many countries, remedial actions are required to enable sites or parts of sites to be reused for other purposes. Remediation has usually been considered as the last in a sequence of decommissioning steps.[29] The goal of nuclear site remediation varies from cost-effective risk reduction and protection of soil and groundwater, restoration to a greenfield site, to clearance for unrestricted use of the land which was previously contaminated.[30]

Social and environmental issues in decommissioning

Social and environmental issues are becoming more important aspects of the decommissioning process. In many cases, the shut-down of nuclear facilities may have negative impacts on the livelihood of the local communities that have developed around these facilities as the community infrastructures may need to be dismantled due to decommissioning. During the decommissioning of nuclear power plants or research reactors, radioactive and non-radioactive pollutants may be discharged to the environment. These social and environmental aspects of decommissioning should be addressed in the regulatory framework. In particular, decommissioning may generate public interest and concern over the social and environmental issues relating to the risk of radioactive releases during decommissioning, waste disposal and the construction of a spent fuel storage facility,

27 Ibid.

28 'Nuclear Site Remediation and Restoration during Decommissioning of Nuclear Installations', A Report by the NEA Co-operative Programme on Decommissioning, OECD 2014 NEA No. 7192, Nuclear Energy Agency and Organisation for Economic Co-operation and Development.

29 Ibid.

30 Ibid, 16.

or an interim radioactive waste storage facility on the site.[31] To address these concerns and to build public confidence in the process, public consultation may be useful. A stakeholder participation plan may be incorporated in the regulatory framework to integrate the stakeholders' views on the important aspects of the decommissioning process.[32]

Conclusion

Decommissioning a nuclear facility may involve new issues and challenges regarding safety, liability, public interest and environmental protection which are quite different from those during operation. In particular, local people surrounding the nuclear facility should be protected from radioactive releases during the decommissioning process, and they should be kept informed about the decommissioning process and about plans for the long-term condition of the site.[33] Decommissioning should be carried out under stringent regulatory regimes in order to ensure that the safety, security, and environmental protection are maintained.

31 'The Regulatory Challenges of Decommissioning Nuclear Reactors' (n 5) 17.
32 Ibid, 26.
33 'The Regulatory Challenges of Decommissioning Nuclear Reactors' (n 5) 25–26.

7 Legal regime on third-party nuclear liability

Introduction

The legal regime on third-party nuclear liability was developed by the international community during the 1960s in order to address potential catastrophic risks associated with the nuclear energy industry. But owing to the magnitude of the risk involved and the characteristics of the type of damage that can be caused by nuclear accident, this liability regime had to depart from the traditional concept of liability, for example liability based on fault,[1] and in respect of nuclear damage, strict and exclusive liability is applied. It is well established that damage caused by nuclear accidents is not usually limited to the state where the accident occurs but also affects neighbouring or more distant states. Transboundary harm is more likely in cases of accidents involving border nuclear installations. Transboundary damage may also occur in the case of transportation of nuclear material through more than one country. Liability can be imposed for nuclear damage which can include loss of life or personal injury caused by nuclear accidents or nuclear wastes. The legal framework on third-party nuclear liability aims to ensure adequate compensation for damage to persons and property resulting from a nuclear accident, and to encourage industry to develop nuclear technology. The development of nuclear liability is treated as one of the cornerstones of public confidence and another pillar of the international nuclear safety regime. The concept of third-party nuclear liability is based on some well-established principles of environmental liability. Liability for environmental damage at international level arises where a state permits activities which cause damage to its own environment; where a state permits activities which cause damage to the environment of another state; and where a state permits damage to the environment in an area beyond its national jurisdiction. Environmental damage encompasses property damage, personal injury and economic damage.[2]

1 Dr Nathalie L.J.T. Horbach, 'Lacunae of International Nuclear Liability Agreements', in Horbach (ed.), *Contemporary Developments in Nuclear Energy Law: Harmonising Legislation in CEEC/NIS* (The Hague, Kluwer Law International 1999) 43.

2 Lucas Bergkamp, *Liability and Environment* (The Hague, Kluwer Law International 2001) 9.

The concept of environmental liability

Environmental liability has emerged as one of the main instruments used to combat environmental pollution. Environmental liabilities refer to the future environmental costs that should be paid for damaging the environment by those that cause the damage. A balanced liability regime should ensure that charges for environmental liability adequately reflect the costs inflicted on the environment and are used to rectify environmental damage. Compensation as a result of liability is a well-established norm under international environmental law.[3] An environmental liability regime has many objectives, such as compensation to victims, an increase in efficiency through cost internalization, as means of penalizing wrongful conduct, a deterrence effect on the polluter that caused environmental damage, an environmental risk-spreading function, and ensuring distributive and corrective justice.[4]

While environmental legislation and international instruments lay down norms and procedures aimed at preserving the environment, liability is a necessary complement to ensure that persons responsible for non-compliance resulting in environmental damage face the prospect of having to pay for restoration of the affected environment or compensating for the damage caused. Under international environmental law, there are two types of liability regime – state liability and civil liability. State liability refers to the liability of a state and other international persons under public international law; whereas, civil liability refers to the liability of any legal or natural person (which may include a state) under the rules of national law adopted pursuant to international treaty obligations establishing harmonized minimum standards.[5] State liability for environmental damage is premised upon breach of an international legal obligation established by treaty, or by a rule of customary international law or possibly under general principles of international law.[6] However, all environmental damage might not give rise to state liability. There are no agreed international standards that establish a threshold for environmental damage that triggers liability. State practice and decisions of international tribunals suggest that environmental damage must be significant or substantial for liability to be triggered.[7] Only a small number of treaties provide for state liability for environmental damage. The main treaties that incorporate state liability include the Convention on International Liability for Damage Caused by Space Objects (1972 Space Liability Convention) and the Law of the Sea Convention 1982. For example, the 1972 Space Liability Convention provides that, subject to some restrictions, a state that launches a space

3 Detlef F. Sprinzl and Steffen von Bünau, 'The Compensation Fund for Climate Impacts' (2013) 5(3) *Journal of Weather, Climate and Society* 1–27.

4 Bergkamp (n 2) 69–77.

5 Philippe Sands and Jacqueline Peel, *Principles of International Law* (3rd edn, Cambridge University Press 2012) 700.

6 Ibid, 705.

7 Ibid, 708.

object is absolutely liable to pay compensation for damage caused by its space object on the surface of the earth or to aircraft in flight. According to Article 235 of UNCLOS, states are responsible for the fulfilment of their international obligations concerning the protection and preservation of the marine environment. They shall be liable in accordance with international law in case of breach of such obligation.

On the other hand, civil liability under international law refers to the liability of actors, under the rules of national law adopted pursuant to treaties, for breach of national civil liability rules or set minimum standards.[8] It entails rules to define the activities or substances (covered), define the damage, channel liability, establish a standard of care, provide for liability amounts, insurance or financial security, identify a court or tribunal to receive the claims, and provide for recognition and enforcement of judgment.[9] Civil liability regimes for environmental damage can be only applied to situations in which (1) there is one or more identifiable actors (polluters), (2) the damage is concrete and quantifiable, and (3) it is possible to establish a causal link between the damage and the actions of the identified polluter(s).[10] As a result, it is much easier to establish personal liability for activities such as industrial accidents, hazardous waste disposal, or water pollution.

The scope of the environmental liability regime has been expanded and elaborated considerably in recent times by both international soft and hard law environmental instruments. The existing environmental soft law instruments, such as the Rio Declaration 1992, requires states to expand environmental liability as a way of integrating environmental costs into the production process and providing compensation to the victims of pollution and other environmental damage.[11]

International environmental treaties that impose liability rules include Conventions on nuclear energy, oil pollution, hazardous waste, transportation of dangerous goods, Antarctic resources and space activities. The liability schemes set forth in these Conventions have certain features in common:

> First, they provide for strict liability, irrespective of any fault of the liable person. Second, they typically impose a cap on liability, and in some instances exclude certain types of damage and compensation may not be available for economic loss or pain and suffering. Third, liability is exclusive in that no other person other than the one identified in the scheme can be held liable. Fourth, the defenses available to defendants are listed exhaustively; these defenses, but no other defenses, may be invoked. . . . Sixth, liability insurance or financial security is often required. Seventh, to supplement compensation

8 Ibid

9 Ibid.

10 European Commission, *White Paper on Environmental Liability* (Feb 2000) http://ec.europa.eu/environment/legal/liability/pdf/el_full.pdf accessed 11 July 2018.

11 The Rio Declaration on Environment and Development, U.N.Doc. A/CONF.151/5/Rev. 1(1992) 31 ILM 874, 879.

> through liability, a fund is established or contracting states are required to contribute.[12]

There are basically two types of civil liability for environmental damage – fault-based and strict liability. Both at the international and national level, existing environmental liability systems include a mix of fault-based and strict, i.e., no fault, liability rules. 'Fault' exists when someone fails to perform a duty or observe a standard.[13] In fault-based liability, generally the cause of damage is exempted from liability if the perpetrator shows that he/she has taken necessary and practicable measures to prevent such damage, i.e., exercised due diligence. If liability is strict, fault need not be established. Absence of intention to violate a duty of care or a norm and absence of negligence need to be shown for a case to prevail. However, strict liability regimes typically provide for some defences; a person may be exonerated from liability if the damage was caused by, for instance, an act of God (or natural disaster), an act of war, or by the interference of a third party. Strict liability has become an increasingly common form of liability for environmental harm. The rationale for strict liability is that an actor that profits from potentially harmful or inherently dangerous activities should be liable for damage that occurred as a result of the harmful activity – an application of the 'polluter pays principle'. Thus, the strict liability rules are necessary to implement the polluter pays principle. According to the polluter pays principle, all external environmental cost caused by an activity must be internalised so that the production cost reflects the full cost.

While fault liability is the normal rule, strict liability in the environmental area is imposed only with respect to certain specific and well-circumscribed activities.[14] However, recent international and national environmental liability laws on ultra-hazardous activities are invariably based on strict, not fault liability.

Several treaties establish rules on civil liability for environmental or related damage, generally with respect to specific activities, such as nuclear installations, oil pollution and hazardous wastes. These include the Convention on Civil Liability for Oil Pollution Damage 1969, the Convention on the Establishment of an International Fund for Compensation for Oil Pollution Damage 1971, the Convention on Civil Liability for Oil Pollution Damage resulting from Exploration for and Exploitation of Seabed Mineral Resources 1977 and the 1996 International Convention on Liability and Compensation for Damage in connection with the Carriage of Hazardous and Noxious Substances by Sea. Most of the treaty regimes provide prevention of transboundary harm, define the activities or substances and the harm covered, the criteria for establishing who is liable, the standard of care that must be exercised to avoid liability, and provide exceptions from liability. Most treaties set limitations on the amount of liability and

12 Bergkamp (n 2) 34.

13 Alexandre Kiss and Dinah Shelton, *International Environmental Law* (3rd edn, Transnational Publishers 2004) 20.

14 Bergkamp (n 2) 5.

provisions for enforcement of judgments. In addition, many of them include provisions on mandatory insurance or other financial guarantees, establish funds, and aim to regulate compensation for victims of accidents involving the transport of hazardous and noxious substances.

In particular, in view of the fact that a nuclear accident may have a transboundary effect, the principle of prevention of transboundary effects is applied by the nuclear liability regime. The 1996 ICJ Advisory Opinion on the *Legality of the Threat or Use of Nuclear Weapons* explicitly stated: 'The existence of the general obligation of States to ensure that activities within their jurisdiction and control respect the environment of other States or of areas beyond national control is now part of the corpus of international law relating to the environment.'

According to Oskar Schachter, there must be four conditions for environmental damage to fall within the definition of trans-boundary environmental harm: First, the harm must be a result of human activity; second, the harm must result from a physical consequence of that human activity; third, there must be transboundary effects and fourth, the harm must be significant or substantial.[15] Environmental harm that may be caused by any potential nuclear accident can meet all these criteria.

Liability regime under nuclear treaties

A nuclear liability regime serves the function of nuclear safety as well as providing compensation to the potential victims after a nuclear accident. An effective and transparent nuclear liability regime is also important from the context of the number of states that aim to build nuclear energy plants for the first time.[16] The nuclear liability regime is based on exceptional risks arising from nuclear activities where common rules may not be appropriate, and secondly, on the potential transboundary impact of such risks. The transboundary nature of nuclear accidents dictates that a nuclear liability regime should be based on the principle of prevention of transboundary harm and burden-sharing by third parties. Although nuclear safety standards have been improved and consequently the risk of an accident is lower, the magnitude of damage that could result to third parties from a nuclear accident is potentially significant. This led to the development of a special legal regime for the nuclear industry to provide for compensation for the victims of a nuclear accident. This special legal regime is different from the ordinary rules of tort and contract. The nuclear liability regime performs several goals: to provide adequate protection to the public from possible damage; to ensure that the growth of the nuclear industry is protected from excessively burdensome liabilities; to facilitate international security market resources to ensure that sufficient financial security is

15 O. Schachter, *International Law in Theory and Practice* (Dordrecht, Martinus Nijhoff 1991) 36–38.

16 Raphael J. Heffron, Stephen F. Ashley and William J. Nuttall, 'The Global Nuclear Liability Regime Post Fukushima Daiichi' (2016) 90 *Progress in Nuclear Energy* 1–10.

available to satisfy potentially large claims; and to ensure that liability and compensation mechanisms address the transboundary nature of nuclear damage.[17]

The nuclear liability regime does not, however, address damage that may be caused by radioactive sources outside of a nuclear installation. The international nuclear liability regime is primarily contained in two sets of instruments: the International Atomic Energy Agency's 1963 Vienna Convention on Civil Liability for Nuclear Damage,[18] which entered into force in 1977, and the OECD's Paris Convention on Third Party Liability in the Field of Nuclear Energy of 1960,[19] which entered into force in 1968. These two instruments have been expanded by protocols and other treaties adopted subsequently to address new challenges that have emerged after nuclear accidents.

Paris Convention on Nuclear Third Party Liability 1960

The Paris Convention is open to any OECD country as of right and to any non-member with the consent of the other contracting parties. Under Article 3 of the Paris Convention, an operator can be liable for certain damage, (1) caused by a nuclear incident in a 'nuclear installation', or (2) involving 'nuclear substances' coming from such installation. The Paris Convention provides for compensation for injury to or loss of life of any person, and for damage to, or loss of any property caused by a nuclear accident in a nuclear installation or during the transport of nuclear substances to and from installations. It does not cover damage to the nuclear installation itself. Facilities which do not involve high levels of radioactivity, such as those for uranium mining and milling and for the production of radioisotopes, are covered by general tort law rather than the Convention.[20] The Paris Convention generally applies when an accident causing damage occurs in the territory of a party and damage from this accident is suffered in the territory of a party, including the territorial sea. The Paris Convention also applies to nuclear substances in transport from one nuclear operator to another.

The Paris Convention aims to harmonise national legislation with regard to third party liability and insurance against the liability of the operator. It applies only to nuclear incidents occurring, and damage suffered by individuals or their property, in the territory of the Contracting States. But states may extend the scope of damage suffered or incidents occurring in the territory of non-Contracting States

17 Nuclear Energy in a Sustainable Development Perspective (200) NEA, OECD 42.

18 Vienna Convention on Civil Liability for Nuclear Damage, opened for signature May 21, 1963, 1063 U.N.T.S. 266, available at https://www.iaea.org/sites/default/files/infcirc500.pdf, accessed 12 July 2018.

19 Convention on Third Party Liability in the Field of Nuclear Energy, opened for signature 29 July 1960, 956 U.N.T.S. 264.

20 Paris Convention on Nuclear Third Party Liability, NEA, https://www.oecd-nea.org/law/paris-convention.html, accessed 12 July 2018.

within their national legislation.[21] It defines 'nuclear installation',[22] 'nuclear incident'[23] and 'operator'[24] of a nuclear installation. The Paris Convention establishes a third party liability regime in the nuclear field for the first time, imposing liability on operators for damage to third parties and requiring operators to maintain financial security to cover such liability.[25]

Brussels Supplementary Convention 1963

It was realized by the State Parties to the Paris Convention that the amount of liability provided for in this Convention would not likely be adequate to cover the damage suffered in the event of a serious nuclear accident. To remedy that deficiency, the Convention Supplementary to the Paris Convention of 29 July 1960 ('Brussels Supplementary Convention') was adopted in 1963 to provide additional funds to compensate for damage as a result of a nuclear incident. Under the Brussels Supplementary Convention additional compensation beyond that provided for under the Paris Convention would be made available to victims through the establishment of a three-tier system: the first tier is provided by the operator; the second tier is provided by the state in which the nuclear installation of the liable operator is situated (unless the national law transfers the obligation to the operator); and the third tier is contributed jointly by all Contracting Parties to the Brussels Supplementary Convention.[26] The Convention, which entered into force on 4 December 1974, is open only to Paris Convention states. According to Article 3, the compensation due in respect of nuclear damage shall be provided up to the amount of €1500 million per incident.[27] No state may become

21 Article 2 of the 1960 Paris Convention and modified by the Protocol to the Convention.
22 Article 1(a)(ii): 'Nuclear installation' means reactors other than those comprised in any means of transport; factories for the manufacture or processing of nuclear substances; factories for the separation of isotopes of nuclear fuel; factories for the reprocessing of irradiated nuclear fuel; facilities for the storage of nuclear substances other than storage incidental to the carriage of such substances; and such other installations in which there are nuclear fuel or radioactive products or waste.
23 Article 1(a)(i): 'A nuclear incident' means any occurrence or succession of occurrences having the same origin which causes damage, provided that such occurrence or succession of occurrences, or any of the damage caused, arises out of or results either from the radioactive properties, or a combination of radioactive properties with toxic, explosive, or other hazardous properties of nuclear fuel or radioactive products or waste or with any of them, or from ionizing radiations emitted by any source of radiation inside a nuclear installation.
24 Article 1(a)(vi): 'Operator' in relation to a nuclear installation is a person designated or recognised by the competent public authority as the operator of that installation and may be a private entity or the state itself.
25 See Arts 4 and 10 of the Paris Convention.
26 'Progress towards a global nuclear liability regime', *Nuclear Law Bulletin* No. 93, OECD 2014 NEA No. 7181.
27 Convention of 31 January 1963 Supplementary to the Paris Convention of 29 July 1960 on Third Party Liability in the Field of Nuclear Energy, as Amended by the Additional Protocol of 28 January 1964, by the Protocol of 16 November 1982 and by the Protocol of 12 February 2004, available at https://www.oecd-nea.org/law/Unofficial%20consolidated%20Brussels%20Supplementary%20Convention.pdf, accessed 14 July 2018.

or remain a Contracting Party to the Brussels Supplementary Convention unless it is already a Contracting Party to the Paris Convention. The Brussels Supplementary Convention will remain in place only for as long as the Paris Convention also remains in force.[28]

Paris Protocol 2004

This Protocol was adopted to bring the Paris Convention more into line with the IAEA Conventions amended in 1997. The principal objective of the Protocol was to provide more compensation to more people for a wider scope of nuclear damage. Under the Paris Protocol, the amount of a nuclear operator's liability is increased to a new minimum of €700 million.[29] In addition, the minimum liability amount applicable to low-risk installations and transport activities is raised to €70 million and €80 million respectively.[30] Another principal amendment to the Paris Convention is the introduction of a broad definition of 'nuclear damage'. In addition to personal injury and property damage, the Protocol includes certain types of economic loss, the cost of measures to reinstate a significantly impaired environment, loss of income resulting from that impaired environment and the cost of preventative measures, including loss or damage caused by such measures.[31]

The Protocol also applies to more nuclear installations, including those that are in the course of being decommissioned and all nuclear installations for the disposal of nuclear substances.[32]

Under the Protocol, more victims will be entitled to compensation as it has also expanded the geographical scope of coverage of the Convention. While under the Paris Convention a nuclear incident must occur in the territory of a Contracting Party and damage must be suffered there before the Convention will apply, the Protocol will also apply to nuclear damage suffered in a non-Convention State if (a) it is a party to the Vienna Convention and the 1988 Joint Protocol, or (b) it has no nuclear installations, or (c) its nuclear liability legislation affords equivalent reciprocal benefits and is based on principles identical to those

28 Brussels Supplementary Convention, NEA, available at https://www.oecd-nea.org/law/brussels-supplementary-convention.html, accessed 12 July 2018.

29 Article 7 of the Protocol, available at https://cil.nus.edu.sg/wp-content/uploads/formidable/14/2004-Protocol-to-Amend-the-Paris-Convention-on-Nuclear-Third-Party-Liability.pdf, accessed 12 July 2018.

30 Ibid.

31 Article 1 of the Protocol.

32 Article 1(ii) of the Protocol: 'Nuclear installation. means reactors other than those comprised in any means of transport; factories for the manufacture or processing of nuclear substances; factories for the separation of isotopes of nuclear fuel; factories for the reprocessing of irradiated nuclear fuel; facilities for the storage of nuclear substances other than storage incidental to the carriage of such substances; installations for the disposal of nuclear substances; any such reactor, factory, facility or installation that is in the course of being decommissioned; and such other installations in which there are nuclear fuel or radioactive products or waste.

contained in the Paris Convention.[33] The Protocol also recognizes the concerns of coastal states which allow maritime shipments of nuclear substances through their waters, by including provisions to ensure that where a nuclear incident occurs in the exclusive economic zone of a Paris Convention State, jurisdiction over claims for nuclear damage arising from that incident shall lie only with the courts of that coastal state.[34]

But the Paris Protocol is not yet in force. As of January 2018, only Switzerland and Norway had ratified the Protocol.

Vienna Convention on Civil Liability for Nuclear Damage 1963

Unlike the Paris Convention which is regional in scope, the Vienna Convention on Civil Liability for Nuclear Damage is a global treaty and establishes a global nuclear liability regime. According to the Convention, each nuclear installation must have an operator. The operator of a nuclear installation shall be exclusively liable for nuclear damage caused by a nuclear incident and such liability shall be absolute.[35] According to Vienna Convention, the upper ceiling for the operator is not fixed but may be limited by legislation by each Contracting Party.[36] The operator will be exonerated from liability only if he proves, for example, that the nuclear incident was directly due to armed conflict, hostilities, civil war or insurrection, or that it resulted wholly or partly either from gross negligence of the victim or from an act or omission of the victim with intent to cause harm.[37] The Convention does not provide a maximum amount of liability but it sets a minimum amount of liability.[38] The Vienna Convention provides that any Installation State may limit the operator's liability in its national legislation. But the minimum amount of the operator's liability by the Installation State may not be less than US$5 million for any one nuclear incident.[39] Any action to realize compensation under this Convention shall be brought within ten years from the date of the nuclear incident.[40] The operator is required to maintain insurance or other financial security covering his liability for nuclear damage but the Installation State shall provide the necessary funds to the extent that the insurance maintained by the operator is inadequate to satisfy such claim.[41] The nature, form and extent of the compensation shall be governed by the law of the competent

33 Article 2 of the Protocol.
34 Article 13 of the Protocol.
35 Articles II(i) and IV(i) of the Convention.
36 See the consolidated text of the Vienna Convention on Civil Liability for Nuclear Damage of 21 May 1963 as amended by the protocol of 12 September 1997, available at https://www.iaea.org/About/Policy/GC/GC41/GC41InfDocuments/English/gc41inf-13-add1_en.pdf, accessed 12 July 2018.
37 Article IV(2) and IV(3) of the Convention.
38 Article V of the Convention.
39 Article V of the Convention.
40 Article VI(I) of the Convention.
41 Article VII(1) of the Convention.

court.[42] Jurisdiction over nuclear damage claims lies only with the courts of the state in which the accident occurred.[43] Although the operator is exclusively liable for compensation, he shall have a right of recourse in two circumstances: (a) if this is expressly provided for by a contract in writing; or (b) if the nuclear incident results from an act or omission done with intent to cause damage.[44]

Vienna Protocol 1997

This Protocol to the 1963 Vienna Convention was adopted in 1997 and came into force in 2003. It provides for a broader scope of nuclear damage, increases the period during which claims may be brought, extends the geographical coverage of damage covered, increases amount of liability of an operator of a nuclear installation and enhanced means for securing adequate compensation. The main features of the Vienna Protocol can be described as the following:

Broader definition of nuclear damage

The definition of 'nuclear damage' is essential for the proper functioning of the regime which aims to provide fair compensation for victims in the event of a nuclear incident. The 1997 Vienna Protocol broadens the definition of nuclear damage. The definition of nuclear damage in the 1963 Convention was too narrow, being simply '(i) loss of life, (ii) any personal injury or any loss of, or damage to, property'. The definition of nuclear damage under the Protocol also includes economic loss arising from death, personal injury or damage to property; the costs of measures of reinstatement of impaired environment; loss of income incurred as a result of significant impairment of that environment and the cost of preventative measures. The preventative measures covered by the definition include all reasonable measures which remain to be taken after the preventative measures, namely clean-up measures aimed at removing the contamination, and restoration measures which are taken after the contamination has been removed in order to reinstate the environment to its condition prior to the nuclear incident.[45]

However, the definition of nuclear damage under the Protocol does not include environmental damage; rather, it contains the costs of measures of reinstatement of impaired environment. 'Measures of reinstatement' encompass any reasonable measures but subject to approval of the competent authorities of the state and the aim of which is to reinstate or restore damaged or destroyed components of the environment.[46] Exclusion of environmental damage from the scope of

42 Article VIII of the Convention.

43 Article XI of the Convention.

44 Article X of the Convention.

45 Vedran Soljan, 'The New Definition of Nuclear Damage in the 1997 Protocol to Amend the 1963 Vienna Convention on Civil Liability for Nuclear Damage', in *Reform of Nuclear Civil Liability*, OECD Budapest Symposium, NEA, 2000.

46 Ibid.

nuclear damage greatly reduces the total number of possible claimants following a nuclear accident.

This definition leaves it to the law of the competent court to decide to what extent these aspects of damage may qualify for compensation. Therefore, the Protocol has broadened the definition of nuclear damage, but at the same time has recognised the existing differences in comparative legislation, leaving the extent of damage to be determined ultimately by the law of the competent court.[47] Such a solution makes compensation for nuclear damage dependent on the interpretation of the law of the competent court on the notions of economic loss, environmental damage and preventative measures.[48]

Definition of 'nuclear incident'

Under the protocol, the definition of 'nuclear incident' was extended to include incidents creating 'a grave and imminent threat' of causing nuclear damage.

Geographical scope

While the 1963 Vienna Convention did not contain an explicit provision on the geographical scope of its application, the Vienna Protocol extended the coverage to nuclear damage 'wherever suffered' and incidents occurring in the European Economic Zone. But there is one exception to this coverage rule: the legislation of the Installation State may exclude damage suffered in the territory of a non-Contracting State which at the time of the incident has a nuclear installation in its territory or in any maritime zones and does not afford 'equivalent reciprocal benefits'.'[49] While the Vienna Protocol does not clarify the exact meaning of 'equivalent reciprocal benefits', it means that victims that are nationals of non-nuclear states, even if they are not party to any international nuclear liability agreement, will have to be compensated equally with other victims. It can be also be inferred that the exclusion of damage suffered in a non-contracting nuclear state is based on the fact that the legislation of that state does not provide for compensation for damage suffered by victims in a State Party to the Vienna Protocol.[50]

Scope of the application

The 1963 Vienna Convention did not clearly state whether it was applicable for nuclear installations used for peaceful purposes only. But the 1997 Vienna

47 Ibid.

48 Vanda Lamm, 'The Protocol Amending the 1963 Vienna Convention' (1998) 63 *Nuclear Law Bulletin* 14.

49 Article 1A.2 and 1A.3.

50 The 1997 Vienna Convention on Civil Liability for Nuclear Damage and the 1997 Convention on Supplementary Compensation for Nuclear Damage- Explanatory Texts (2007) *IAEA International Law Series No. 3*, Vienna, IAEA 30.

Protocol explicitly excludes its application to nuclear installations used for non-peaceful or military purpose. It means that victims of damage resulting from the nuclear installations for military purposes will be deprived of benefit from the international liability regime, which remains one of the weaknesses of the Vienna Protocol.[51]

The Vienna Protocol has also broadened the definition of 'nuclear installation'. The Vienna Convention defines it as any nuclear reactor, any factory using nuclear fuel for the production of nuclear material and any nuclear storage facility.[52] This definition excluded additional types of installation which may involve risks of a considerable magnitude, such as radioactive waste disposal facilities. But the 1997 Protocol added 'such other installations in which there are nuclear fuel or radioactive products or waste as the Board of Governors of the International Atomic Energy Agency shall from time to time determine'.[53]

Amendment of liability amount

The existing liability limit under the 1963 Vienna Convention was grossly inadequate, particularly in the absence of a system of supplementary compensation whereby public funds could be made available to compensate for damage in excess of that amount. It also appeared to be too low to cover all possible losses arising from a nuclear incident. The 1997 Vienna Protocol substantially increases the liability limit for any nuclear incident up to at least 300 million SDRs from the previous limit of US$5 million. However, the Installation State can limit the operator's liability either to that amount or to an amount of at least 150 million SDRs, provided that it makes public funds available to compensate damage in excess of that amount up to 300 million SDRs.[54]

Exoneration

The Vienna Convention provided for possible exoneration of the operator's liability in case of an exceptional natural disaster. But under the Vienna Protocol the possible exoneration of operator's liability in case of a grave natural disaster of an exceptional character is omitted, taking into account the technological progress in design and construction of nuclear installations which no longer justify such exoneration.[55]

Change in prescription periods

The time period for submitting claims of compensation was extended to 30 years in respect of physical injury and 10 years in respect of other types of damage.

51 Ibid, 80.
52 Article 1.1(j) of the 1963 Vienna Convention.
53 Article 1.1.(j)(iv) of the Protocol.
54 Article V(1) of the Protocol.
55 Horbach, 'Lacunae of International Nuclear Liability Agreements' (n 1) 67.

Such time extension was a reflection of the experience with the Chernobyl accident and the latent injuries which are expected to be revealed even 30 years after its occurrence. The increase in the operator's liability limit was accordingly necessary to reflect the considerable increase in possible claims for nuclear damage.[56]

Both the 1997 Vienna Protocol and the 2004 Paris Protocol extend the ten-year time limit for claims to 30 years for loss of life and personal injury. For example, under the Paris Protocol, victims have more time in which to make their claims as it provides that prescription and extinction periods for nuclear damage claims will be extended to 30 years for actions in respect of loss of life and personal injury. On standing, the revised Vienna Convention provides that the state may bring an action on behalf of victims. Liability under the 1997 Vienna Protocol is strict, but there is an exemption for nuclear damage caused by an act of armed conflict, hostilities, civil war or insurrection, and damage caused by a grave natural disaster of an exceptional character.

These Conventions and Protocols are based on the following overarching principles:

Absolute liability

The liability of the operator is absolute, i.e. the operator is held liable irrespective of fault. Due to the complex techniques used in respect of the production of nuclear energy, it was considered to be too difficult to prove the existence of fault. Proof of damage causally linked to the nuclear incident was sufficient; who caused the nuclear incident is no longer relevant in respect of the strict liability of the operator. However, the liability was limited in both temporal and financial aspects. The Conventions make provision for payment up to the prescribed limit of liability which is supported by compulsory insurance or security held by the operator and guaranteed by the state-funded compensation schemes. Under the Vienna Convention, it may be limited to not less than US$5 million (value in gold on 29 April 1963), but an upper ceiling is not fixed. The Paris Convention sets a maximum liability of 15 million SDRs, provided that the Installation State provides for a greater or lesser amount but not less than 5 million SDRs taking into account the availability of insurance coverage. The Brussels Supplementary Convention established additional funding beyond the amount available under the Paris Convention up to a total of 300 million SDRs, consisting of contributions by the Installation State and Contracting Parties. Liability is also limited in time. Compensation rights are extinguished under both Conventions if an action is not brought within ten years from the date of the nuclear incident. Longer periods are permissible if, under the law of the Installation State, the liability of the operator is covered by financial security. National law may establish a shorter time limit, but

56 Dr Nathalie L.J.T. Horbach, 'Nuclear Safety and Liability Conventions', in Nathalie L.J.T. Horbach (ed.), *Contemporary Developments in Nuclear Energy Law: Harmonising Legislation in CEEC/NIS* (The Hague, Kluwer Law International 1999) 7.

not less than two years (the Paris Convention) or three years (the Vienna Convention) from the date the claimant knew or ought to have known of the damage and the operator liable. The operator must maintain insurance or other financial security for an amount corresponding to his liability; if such security is insufficient, the Installation State is obliged to make up the difference up to the limit of the operator's liability. Jurisdiction over actions lies exclusively with the courts of the Contracting Party in whose territory the nuclear incident occurred. The Conventions also ask States Parties to apply the principle of non-discrimination of victims on the grounds of nationality, domicile or residence.

Exclusive liability: the principle of channelling of liability to operator

One of the key principles of present nuclear liability regimes is the channelling principle, whereby all liability is channelled exclusively to one person – the operator of the nuclear installation or ship. Generally, the 'operator' of a nuclear power plant is the company designated or recognized or a licence-holder who is required by the competent public authority and regulation of a country to hold the necessary financial protection to meet third-party liability risks.[57] The principle of legal channelling of liability pervades all the international legal instruments on nuclear liability and remains the cornerstone of the international nuclear liability regime aimed at ensuring that liability is legally channelled to the operator. This principle aims to ensure that liability claims of victims in respect of nuclear damage are to be adequately and rapidly settled without hampering the commercial development of nuclear industry and avoiding complexity of legal process.[58]

Suppliers to nuclear power plants enjoy a large degree of protection in European countries.

The channelling principle is best expressed in the Vienna and Paris Conventions in the following way: 'Except as otherwise provided in this Convention, no person other than the operator shall be liable for nuclear damage.' In essence, it follows that a nuclear operator will be solely liable for the accident. The choice of the operator to channel all liability rather than any other potential defendant is based on three grounds. First, it is desirable to avoid difficult and lengthy questions of complicated legal process to establish who is legally liable in individual cases. Second, such channelling obviates the necessity for all those who might be associated with construction or operation of a nuclear installation other than the operator himself to take out insurance, and thus allows a concentration of the insurance capacity available.[59] Third, it aims to obviate the potential liability

57 Evelyne M. Ameye, 'United States and India: Two Nuclear States with Legislation that Truly Holds Responsible Parties Liable in Case of a Nuclear Accident' (2015) 18 (8) *Journal of Risk Research* 1070–1082, 1071.

58 Ibid, 44.

59 OECD/NEA, Revised text of the *Exposé des Motifs* of the Paris Convention, approved by the OECD Council on 16 November 1982, para. 15, available at www.oecd-nea.org/law/nlparis_motif.html, accessed 12 July 2018.

of suppliers of equipment and services to nuclear installations. It is assumed that potential liability of these persons, or those working in a nuclear installation, would hamper the development of nuclear industry.[60] In this way, this principle favours the manufacturer, supplier or carrier of the material or equipment since it obviates the necessity for them to take out insurance.

Channelling liability is not a new concept. It is found in a number of environmental treaties. For instance, the liability for oil pollution damage of the sea is channelled through the owner of the ship from which the oil originates.[61] Now this concept of channelling is predominantly used in international nuclear law. The operator is required to have and maintain insurance or other financial security to cover his liability. Such insurance is generally provided by way of establishing nuclear insurance pools.

In the nuclear energy field, the concept of channelling of liability had its origin in the hold-harmless clause of the contracts between the US Atomic Energy Commission (AEC) and private European companies by which the AEC had full liability for damage to third parties. This hold-harmless clause became a standard clause in contracts between US suppliers and their European customers. According to a Harvard report,[62] this principle had been introduced in the USA for the following reasons: first, in case of a nuclear accident, the suppliers feared being prosecuted instead of or jointly with the nuclear operator, because the victim of a nuclear incident could be compelled to sue as many as companies as possible. Second, it would be unfair to hold the suppliers liable, since after the delivery of goods and services they generally lose control thereof. The operator is thus in a better position to control the risk than are the different suppliers. This could also be referred to as an argument of fairness. Because the suppliers no longer have control over the reactor, it is fair that they will not be held liable in case of a nuclear accident. Third, it was considered that the operators were more capable of obtaining insurance. By concentrating liability in the operator, pyramidal insurance costs can be avoided. This means that if every supplier had to obtain a separate insurance coverage, it would result in disproportionately high premiums. The concentration of liability at the level of the operator would minimize not only the procedural costs but also the insurance costs.[63] As a result, this principle would lead to lower procedural and insurance costs, to legal security and justice. However, the USA has subsequently introduced economic channelling of liability for the suppliers and operators through its nuclear energy legislation.

60 Ibid, 43–44.

61 Tom vanden Borre, 'Channelling of Liability: A Few Juridical and Economic Views on an Inadequate Legal Construction' in: Nathalie L.J.T. Horbach (ed.), *Contemporary Developments in Nuclear Energy Law: Harmonising Legislation in CEEC/NIS* (The Hague, Kluwer Law International 1999) 13.

62 'International Problems of Financial Protection against Nuclear Risk', study under the auspices of Harvard Law School and Atomic Industrial Forum, 1959, New York, Atomic Industrial Forum.

63 vanden Borre (n 61) 20.

Article 6 of the Paris Convention contains detailed rules on the legal channelling of liability. This definition contains two elements. First, the operator can only be held liable in case of a nuclear incident; and secondly, no one other than the operator is liable. This means that the suppliers of the operator are immune against third-party claims and cannot be sued. Under this principle, a victim of a nuclear incident can only sue the operator of the nuclear installation to the exclusion of all other possible defendants. This principle would avoid lengthy litigation to determine who is liable[64] The policy reasons for legal channelling of liability are also centred around simplification of procedure for victims and cost effectiveness, as it limits the potential problems arising from multiple law suits.[65]

The legal channelling of liability has been criticized on the ground that it would lead to absolute immunity of the supplier of the operator and the operator of a nuclear installation has in principle no right of recourse for amounts paid by it or its insurer to victims of a nuclear incident.[66] The concept of 'right of recourse' operates as a limited exception to this principle. Such a right enables the operator to recover the amount of compensation from the responsible party after the operator has paid it. In order to make channelling effective, it was thus necessary to ensure that the right of recourse is limited to restrictive circumstances. Two grounds for recourse are generally accepted in the international regime: firstly, when such recourse is contractually stipulated, and secondly, when the damage is caused by an 'individual' with the intent to cause damage.[67] Thus, a supplier can be subjected to a contractual claim from the operator.

Legal channelling of liability is different from economic channelling of liability. Insurance could be regarded as a form of economic channelling of a certain risk and it is indeed the insurer who carries the liability risk.[68] In the USA, the nuclear liability legislation does not channel the damage resulting from a nuclear incident to the operator of a nuclear installation. An American nuclear insurer offers two types of insurance policy: the first insurance policy for commercial nuclear installations is concluded per installation; a second insurance policy is specifically directed towards the suppliers and transporters of nuclear material. Because of the absence of legal channelling of liability within US nuclear law, a victim of a nuclear accident can sue everyone who, according to his view, caused the incident.[69]

In the USA, the suppliers are to contribute to the pool fund for victim compensation. The scheme in the USA, based upon the 1957 Price Anderson Act, provides for a framework where the supplier or other party can be held legally liable; however, the compensation amount is covered by the insurance scheme

64 Ayushi Sutaria, 'Placing the Indian Civil Nuclear Liability Regime in Context: The Extent of Supplier's Liability (2014) 17(1) *Journal of Risk Research* 99.

65 Ibid, 101.

66 vanden Borre (n 61) 22.

67 vanden Borre (n 61).

68 vanden Borre (n 61) 27.

69 vanden Borre (n 61) 35.

taken by the operator (commonly referred to as the 'first tier of compensation'), or by the fund pool collectively provided by all the licensed operators (the second tier of compensation) if the compensation exceeds a certain amount. The legal liability of the supplier can be triggered either by the victims directly or through a recourse action exercised, for example, by the insurer of the nuclear operator. The recent change in the framework, *vis-à-vis* supplier liability, has been due to the enactment of the Energy Independence and Security Act 2007.

The justification for the channelling of liability and an extremely restricted right of recourse has not gone uncontested. Given the increasingly complex designs of the new generations of nuclear power plants, it may now have become realistically incorrect to maintain the heavy burden of legal channelling upon the operator.[70]

The minimum liability borne by the operator

The Contracting Parties to international nuclear liability treaties (both the Paris Convention and the Vienna Convention) shall provide under their legislation an amount of liability which shall not be less than the minimum amount provided by the international Convention.[71] In most countries the operator's nuclear liability is limited to a specified amount. Only a few countries at present have provided for unlimited liability under their nuclear liability legislation.[72] In fact, the liability regime differs in different countries in terms of the operator's and the public fund liability amount.

The obligation on the operator to have and maintain financial security

International nuclear treaties require the operator of a nuclear installation to maintain financial security up to its liability amount or, in the case of unlimited liability, up to the amount required by law, which cannot be less than the minimum liability amount required under the relevant treaty adopted by the state where the operator's installation is situated.[73]

Competent jurisdiction and enforcement of judgments

In the case of a nuclear incident a potential plaintiff may have the choice of various jurisdictions using various applicable laws. But these Conventions have established that jurisdiction over nuclear damage claims lies only with the courts of the state in which the accident has occurred. The judgments rendered by the competent court are enforceable in any Contracting State.[74] This exclusive jurisdiction

70 Sutaria (n 64) 102.
71 'Progress Towards a Global Nuclear Liability Regime' (n 26).
72 Ibid.
73 Ibid.
74 Ibid.

has two effects; firstly it prevents what is known as jurisdiction shopping, whereby claimants try and find courts and national legislation more friendly to their claims, thus offering nuclear operators a degree of certainty and protection. Secondly it locates the competent court close to the source of the damage, so that victims do not have to travel far in order to lodge claims.[75] Another reason for establishing one exclusive competent court seems to be to ensure that the maximum amount of liability will not be exceeded and if the claims with respect to one nuclear incident could be made before different courts, it might exceed the maximum amount.[76]

Applicable law and non-discrimination

The courts having jurisdiction will apply the relevant Convention (if the state has adhered to one of them) and their own national law over claims arising out of a nuclear accident, and that law shall apply to all matters both substantive and procedural and to all victims, without discrimination based upon nationality, domicile or residence.[77]

Joint Protocol Relating to the Application of the Vienna Convention and the Paris Convention 1988

After the Chernobyl accident and its catastrophic effects, the IAEA started to improve all aspects of nuclear liability with a view to improving the Paris and Vienna Conventions and establishing a comprehensive liability regime. Although these two Conventions are based on very similar basic principles, there are a number of substantive differences between them, in particular regarding the different limits envisaged for the amount of the operator's liability. In 1988, this Joint Protocol Relating to the Application of the Vienna Convention and the Paris Convention was adopted as a result of joint efforts by the IAEA and OECD/NEA to solve the problems arising from the very existence of distinct treaty regimes that have different Contracting Parties. The Joint Protocol established a link between the two Conventions, combining them into one expanded liability regime.[78] The Joint Protocol is an international treaty, distinct from the Vienna Convention and the Paris Convention but additional to both. But the Joint Protocol is not a free-standing international agreement as it is open only to States which are already Parties to either the Vienna Convention or the Paris Convention. The Joint Protocol is not an amending treaty in respect of either the Vienna Convention or the

75 Liability for Nuclear Damage, available at http://www.world-nuclear.org/information-library/safety-and-security/safety-of-plants/liability-for-nuclear-damage.aspx, accessed 12 July 2018.

76 vanden Borre (n 61) 17.

77 'Progress Towards a Global Nuclear Liability Regime' (n 26).

78 The Joint Protocol is available at https://www.iaea.org/sites/default/files/infcirc402.pdf, accessed 12 July 2018.

Paris Convention, whose provisions remain thereby formally unaffected,[79] but acts as a bridge between the Paris and Vienna Conventions, effectively extending the benefits provided by one Convention to victims in countries that have joined the other Convention. The Joint Protocol aims to enhance the civil liability regime of the Paris Convention and the Vienna Convention by harmonizing the application of the two Conventions. In other words, the Joint Protocol has two objectives: (a) elimination of conflicts of law which might arise from simultaneous application of the two Conventions, in the event of a nuclear accident involving Parties to both Conventions; and (b) mutual extension of the civil liability regime established under each Convention for the wider application of victims of a nuclear accident.[80]

As was explained in the 1987 Explanatory Note, it can therefore be said that the Joint Protocol has a 'dual purpose' and is based on two underlying principles. The first principle, which underlines Articles II and IV of the Joint Protocol, is 'to create a link or "bridge" between the two Conventions by abolishing the distinction between Contracting Parties and non-Contracting States as regards the operative provisions of either Convention'. The second principle, which underlines Article III of the Joint Protocol, consists in making either the Vienna Convention or the Paris Convention exclusively apply to a nuclear incident by means of an 'appropriate conflict rule'.[81]

This mutual extension of the territorial scope of the operator's liability does not, however, otherwise affect that liability as determined by the applicable Convention: the operator remains liable under the Convention to which the State in which his installation is situated is a Party, and the amount of his liability is still determined by the legislation of that State pursuant to that Convention.[82]

The Convention on Supplementary Compensation for Nuclear Damage (CSC) 1997

This Convention is a global and independent treaty to which all States may be Parties irrespective of whether or not they have signed or ratified the existing

79 In the Preamble, the Contracting Parties to the Joint Protocol declare themselves 'desirous to establish a link' between the Paris Convention and the Vienna Convention on the basis, on the one hand, of the consideration that no State was a Party to both Conventions at the time of its adoption (a fact that has since remained unchanged) and, on the other, of their conviction that 'adherence to either Convention by Parties to the other Convention could lead to difficulties resulting from the simultaneous application of both Conventions to a nuclear incident'.

80 Horbach 'Lacunae of International Nuclear Liability Agreements' (n 1) 50.

81 The 1988 Joint Protocol relating to the application of the Vienna Convention and the Paris Convention – Explanatory Text, IAEA International Law Series no. 5, IAEA, Vienna, 2013, 14, available at https://www-pub.iaea.org/MTCD/Publications/PDF/Pub1593_web.pdf, accessed 12 July 2018.

82 Ibid, 16.

nuclear liability Conventions or have nuclear installation on their territories.[83] The CSC is a stand-alone Convention, in the sense that any country can join the Convention without having to be a Party either to the Paris or the Vienna Convention. It aims to enhance the existing international nuclear liability regime and establish a global compensation scheme for nuclear damage by providing for an additional funding system supplementing the compensation available under relevant national legislation of States Parties. Even states which differ in respect in respect of channelling liability or the scope of nuclear damage may become Parties to this Convention. The Supplementary Convention came into force in 2015.

The Preamble to the CSC recognizes the importance of the Paris Convention and Vienna Convention as well as national legislation on compensation for nuclear damage consistent with the principles of these Conventions. In order to supplement national compensation, the Convention also establishes an international fund, to which Contracting Parties will be expected to contribute in the event of a nuclear accident. The CSC focuses not only on providing legal certainty on the treatment of legal liability for nuclear damage resulting from a nuclear incident, but also, in the unlikely event of a nuclear incident, on assuring the prompt availability of meaningful compensation with a minimum of litigation and other burdens.[84]

The CSC requires each Member State to have national law on nuclear liability that is based on the Paris Convention or the Vienna Convention. This requirement ensures that the national law of each Member State will reflect the basic principles of nuclear liability law, which include: (1) channelling all legal liability for nuclear damage exclusively to the operator; (2) imposing liability on the operator without the need to demonstrate fault, negligence or intent; (3) granting exclusive jurisdiction to the courts of the state where the nuclear incident occurs; (4) permitting liability to be limited in amount and in time; and (5) compensating damage without any discrimination based upon nationality, domicile or residence.[85]

Definition of nuclear damage

The CSC requires Member States to adopt a broad definition of nuclear damage. The CSC provides that nuclear damage must include not only personal injury and property damage, but also certain categories of damage relating to cost of reinstatement of impaired environment, the cost of preventative measures, loss

83 Convention on Supplementary Compensation for Nuclear Damage, opened for signature 12 Sept. 1997, 36 I.L.M 1473, available at http://www.iaea.org/Publications/Documents/Conventions/supcomp.html, accessed 12 July 2018.

84 Ben McRae, 'The Convention on Supplementary Compensation for Nuclear Damage: Catalyst for a Global Nuclear Liability Regime', available at https://www.oecd-nea.org/law/nlb/nlb-79/017-035%20-%20Article%20Ben%20McRae.pdf, accessed 12 July 2018.

85 Ibid.

of income and economic losses arising from loss of life or damage to property.[86] However, the extent of the costs of reinstatement of impaired environment, preventative measures and certain economic losses will be determined by the national law of the states whose courts have jurisdiction over a particular nuclear accident.[87]

However, 'measures of reinstatement' or 'preventative measures' must be reasonable.[88] 'Reasonable measures' is defined in the CSC as those which are found under the law of the competent court to be appropriate and proportionate' taking into account the nature and extent of the damage incurred and relevant scientific and technical expertise.[89]

Amount of national compensation

According to the CSC, the Installation State shall ensure the availability of compensation up to 300 million Special Drawing Rights (SDRs) or a greater amount in respect of nuclear damage for one near incident.[90] However, it is not clear on what basis the Installation State must ensure the availability of this national compensation amount. The Installation State may establish the limit of the operator's liability at 300 million SDRs or at a lower limit, and this is generally to be provided by the operator liable through insurance or other financial security. This is also called the first tier of compensation. This national amount of compensation corresponds to the minimum amount envisaged in the 1997 Protocol to amend the Vienna Convention. Beyond this amount of 300 million SDRs, supplementary compensation is to be provided by the States Parties to this Convention through public funds according to the specified formula under Article IV. Thus, to the extent funds from the liable operator are insufficient to cover the first tier amount, the CSC requires the Installation State to make public funds available to cover the difference. The State may also establish transitional amount of 150 million SDRs for a maximum period of ten years from the date of the opening for signature of this Convention.[91] The first tier amount is to be distributed on a non-discretionary basis, i.e., to compensate damage suffered both within and outside the territory of the Installation State, although a state may exclude nuclear damage suffered in a non-Contracting State subject to obligations of that state under the Vienna or Paris liability agreements.[92]

International fund

The CSC provides for system of an international fund to supplement the amount of national compensation, if it is inadequate to ensure the payment of all claims

86 Article 1(f) of the Convention.
87 Ibid.
88 Article 1(g) and (h) of the Convention.
89 Article 1(l) of the Convention.
90 Article III(a) of the Convention.
91 Article III(a)(ii) of the Convention.
92 Article III(2) of the Convention.

for compensation for nuclear damage. This is called the second tier of compensation. To establish this supplementary compensation fund, all the Contracting Parties are obliged to make available additional public funds according to the formula for the calculation of contribution under Article IV. According to the formula, the contribution of a Contracting Party to this international fund is calculated, firstly, on the basis of its installed nuclear capacity, and secondly, on the amount determined by applying the ratio between the UN rate of assessment for that Contracting Party and the total of such rates for all Contracting Parties, which constitutes 10 per cent of the part calculated on the basis of installed nuclear capacity.[93] The Member States that have no nuclear installations must contribute on the basis of their UN rate of assessment only.[94] The CSC limits the use of the international fund to compensate nuclear damage that occurs in a geographic scope that is precisely defined and that excludes non-Member States. Contributions to the international fund are based on a formula under which more than 90 per cent of the contributions will come from nuclear power-generating Member States on the basis of their installed nuclear capacity, while the remaining portion comes from all Member States to the CSC on the basis of their UN rate assessments.[95] According to Article IV(2), only 'nuclear reactors', as opposed to all 'nuclear installations', are to be taken into account in order to calculate a Party's contribution on the basis of its installed nuclear capacity. For the purpose of calculating contribution, the Convention requires all States Parties to provide a complete listing of all nuclear installations to the Depositary of the Convention.[96]

Compensation for transboundary damage

According to the CSC, the national compensation amount has to be made available to compensate claims suffered both in and outside the Installation State. Article XI provides that 50 per cent of the national funds will be used to compensate damage suffered both inside and outside the territory of the Installation State and the remaining 50 per cent will be exclusively used to compensate damage suffered outside the territory of the Installation State, to the extent that it has not already been compensated. Thus, about 150 million SDRs would be reserved exclusively for compensation for transboundary damage.

Geographical scope

The national compensation funds (up to 300 million SDRs) shall apply to nuclear damage suffered both in the territory of a Contracting Party (place of a nuclear incident) and by a national of a Contracting Party (place where the nuclear damage

93 Article IV of the Convention.
94 Article IV of the Convention.
95 Article IV(1)(ii) of the Convention.
96 Article VIII of the Convention.

is suffered).[97] But where the damage exceeds the national compensation amount, the additional funds will not be used to cover damage suffered in the territory of non-Contracting States.[98]

Jurisdiction and applicable law

The CSC aims at establishing uniform rules regarding jurisdiction for all States Parties. Jurisdiction over actions concerning nuclear damage from a nuclear incident lies with the courts of the Contracting Party within whose territory the incident took place. However, if nuclear incidents occur in the exclusive economic zone (EEZ), jurisdiction over such action also lies with the courts of that Contracting Party.[99] This rule on jurisdiction is similar to those established under the 1997 Protocol in respect of the EEZ. Article X(2) states that 'Each Contracting Party shall ensure that persons suffering damage may enforce their rights to compensation without having to bring separate proceedings according to the origin of the funds provided for such compensation.' This jurisdictional uniformity allows fair treatment of victims and prevents 'forum shopping' by victims wishing to bring claims in different courts. As to which is the applicable civil liability to a nuclear incident, the Convention states that either the Vienna Convention or the Paris Convention or the Annex to the Convention shall be applied and consequently the domestic law incorporating that Convention shall be applied by the court as the applicable law.[100]

Grandfather clause

The CSC contains an Annex, which is an integral part of the Convention. One of the purposes of the Annex is to allow participation of states that adhere to a nuclear liability regime based on economic rather than legal channelling of liability without changing their legislation. This is popularly referred to as the 'grandfather clause'. States are required to bring their national legislation on compensation for nuclear damage in line with the liability provisions laid down in the Annex. The USA is the only country that follows the economic channelling of liability principle. The grandfather clause provides, however, that national legislation is deemed to be in conformity with the basic liability provisions of the Annex if it provided, as of 1 January 1995, for inter alia strict liability for substantial off-site nuclear damage, indemnification of any person other than the operator liable for nuclear damage and the availability of at least 1 billion SDRs in respect of a civil nuclear power plant and at least 300 million SDRs in respect of other civilian nuclear installations for such indemnification. In fact, the clause refers to a

97 Article V of the Convention.

98 The 1997 Vienna Convention on Civil Liability for Nuclear Damage and the 1997 Convention on Supplementary Compensation for Nuclear Damage- Explanatory Texts (n 50), 74.

99 Article XIII of the Convention.

100 Article XIV of the Convention.

state whose domestic law contained certain provisions on 1 January 1995 and the USA is the only state whose legislation contained those provisions on that date. Since the USA is the only state that can meet these requirements, the grandfather clause can be applied to it only.[101] Accordingly, the USA is not required to apply the operator's liability, the liability amount and the financial security which the operator is required to have and maintain. Furthermore, this grandfather clause allows the USA a definition of 'nuclear damage' wider than the one described in Article 1.1(f) of the Convention.

Convention relating to Civil Liability in the Field of Maritime Carriage of Nuclear Material 1971

This Convention supplements both the Vienna and Paris Conventions in relation to maritime transport, and was developed under the auspices of the OECD, the IAEA and the International Maritime Organization. The preamble to the Convention explicitly refers to the desire of the Contracting Parties to hold the operator of a nuclear installation exclusively liable for damage resulting from any incident occurring during the maritime carriage of nuclear material. This Convention is of a rather supplementary nature, and will not apply if either the 1960 Paris Convention or the 1963 Vienna Convention or applicable national law covers the damage caused by such nuclear material.[102] To this extent, the Convention provides that a person who by virtue of an international Convention or national law might be held liable for damage caused by a nuclear incident occurring in the course of maritime carriage of nuclear material, will be exonerated from such liability if the operator of a nuclear installation is liable for such damage under the Paris or the Vienna Convention.[103]

Conclusion

From the above it is clear that international treaties on civil liability for nuclear damage are mostly based upon principles of the operator's exclusive channelling, strict liability for nuclear damage, mandatory financial coverage, and compensation to the victims without discrimination. Both the 1963 Vienna Convention and the1960 Paris Convention were revised substantially in 1997 and 2004 respectively to address the concerns raised by the Chernobyl incident. The scope of application of the revised Conventions was extended to ensure that more victims will be entitled to compensation than in the past.

Although the current liability regime has significantly improved the efficiency of the nuclear safety system, it has been widely criticized. According to one author, 'The international nuclear liability regime is extremely patchy,

101 The 1997 Vienna Convention on Civil Liability for Nuclear Damage and the 1997 Convention on Supplementary Compensation for Nuclear Damage- Explanatory Texts (n 51) 71.

102 Article 1 of the Convention.

103 Article 2 of the Convention.

complicated and features sparse participation.'[104] The liability regime also has other limitations, such as the inadequacies of the system to include the lack of a neutral tribunal, the general requirement that claimants are to file claims in the courts where the nuclear installation is located, and concerns about the neutrality of the applicable law and limitations on recoverable damages.[105] Another limitation of the existing liability Conventions in general and the Joint Convention in particular is that they are primarily designed to apply to accidents likely to occur during the operation of large nuclear installations and they do not address the issue of liability associated with the long-term management and disposal of radioactive waste. Although the recent amendments to the Vienna and Paris Conventions are much appreciated, they contain many exceptions and the amended Protocols enjoy even sparser participation than the original Conventions.[106] Even under the revised system, no neutral tribunal is provided and claimants are generally required to file claims in the courts where the nuclear installation is located.

Other criticism includes the limits on liability; the imposition of liability primarily on the operator and exempting others; the short statute-of-limitation periods; and the sparse state participation as parties in these instruments.[107] But the most serious lacuna of the nuclear liability regime is one of its basic principles: the Installation State avoids any responsibility for the consequences of its actions or omissions. The current liability regime does not recognize state responsibility for nuclear damage and as such Installation States can avoid claims for compensation. Although operators are exclusively liable for nuclear damage, they do not function independently of any government control.[108] Responsibility for any damage that may arise from nuclear installations operating under state jurisdiction or control should be attributed to that state.[109] States should be responsible under international law for any failure to exercise due diligence over the siting and operation of nuclear facilities and the transport and disposal of nuclear wastes.[110]

104 Duncan E.J. Currie, 'The Problems and Gaps in the Nuclear Liability Conventions and an Analysis of How an Actual Claim Would be Brought under the Current Existing Treaty Regime in the Event of a Nuclear Accident' (2006) 35(1) *Denver Journal of International Law and Policy* 85–127, 85.

105 Ibid.

106 Ibid.

107 Ved P. Nanda and Jon M. Van Dyke, 'International Nuclear Law: An Introduction' (2006) 35(1) *Denver Journal of International Law and Policy* 1–12.

108 Horbach, 'Lacunae of International Nuclear Liability Agreements' (n 1) 84.

109 Ibid, 85.

110 See Alexandre Kiss, 'State Responsibility and Liability for Nuclear Damage' (2006–2007) 35 *Denver Journal of International Law and Policy* 67.

8 Notification, emergency preparedness and response to nuclear accident

Introduction

The issue of prior notification, exchange of information and emergency preparedness in the case of nuclear accident is considered essential to mitigate the negative impact of nuclear accidents that can cause a radiological emergency. There existed no legally binding instruments providing a mechanism for international action that might be necessary for dealing effectively with such emergencies.[1] As a result of the Chernobyl accident, the need for an international instrument creating an obligation for early notification of a nuclear accident and the need for an international framework for rendering assistance, upon request, in case of such an accident was addressed through the adoption of two treaties.[2] These two treaties deal with the issues relating to notification, emergency preparedness and response to nuclear accident.

The Convention on Early Notification of a Nuclear Accident 1986

The Convention on Early Notification of a Nuclear Accident 1986 imposes a duty on a State Party to notify other states likely to be affected by transboundary releases of radioactive material. The duty of a state to inform the public is an established principle of international law.[3] In case of transboundary radioactive release, this Convention requires immediate notification of IAEA Member States and neighbouring states. Article 1 delineates the scope of application of the Convention. It states that this Convention shall apply in the event of any accident involving facilities or activities of a State Party or of persons or legal entities under its jurisdiction from which a release of radioactive material occurs and which has resulted or may result in an international transboundary release that could be of

1 A.O. Adede, *The IAEA Notification and Assistance Conventions in Case of a Nuclear Accident* (London, Graham and Trotman/Martinus Nijhoff Publishers 1987) xx.

2 Ibid, 1.

3 Daniel G. Partan, 'The Duty to Inform in International Environmental Law' (1988) 6 *B.U. International Law Journal* 43, 44.

radiological safety significance for another state. Article 1(2) contains a list of the facilities and activities to which this Convention applies. The facilities and activities include any nuclear reactor, nuclear fuel cycle facility; radioactive waste management facility; the transport and storage of nuclear fuels or radioactive wastes; the manufacture, use, storage, disposal and transport of radioisotopes for agricultural, industrial, medical and related scientific and research purposes; and the use of radioisotopes for power generation in space objects.[4] This Article does not cover nuclear accidents involving military facilities. However, Article 3 allows notification in the event of nuclear accidents other than those specified in Article 1(2). Although Article 3 does not specifically mention nuclear weapons or testing, it is clear that it is intended to apply to accidents involving military facilities.[5] The scope of the Convention is broad as it covers nuclear accidents specified as well as 'other nuclear accidents' which are not specified.[6] Apart from accidents involving military facilities, these 'other nuclear accidents' can also occur outside the nuclear fuel cycle, such as accidents in large radio-pharmaceutical plants, fires in large irradiation units, transport accidents and even thefts of plutonium.[7] However, one important limitation is that the Convention leaves it to the country of origin to decide whether an accident is significant and release of radioactive material is transboundary in nature. Thus, a failure to notify may therefore be excused on the ground that the state in which the accident occurred does not consider the release to be 'significant'.[8] Furthermore, purely domestic releases are not covered in the Convention, nor are releases over areas such as the high seas, which are not subject to the sovereignty or jurisdiction of any state.[9] The Convention does not define a 'nuclear accident'. Rather it has taken a result-oriented approach that an actual or potential release of radioactive material should be 'of radiological safety significance for another State'.

Duty of notification

The Convention makes clear provision for the manner of notification and the kind of information to be provided. Article 2 provides that, in the event of a nuclear accident as specified in the Convention, the State Party shall notify the affected states and IAEA of the nature of the nuclear accident, the time of its occurrence and its exact location. The notifying State Party shall also 'promptly' provide the affected states and the IAEA with available information relevant to minimizing the radiological consequences in those states. Information to be provided by the

4 Article 1(2) of the Convention.

5 Peter Cameron, 'The Vienna Conventions on Early Notification and Assistance', in Peter Cameron, Leigh Hancher, Wolfgang Kuhn, *Nuclear Energy Law after Chernobyl* (London, Graham and Trotman and International Bar Association) 23.

6 Article 3 of the Convention.

7 A.O. Adede (n 1) 5–6.

8 Cameron (n 5) 24.

9 Ibid.

notifying state shall comprise the following data: (a) the time, exact location and the nature of the nuclear accident; (b) the facility or activity involved; (c) the assumed or established cause and the foreseeable development of the nuclear accident relevant to the transboundary release of the radioactive materials; (d) the general characteristics of the radioactive release, the nature, probable physical and chemical form and the quantity, composition and effective height of the radioactive release; (e) information on current and forecast meteorological and hydrological conditions, necessary for forecasting the transboundary release of the radioactive materials; (f) the results of environmental monitoring relevant to the transboundary release of the radioactive materials; (g) the off-site protective measures taken or planned; (h) the predicted behaviour over time of the radioactive release.[10] Such information received may be used without restriction, except when such information is provided in confidence by the notifying State Party.[11]

The notification can be made either directly to the potentially affected states or it can be made to the IAEA. Once it has received such notification, the IAEA shall immediately inform other states and relevant international organizations.[12]

Duty of consultation

Article 6 states that a State Party providing information shall respond 'promptly' to a request for further information or consultations sought by an affected State Party with a view to minimizing the radiological consequences in that state.

Point of contact

Article 7 requires that each State Party shall make known to the Agency and to other States Parties its competent authorities and point of contact responsible for issuing and receiving the notification and information. Such points of contact shall be available continuously. Article 7(2) requires each State Party to promptly inform the Agency of any changes that may occur in the information. The Agency shall maintain an up-to-date list of such national authorities and points of contact, as well as points of contact of relevant international organizations, and shall provide this to States Parties and Member States and to relevant international organizations.[13]

Radiation monitoring

If requested by a State Party, the IAEA can investigate the feasibility and establishment of a suitable radiation monitoring system for preventing nuclear accidents

10 Article 5 of the Convention.
11 Article 5(2) of the Convention.
12 Article 4 of the Convention.
13 Article 7(3) of the Convention.

and minimizing the consequences of any such accident.[14] States Parties may conclude bilateral or multilateral arrangements relating to the duty of notification and consultation in the case of a nuclear accident.[15] Article 11 contains dispute settlement procedure. It states that in the event of a dispute between States Parties, or between a State Party and the Agency, concerning the interpretation or application of this Convention, it shall be settled by consultation or negotiation. If such peaceful means fails, the dispute can be submitted to the ICJ for judicial decision.

The Early Notification Convention improves nuclear safety by minimizing the potential damage from accidents. Although it does not prevent accidents from occurring, it does improve overall safety by assuring adequate response to nuclear accidents. The Early Notification Agreement has been invoked on more than one occasion. The effectiveness of the agreement is evidenced by the fact that a leak from a power plant at Sosnovy Bor in Russia, a signatory to the agreement, was promptly announced to the international community. The Agreement was also invoked in 1999, regarding an allegedly missing source in Turkey, and the IAEA notified neighbouring states and provided information to all Member States.

This Convention has been followed by many subsequent bilateral and regional treaties. One important instance of a notification agreement is the Joint Agreement on Notification of Nuclear Accidents of 1993 between Norway and Russia, by which Russia will ensure early notification in the event of a nuclear incident, which is crucial for Norway's emergency preparedness.. In 2015, Norway and Russia agreed Joint Notification procedures in the event of a nuclear accident.

Convention on Assistance in the Case of Nuclear Accident or Radiological Emergency 1986

This Convention was adopted to create a framework for providing prompt assistance by States Parties or the IAEA or both to any requesting state in the event of a nuclear accident or radiological emergency. Article 1 of the Assistance Convention sets out two objectives of such assistance: to minimize the effects of a nuclear accident or radiological emergency and to protect life, property and the environment from the effects of radioactive releases. The Convention provides for a duty of cooperation between Member States in the case of a nuclear accident or radiological emergency and such cooperation can be facilitated by States Parties through concluding bilateral or multilateral arrangements.[16] The IAEA shall be the focal point to facilitate and support such cooperation.

Provisions on assistance

Article 2 deals with the scope and manner of provision of assistance. If a State Party needs assistance in the event of a nuclear accident or radiological emergency,

14 Article 8 of the Convention.
15 Article 9 of the Convention.
16 Article 1 of the Convention.

it may call for such assistance from any other State Party and the IAEA specifying the scope and type of assistance required. The states which may request assistance include those affected by a nuclear accident or radiological emergency, which has originated in the territory of the requesting state or another state or otherwise from a source beyond its control.[17] The affected state shall also provide necessary information to the requested state so that the latter can determine the extent to which it is able to meet the request.[18] The requested state shall promptly notify the requesting State Party whether it is in a position to render the assistance requested and the scope and type of assistance that might be rendered.[19] The Convention requires Parties to inform the IAEA of their experts and equipment available for the assistance so that the IAEA can coordinate such assistance. However, one of the main weaknesses of the Convention is that at no point does it impose obligation upon States Parties to provide or accept assistance.

Any State Party may request assistance relating to medical treatment or temporary relocation of people involved in a nuclear accident or radiological emergency into another State Party.[20] In case of request for assistance in the event of a nuclear accident or radiological emergency, the IAEA shall respond by (a) making available appropriate resources; (b) promptly transmitting the request to other states and international organizations; and (c) coordinating the assistance at international level.[21]

However, the overall direction, control, coordination and supervision of the assistance shall be the responsibility within territory of the requesting state.[22] If assistance involves personnel, the assisting state shall designate the person who should be in charge of operational supervision over the personnel and the equipment provided by it and the requesting state shall provide local facilities and service for the proper and effective administration of the assistance.[23] The requesting state shall also ensure the protection of personnel, equipment and materials brought into its territory and their return to the assisting state shall be ensured.[24]

Each State Party under the Convention shall inform the IAEA and other States Parties about its competent authorities and point of contact authorized to make and receive requests for and to accept offers of assistance.[25] Such points of contact and a focal point within the Agency shall be available continuously. Each State Party shall promptly inform the IAEA of any changes that may occur in the information relating to points of contact and focal point.[26]

17 Article 2(1) of the Convention.
18 Article 2 of the Convention.
19 Ibid.
20 Article 2(5) of the Convention.
21 Article 2(6) of the Convention.
22 Article 3 of the Convention.
23 Ibid.
24 Ibid.
25 Article 4 of the Convention.
26 Ibid.

Role of the IAEA

Article 5 deals with functions of the IAEA regarding assistance. The IAEA shall collect and disseminate to States Parties and Member States information concerning: (i) experts, equipment and materials which could be made available in the event of nuclear accidents or radiological emergencies; (ii) methodologies, techniques and available results of research relating to response to nuclear accidents or radiological emergencies. If it is requested by a State Party or a Member State, the IAEA shall also assist that State Party or Member State in (i) preparing plans in the case of nuclear accidents and radiological emergencies and the appropriate legislation; (ii) developing appropriate training programmes for personnel to deal with nuclear accidents and radiological emergencies; (iii) transmitting requests for assistance and relevant information in the event of a nuclear accident or radiological emergency; (iv) developing appropriate radiation monitoring programmes, procedures and standards; (v) conducting investigations into the feasibility of establishing appropriate radiation monitoring systems. In the case of a request for assistance, the IAEA shall conduct an initial assessment of the accident or emergency; offer its good offices to the requesting states; and establish and maintain liaison with relevant international organizations for the purposes of obtaining and exchanging relevant information and data.[27]

Confidentiality of information

The Convention asks both the requesting state and the assisting state to protect the confidentiality of any information that becomes available to either of them in connection with such assistance and such information shall be used exclusively for the purpose of the assistance agreed upon.[28] Information relating to such assistance can be made public by the assisting state. But the assisting party shall make every effort to coordinate with the requesting State before releasing information to the public on the assistance provided in connection with a nuclear accident or radiological emergency.[29]

Reimbursement of costs of assistance

Generally an assisting party may offer assistance without costs to the requesting state. When assistance is provided wholly or partly on the basis of reimbursement of cost of assistance, the requesting state shall reimburse the cost of assistance promptly to the assisting party.[30] In the case of such reimbursement, the assisting party shall take into account: (a) the nature of the nuclear accident or

27 Article 5 of the Convention.
28 Article 6(1) of the Convention.
29 Article 6 (2) of the Convention.
30 Article 7(2) of the Convention.

radiological emergency; (b) the place of origin of the nuclear accident or radiological emergency; (c) the needs of developing countries; (d) the particular needs of countries without nuclear facilities; and (e) any other relevant factors.[31] However, the assisting party may at any time waive the reimbursement in whole or in part. In considering such waiver or postponement, assisting parties shall give due consideration to the needs of developing countries.[32]

Privileges, immunities and facilities

The requesting state shall afford to personnel of the assisting party the necessary privileges, immunities and facilities for the performance of their assistance functions.[33] The requesting state shall afford the following privileges and immunities to personnel of the assisting party (a) immunity from arrest, detention and legal process of the requesting state, in respect of acts or omissions in the performance of their duties; and (b) exemption from taxation, duties or other charges in respect of the performance of their assistance functions.[34] The requesting state shall afford the assisting party exemption from taxation, duties or other charges on the equipment and property brought into the territory of the requesting state and provide immunity from seizure, attachment or requisition of such equipment and property.[35] The requesting state shall also ensure the return of such equipment and property. Article 9 requires that each State Party shall, at the request of the requesting state or the assisting party, facilitate the transit through its territory of personnel, equipment and property involved in the assistance. The personnel, equipment and property for which transit is to be facilitated must be duly notified to the transit state.[36]

Claims and compensation

The Convention urges the States Parties to cooperate closely in order to facilitate the settlement of legal proceedings and claims for compensation. There are three main obligations imposed upon the requesting state for damage caused during the provision of assistance. First, in the case of the death of or of injury to persons, damage or loss of property, or damage to the environment caused to the requesting state in the course of providing the assistance, the requesting state shall not bring any legal proceedings against the assisting party.[37] Second, the requesting state shall assume responsibility for legal proceedings and claims brought by third parties against the assisting party and hold the assisting party

31 Article 7 of the Convention.
32 Article 7(3) of the Convention.
33 Article 8(1) of the Convention.
34 Article 8(2) of the Convention.
35 Article 8(3) of the Convention.
36 Article 9(2) of the Convention.
37 Article 10(2)(a) of the Convention.

harmless in respect of such legal proceedings and claims.[38] Third, it shall also compensate the assisting party for death of or injury to personnel of the assisting party; loss of or damage to equipment or materials related to the assistance.[39] However, a State Party can make a reservation to this clause that it will not apply in cases of gross negligence by the individuals who caused the death, injury, loss or damage.[40]

This provision is based on two approaches: the hold harmless approach (instituting no claim against the relevant party) and the indemnification approach.

Termination of assistance

The requesting state or the assisting party may at any time, after appropriate consultations and by notification in writing, request the termination of providing such assistance. Once such a request has been made, the parties involved shall consult with each other to make arrangements for the proper conclusion of the assistance.[41]

Dispute settlement

The provision relating to dispute settlement is similar. But both the Conventions have provisions for making reservation by the States Parties to the dispute settlement clause to avoid it. In fact, reservations have been made by many States Parties to the provisions on dispute settlement in both Conventions.

The Assistance Convention has been invoked a few times to respond to requests from Member States. The Convention was invoked in 1999 in response to emergencies in Peru, Ghana, and Turkey, and it was invoked in response to requests by Georgia and Thailand. The fact that the Assistance Convention is invoked relatively frequently confirms the need for strong international and national response teams.[42] However this Convention is criticized for emphasizing the protection of the assisting state.[43]

Conclusion

The two Conventions have some important limitations as they did not define the term 'radiological safety significance'; contain provisions on intervention level which may be a trigger factor for notification of accidents; and address the

38 Article 10(2)(b)of the Convention.
39 Article 10(2)(d) of the Convention.
40 Article 10(5)(b) of the Convention.
41 Article 11 of the Convention.
42 Karen McMillan, 'Strengthening the International Legal Framework for Nuclear Energy' (2001) 13 *Georgetown International Environmental Law Review* 983–1031, 992.
43 Philippe Sands and Jacqueline Peel, *Principles of International Law* (3rd edn, Cambridge University Press 2012) 543.

question of state responsibility and compensation for nuclear damage.[44] Despite some limitations of these two Conventions, they have contributed to improve overall nuclear safety by reducing the likelihood of transboundary harm or by minimizing effects resulting from nuclear accidents or radiological emergency. These two Conventions can also minimize international environmental harm caused by nuclear accidents. Apart from the legal significance of the two Conventions, the political significance of the Convention on Early Notification is that all five nuclear weapon states have accepted the legal obligations to notify and to give detailed information on all accidents. Many bilateral agreements have been concluded by the States Parties to address a number of issues covered under the Conventions.

44 Edith Brown Weiss, Daniel Barstow Magraw, Stephen C. McCaffrey, Stephanie Tai and A. Dan Tarlock, *International Law for the Environment* (West Academic Publishing 2016) 341.

9 Institutional framework of regulation of nuclear energy

Introduction

The International Atomic Energy Agency (IAEA), Nuclear Energy Agency (NEA), and EURATOM are three main organizations that deal with standard-setting, inspection and technology transfer in nuclear energy. These specialized organizations were created to set technical standards and regulation of nuclear energy which is highly risky and requires special safety measures. Apart from these three main intergovernmental organizations, there is one important non-governmental organization: the International Commission for Radiological Protection (ICRP), and two other intergovernmental organizations, the International Labour Organization (ILO) and the World Health Organization (WHO), which are also concerned with radiation protection.

IAEA

The IAEA was established in 1957 to promote the peaceful development and use of nuclear energy. It is a specialized agency of the UN but works independently as an intergovernmental forum for the scientific and technical cooperation in the field of nuclear energy. The Agency exercises power and functions derived from its mandate under the IAEA Statute and the nuclear treaties which have assigned to it specific responsibilities. The IAEA also has law-making power to set standards and recommendations. Thus, the IAEA has both statute-based and treaty-based functions. Since its establishment, the IAEA has issued standards, codes, voluntary guidelines regarding all aspects of nuclear energy and these enjoy widespread acceptance among states. The IAEA has established institutions such as the Radiation Protection Advisory Team (RAPAT), Operational Safety Review Team (OSART), Assessment of Safety Significant Events Team (ASSET), Waste Management Advisory Programme (WAMAP) and Waste Management Assessment and Technical Review Programme (WATRP) to implement its mandate.

The functions of the IAEA can be described in the following way:

Setting standards on nuclear safety

Since its establishment, the IAEA has been instrumental in setting and promoting the application of international safety standards for the management and regulation of activities involving nuclear and radioactive materials. The IAEA covers the safety of nuclear installations, radioactive sources, radioactive materials in transport, and radioactive waste. Although regulating nuclear safety is largely a national responsibility, the IAEA has been instrumental in developing many legally binding nuclear safety principles and non-binding safety standards in the form of recommendations and guidelines. Many Member States of the IAEA have adopted its safety standards for use in their national regulations. The standards are also applied by designers, manufacturers and operators around the world to enhance nuclear and radiation safety in power generation, medicine, industry, agriculture, research and education.[1] The IAEA Nuclear Safety Standards (NUSS) cover the following five areas: governmental organization of the regulation of nuclear power plants; safety in nuclear power plant siting; safety in the design of nuclear power plants; safety in nuclear power plant operation; and quality assurance for safety of nuclear power plants. In order to disseminate information on unusual events related to nuclear safety, a special system known as the Incident Reporting System (IRS) was created by the IAEA.

Safety measures have the aim of protecting human life and health and the environment. While the principal users of safety standards in IAEA Member States are regulatory bodies and other relevant national authorities, they are also used by co-sponsoring organizations and by many organizations that design, construct and operate nuclear facilities, as well as organizations involved in the use of radiation and radioactive sources. They can be used by states as a reference for their national regulations in respect of facilities and activities. The IAEA's Statute makes the safety standards binding on the IAEA in relation to its own operations and also on states in relation to IAEA-assisted operations. The IAEA safety standards also form the basis for the IAEA's safety review services, and are used by the IAEA in support of competence-building, including in the development of educational curricula and training courses.[2]

For the States Parties to the various international safety Conventions, IAEA standards provide a consistent, reliable means of ensuring the effective fulfilment of obligations under the Conventions. The standards are also applied by designers, manufacturers and operators around the world to enhance nuclear and radiation safety in power generation, medicine, industry, agriculture, research and education.[3]

IAEA role in non-proliferation of nuclear weapons

The IAEA is concerned not only with ensuring the peaceful use of nuclear energy through multilateral and bilateral agreements, but also seeks non-proliferation of nuclear weapons by means of mechanisms developed by it under the international

1 'IAEA Safety Standards, Classification of Radioactive Waste', General Safety Guide IAEA Safety Standards Series No. GSG-1, IAEA, Vienna, 2009.

2 Ibid.

3 Ibid.

instruments. A country undertaking a nuclear power programme should have a clear commitment to its international non-proliferation obligations and safeguards agreement with the IAEA. In addition to establishing standards and recommended practices in radiation protection, nuclear safety and waste management, the IAEA has developed a safeguard system by which, at the request of a state, it can send experts to inspect the facilities of radiation protection, nuclear safety and waste management in that state. Its functions have been described as both positive and negative,[4] the positive function being to 'seek to accelerate and enlarge the contribution of atomic energy to peace, health and prosperity throughout the world', and the negative function 'ensuring that assistance provided by it or at its request or under its supervision or control, is not used in such a way as to further any military purpose'.[5] International verification through IAEA safeguards remains the cornerstone of non-proliferation efforts.[6]

The IAEA established its first 'safeguards system' in 1961, consisting of procedures for safeguarding small research reactors[7] but its comprehensive safeguard system was set up only after adoption of the NPT, which obliges non-nuclear weapons states (NNWS) that are party to the treaty to accept safeguards as set forth in an agreement to be concluded with the IAEA. Since that time, the safeguard system has evolved and been strengthened by the IAEA to take into account the changing perception of the nuclear threat and risk factors, as well as technological development.

The IAEA Department of Safeguards promotes non-proliferation on two ways: by providing credible assurance that states are complying with their international obligations, thus helping to build international confidence; and by being able to detect early any misuse of nuclear material or technology, thereby alerting the world to potential proliferation.[8] In order to achieve this, the Department applies various technical measures to verify the correctness and the completeness of the declarations made by states about their nuclear material and activities.[9] Non-nuclear weapons States Parties to the NPT agree to accept technical safeguards measures applied by the IAEA. These require that operators of nuclear facilities maintain and declare detailed accounting records of all movements and transactions involving nuclear material.[10] These records are verified and audited by regular inspections by the IAEA.

4 Bernhard G. Bechhoefer and Eric Stein, 'Atoms for Peace: The New International Atomic Energy Agency' (1957) 55(6) *Michigan Law Review* 747–798.
5 Article II of the Statute.
6 Laura Rockwood, 'The IAEA and International Safeguards' in Joseph F. Pilat and Nathan E. Busch (eds) *Routledge Handbook of Nuclear Proliferation and Policy* (Routledge 2018) 142–157.
7 Ibid, 144.
8 Nasiru Imam Zakariya and M.T.E. Kahn, 'Safety, Security and Safeguard' (2015) 75 *Annals of Nuclear Energy* 292–302.
9 Ibid, 297.
10 Ibid, 298.

Although safeguards are technical means of verifying compliance with legal obligations relevant to the peaceful uses of nuclear energy, their objectives are political in the sense that they assure the international community of the peaceful nature of safeguarded nuclear activity by deterring diversion or misuse of safeguarded materials or facilities through the risk of early detection.[11] The system has a number of basic features: first, the application of safeguards is primarily but not exclusively based on information provided by the state as to the existence of nuclear material or equipment that should be subject to safeguards. Second, safeguards cannot themselves prevent a violation by a state of its obligations not to divert nuclear material from peaceful purposes. Rather, the safeguard system is designed as an early warning mechanism to initiate the necessary procedures for remedial action in case of violation.[12] But the IAEA has only limited power to act as an international nuclear inspectorate under its statute. Compulsory inspection is possible only where an assistance agreement is in force.[13] Under the IAEA statute, any non-compliance with safeguards obligations is to be reported to the UN Security Council for appropriate action.

There are three different types of safeguard agreements: first, the NPT requires non-nuclear-weapons States Parties to the treaty to enter into legally binding agreements with the IAEA, known as comprehensive safeguards agreements (CSAs). Denuclearization treaties also require their States Parties to enter into CSAs with the IAEA. Under a CSA, the States Parties accept IAEA safeguards on all nuclear material in all peaceful activities in the state. Second, under the NPT five of the nuclear weapon states (NWSs) – China, France, Russia, the UK and the USA – have entered into 'voluntary offer agreements' (VOAs) with the IAEA. Under a VOA, the IAEA applies safeguards to nuclear material in facilities that the NWS has 'offered' for safeguards. Third, an 'item-specific safeguards agreements' that is applied by the IAEA to nuclear material, facilities and other items specified in the agreement. This type of safeguards agreement is currently implemented by the IAEA in three states–India, Israel and Pakistan – which are not party to the NPT.[14]

In order to strengthen and extend the existing safeguards system, a new modality called the 'Additional Protocol' was developed by the IAEA Board of Governors in 1997. This enhanced the IAEA's ability to detect undeclared nuclear activities.[15] The Additional Protocol must be agreed with the IAEA by each NWS, as a supplement to their existing comprehensive safeguards agreement. Under the

11 Mohamed El Baradi, Edwin Nwogugu and John Rames, 'International Law and Nuclear Energy: Overview of the Legal Framework' (1995) 3 *IAEA Bulletin* 22.

12 Ibid.

13 Patricia Birnie and Alan Boyle, *International Law and the Environment* (2nd edn, New York, Oxford University Press 2002) 458.

14 'IAEA Safeguards: Serving', *IAEA Bulletin*, June 2016, 5.

15 'Safeguards to Prevent Nuclear Proliferation', available at http://www.world-nuclear.org/information-library/safety-and-security/non-proliferation/safeguards-to-prevent-nuclear-proliferation.aspx, accessed 16 July 2018.

Additional Protocol, the IAEA is given considerably more information on nuclear and nuclear-related activities, and nuclear-related imports and exports; and IAEA inspectors have greater rights of access.[16] This includes any suspect location, can be at short notice, and the IAEA can deploy environmental sampling and remote monitoring techniques to detect illicit activities.[17] However, the purpose of the Additional Protocol is to provide the IAEA with information on nuclear supply to, and cooperation with, NWS. Many states that have a CSA, also have an additional protocol to their CSA. An additional protocol provides the IAEA with a broader scope of access to information and locations in a state, increasing the IAEA's ability to verify the peaceful use of all nuclear material in that state.[18]

However, many countries which have not joined the NPT are outside the safeguard system.

IAEA role in environmental protection

The scope of the IAEA's involvement in the environmental sphere lies in the sustainable use and management of natural resources, and the protection and understanding of the environment through nuclear technology, and protecting humans and ecosystems from ionizing radiation. The IAEA is actively involved in ensuring the proper operation, closing and decommissioning of nuclear facilities and the proper handling of other radioactive materials, thereby limiting the release of radioactivity into the environment.

Although the IAEA Statute does not specifically provide for environmental protection from radioactive pollution, the Agency's activities in that area are based on its Statute, in particular on its provisions relating to matters of health and safety. The fact that the drafters of the IAEA Statute did not include a specific provision on environmental protection is not surprising, as the initial concern of the international community was ensuring the peaceful uses of nuclear energy.[19] However, currently more than 80 per cent of the activities of the IAEA are in the area of nuclear safety, and about half of those are in the fields of nuclear power, the nuclear fuel cycle, and nuclear applications, which support environmental objectives.[20]

Technical assistance to Member States

The IAEA provides technical assistance to its Member States, particularly developing countries, in formulating their nuclear legislation, organizing training courses on regulatory and technical aspects of nuclear energy in order to enhance capacity-building of the concerned officials. The IAEA assistance and cooperation

16 Ibid.

17 Ibid.

18 'IAEA safeguards: Serving' (n 12) 5–6.

19 Elena Molodstova, 'Nuclear Energy and Environmental Protection: Responses of International Law' (1994) 12(1) *Pace Environmental Law Review* 201.

20 International Atomic Energy Agency: Highlights of Activities 24 (1990).

programmes are implemented through the conclusion of bilateral or other types of agreement. In order to protect the environment and avoid health hazards, the Agency assists its Member States in planning the management and disposal of radioactive wastes, and provides research and scientific support to developing countries at their request.[21]

The IAEA also provides technical assistance to Member States to improve the safety of existing nuclear installations. However, states which receive technical assistance or reactor project assistance must sign an agreement with the IAEA by which they undertake to apply to the assisted operations the Agency's safety standards and measures that are specified in the agreement.

In addition, the IAEA promotes harmonization of nuclear energy legislation worldwide through the conclusion of bilateral agreements with State Parties and the adoption of multilateral agreements, guidelines, standards and codes of practice, which are implemented in national legislation.[22]

The IAEA has introduced a programme called 'Milestones in the Development of a National Infrastructure for Nuclear Power', to provide technical support to the countries which are undertaking their first nuclear power plant. The 'Milestones Approach' supports a sound development process for a new nuclear power programme, enabling a country to understand, and prepare for, the commitments and obligations associated with developing a safe, secure and sustainable nuclear power programme.[23] The infrastructure needed to support the implementation of a nuclear power plant covers not only the physical facilities and equipment but also the facilities for handling the radioactive waste material, necessary legal and regulatory framework, and the human and financial resources to implement the required activities.[24] The IAEA provides the required infrastructure to support a nuclear power programme in three phases:

phase 1: considerations before a decision to undertake a nuclear power programme such as a Pre-Feasibility study;

phase 2: preparatory work for the contracting and construction of a nuclear power plant after a policy decision has been taken. It includes establishment of legal and regulatory framework.

Phase 3: activities to implement the first nuclear power plant.[25]

21 Atomic Energy and the Environment, Fact sheet of IAEA, Vienna.

22 Dr Natalie L.J.T. Horbach, 'Assistance Programmes of the International Atomic Energy Agency to CEEC/NIS', in Nathalie L.J.T. Horbach (ed.), *Contemporary Developments in Nuclear Energy Law: Harmonising Legislation in CEEC/NIS* (The Hague, Kluwer Law International 1999) 439.

23 'IAEA Milestones Approach: Developing the National Infrastructure for Nuclear Power' IAEA, https://www.iaea.org/sites/default/files/18/01/developing-the-national-nuclear-infrastructure-for-nuclear-power.pdf, accessed 18 April 2018.

24 See 'Milestones in the Development of a National Infrastructure for Nuclear Power,' IAEA Nuclear Energy Series No. NG-G-3.1 (Rev. 1) 2015, IAEA, Vienna, https://www-pub.iaea.org/MTCD/Publications/PDF/Pub1704_web.pdf, accessed 16 July 2018.

25 Ibid 21.

The completion of each phase is marked by a specific milestone at which the progress of the development effort can be assessed and a decision can be made to move on to the next phase. These milestones are:

Milestone 1: Ready to make a knowledgeable commitment to a nuclear power programme;
Milestone 2: Ready to invite bids/negotiate a contract for the first nuclear power plant;
Milestone 3: Ready to commission and operate the first nuclear power plant.[26]

The IAEA is currently providing infrastructure support under this programme in Turkey, Poland, Jordan and Bangladesh, which are constructing their first nuclear power reactors.

Based on the Milestones Approach, the IAEA launched the Integrated Nuclear Infrastructure Review (INIR) service in 2009 to both new-comer countries and those that are expanding their nuclear power programme. This service helps ensure that the infrastructure required for the safe, secure and sustainable use of nuclear power is developed and implemented in a responsible and orderly manner.[27] Since its launch in 2009, the INIR service has been widely used by countries in the development or expansion of their nuclear power programmes.[28]

Radiation protection regulation

IAEA has adopted 'Basic Safety Standards for Radiation Protection' which aim to protect human beings from the effects of radiation, but do not contain measures for the protection of the environment.[29] The core of the regulation is the limitation of exposure from controllable sources as it sets out maximum permissible doses of radiation exposure for three categories of human being: workers, individual members of the public, and the whole population. However, the regulation does not set limits of radioactive emissions, and does not identify principles for monitoring and control. Limits for the release of radioactive materials are set out in its 'Principles for Limiting Releases of Radioactive Effluents into the Environment' of 1986[30] and 'The Application of the Principles for Limiting Releases of Radioactive Effluents in the Case of Mining and Milling of Radioactive Ores'.[31]

26 Ibid.
27 'IAEA Milestones Approach: Developing the National Infrastructure for Nuclear Power' IAEA, available at https://www.iaea.org/sites/default/files/18/01/developing-the-national-nuclear-infrastructure-for-nuclear-power.pdf, accessed 16 July 2018.
28 Ibid.
29 Molodstova (n 17) 207–208.
30 See http://www.iaea.org/inis/collection/NCLCollectionStore/_Public/17/072/17072661.pdf?r=1, accessed 19 July 2018.
31 See https://www-pub.iaea.org/books/IAEABooks/3644/The-Application-of-the-Principles-for-Limiting-Releases-of-Radioactive-Effluents-in-the-Case-of-the-Mining-and-Milling-of-Radioactive-Ores, accessed 19 July 2018.

Regulating nuclear waste

The Agency has issued a number of recommendations concerning standards and criteria for high-level waste disposal and for low-level waste disposal. For example, in 1989, the Agency published 'Safety Principles and Standards for the Underground disposal of high-level radioactive waste'. In order to deal with the transboundary movement of nuclear wastes, in 1990 the Agency established a Code of Practice on the International Transboundary Movements of Radioactive Waste. The provisions of the Code are designed to be included within bilateral, multilateral or regional agreements of states on management of high-level radioactive waste.[32] The IAEA also established the Radioactive Waste Safety Standards (RADWASS) programme in 1991 to take a harmonized approach to the safe management of radioactive waste at international level.

Nuclear Energy Agency (NEA)

The Nuclear Energy Agency (NEA) is an intergovernmental agency under the OECD that facilitates scientific cooperation among developed countries with advanced nuclear technology, exchange of information, and harmonization of nuclear legislation in the OECD countries. The main functions of the NEA are:

- to undertake programmes and projects and promote studies and research on the use of nuclear energy for peaceful purposes;[33]
- to promote the formation of joint undertakings for the production of nuclear energy'[34]
- to establish a security control to prevent proliferation of nuclear weapons;[35]
- to promote the safety of nuclear installations, and protect the public and workers against the hazards of ionizing radiation, preservation of the environment;
- to promote third-party liability and insurance with respect to nuclear damage, development of nuclear industry; and
- to disseminate information in the field of nuclear energy.[36]

The NEA is also mandated to collaborate with the IAEA and EURATOM in activities relating to nuclear energy. The specific areas of competence of the NEA include safety and regulation of nuclear activities, radioactive waste management, radiological protection, nuclear science, economic and technical analyses of the nuclear fuel cycle, nuclear law and liability, and public information on nuclear energy. The NEA carries out these functions through a Steering Committee

32 Molodstova (n 17) 217.
33 Article 4 of the Statute.
34 Article 5 of the Statute.
35 Article 6 of the Statute.
36 Article 8 of the Statute.

composed of representatives of all governments, which can adopt a 'decision' or recommendation regarding any matter within its competence.[37] Decisions are binding on the Member States.

Nuclear safety

The NEA assists member countries in ensuring high standards of safety in the use of nuclear energy, by supporting the development of effective and efficient regulation and oversight of nuclear installations, and by helping to maintain and advance the scientific and technological knowledge base.[38] These functions are carried out through two committees: the Committee on the Safety of Nuclear Installations (CSNI) and the Committee on Nuclear Regulatory Activities (CNRA). It also undertakes joint projects related to nuclear safety. It set up the first international Incident Reporting System (IRS) between national nuclear regulatory organizations for systematically collecting and disseminating information on reactor operating experience.

Radioactive waste management and decommissioning

The NEA also assists its Member States in developing safe, sustainable and socetially acceptable strategies for the management of all types of radioactive waste. In 1975 it established the Radioactive Waste Management Committee (RWMC), which comprises senior representatives from regulatory authorities, radioactive waste management and decommissioning organizations, policy-making bodies, and research and development institutions from the NEA states. The RWMC maintains strong ties with national high-level advisory bodies to governments and with transnational bodies such as the International Commission on Radiological Protection. The purpose of the RWMC is to support international cooperation in the management of material from nuclear installations, including facility decommissioning and long-term waste management. The Committee implements a programme of work that fosters a shared and broad-based understanding of the state-of-the-art and emerging issues; facilitates the elaboration of waste management strategies that respect societal requirements; helps to provide common bases to the national regulatory frameworks; enables the management of radioactive waste and materials to benefit from the progress of scientific and technical knowledge, for example through joint projects and specialist meetings; contributes to knowledge consolidation and transfer, for example through the publication of technical reports, consensus statements and short flyers; and helps to advance best practice, for example by supporting international peer reviews.

37 Articles 9 and 10 of the Statute.

38 'Nuclear Safety and Regulation', available at https://www.oecd-nea.org/nsd/, accessed 16 July 2018.

Overall, the RWMC is a unique multinational committee of specialists at the forefront in addressing both the technical and societal requirements for durable and sustainable waste management and decommissioning solutions.[39]

Radiological protection

The NEA assists Member States in the regulation and implementation of the system of radiological protection by identifying and addressing conceptual, scientific, policy, regulatory, operational and societal issues and clarifying their implications. It also identifies emerging issues in radiological protection science and improves the implementation of scientific knowledge for practical uses; and assists policy-makers in developing and improving policies to best reflect state-of-the-art science and technology, as well as modern approaches to risk governance. It facilitates the improvement of Member States' operational radiological protection capabilities.

The Committee on Radiological Protection and Public Health (CRPPH) addresses two areas: conceptual and policy issues, and operational radiation protection. The CRPPH works in close collaboration with the IAEA in the area of radiation protection, and the two agencies' programmes of work are complementary. Results of these programmes are made available to the international nuclear community.

One important aspect of the NEA's work focuses on the role of civil society and how to best to involve stakeholders in the decision-making process.

European Atomic Energy Community (EURATOM)

EURATOM was established by the Treaty of Rome of 1957 alongside the European Economic Community (EEC). According to the Treaty, the specific tasks of EURATOM are to promote research and to ensure the dissemination of technical information; to establish uniform safety standards to protect the health of workers and of the general public and ensure that they are applied; to facilitate investment and ensure the establishment of the basic installations necessary for the development of nuclear energy in the EU; and to ensure that all users in the EU receive a regular and equitable supply of ores and nuclear fuels. Supplies of ores, source materials and special fissile materials are ensured by means of a common supply policy based on the principle of equal access to sources of supply.

EURATOM is a part of the European Union and has the same members as the European Union. It is governed by the Commission and Council, operating under the jurisdiction of the European Court of Justice. EURATOM regulates the European civil nuclear industry, which produces almost 30 per cent of energy in the EU. In order to regulate the common nuclear market, the EURATOM

39 'Radioactive Waste Management and Decommissioning', https://www.oecd-nea.org/rwm/, accessed 16 July 2018.

Supply Agency (ESA) was established under Article 52 of the Treaty. It is an independent commercial body with legal personality and financial autonomy, even though it was to operate under the Commission's supervision. It aims to ensure a regular and equitable supply of nuclear fuels to EU users. To this end, the ESA applies a supply policy based on the principle of equal access of all users to ores and nuclear fuel.[40] The ESA works on enhancing the security of supply for users located in the European Union, and in order to achieve this it recommends that EU utilities operating nuclear power plants maintain stocks of nuclear materials and cover their needs by entering into long-term contracts with diverse sources of supply. It also monitors the common nuclear market to ensure that the market activities of individual users reflect the values set out in the treaty.[41]

The EURATOM Treaty contains stringent provisions on health and safety, and on safeguards for the peaceful use of nuclear energy. The Treaty provisions are implemented through making regulations, issuing directives, taking decisions and making recommendations through the Council and the Commission.[42] While a regulation is binding on all Member States, a directive is binding on the State Party to whom it is addressed, with the choice of form and method being left to Member States. On the other hand, a decision is binding upon those states to whom it is addressed.[43] Generally, EURATOM's regulations cover issues on nuclear safeguards, certain requirements concerning investments in nuclear activities or certain basic definitions of nuclear materials.[44] EURATOM's directives are concerned with 'basic standards' on specific areas of radiation protection such as radiation protection in nuclear medicine and radiology, in the shipment of radioactive substance, etc. On the other hand, decisions have been adopted in specific areas such as the exchange of information in the case of radiological emergency or nuclear safety.[45] The recommendations are adopted in specific areas, such as guidelines for the application of certain EURATOM Treaty provisions, radioactive waste classification and disposal.[46]

As with the IAEA and the NEA, the protection of health and safety from radiation is an important objective of EURATOM. According to the EURATOM Treaty, it is the responsibility of the Commission to establish Basic Safety Standards. Article 30 of the Treaty defines the phrase 'basic standards' to mean: '(a) maximum permissible doses compatible with adequate safety; (b) maximum permissible levels of exposure and contamination; (c) the fundamental principles governing the health surveillance of workers.' This definition covers only matters of

40 EURATOM Supply Agency, see http://ec.europa.eu/euratom/mission.html, accessed 16 July 2018.

41 Ibid.

42 Article 161 of the Treaty.

43 Ibid.

44 Fabrizio Nocera, *The Legal Regime of Nuclear Energy: A Comprehensive Guide to International and European Union Law* (Antwerpen-Oxford, Intersentia 2005) 43.

45 Ibid, 44.

46 Ibid.

radiation protection and does not address nuclear safety. The Council first adopted the Basic Safety Standards in 1959, in the form of the Council's Directive. It adopted the latest Basic Safety Standards in 2013 and repealed earlier directives for protection against the dangers arising from exposure to ionizing radiation to reflect the scientific developments in the area of radiation protection. This Directive establishes uniform basic safety standards for the protection of the health of individuals subject to occupational, medical and public exposures against the dangers arising from ionizing radiation.[47] It applies to any planned, existing or emergency exposure situation which involves a risk from exposure to ionizing radiation which cannot be disregarded from a radiation protection point of view or with regard to the environment in view of long-term human health protection.[48]

Unlike the IAEA Statute, the EURATOM Treaty contains provisions on environmental protection from radiation. Article 34 of the treaty requires the assent of the Commission when the effects of 'particularly dangerous experiments' are liable to affect the territories of other Member States. This provision addresses possible transnational environmental harm. Legal requirements and regulatory control of radiation protection under EURATOM are based on the principles of justification, optimization and dose limitation.[49] The implementation and enforcement of the Basic Safety Standards are in the hands of the Member States. Each Member State lays down appropriate provisions, whether by legislation, regulation or administrative action, to ensure compliance with the basic standards established by the Treaty. Each Member State shall establish the facilities to carry out continuous monitoring of the level of radioactivity in the air, water and soil. The Commission has a right of inspection of the monitoring facilities of the Member States in order to ensure their compliance with the Basic Safety Standards.[50] The Commission reserves the power to initiate legal proceedings in the case of non-compliance with the Uniform Safety Standards Directive. Articles 35 and 36 of the EURATOM Treaty provide for the regular monitoring and transmission of information on the levels of radioactivity to which the public is exposed. According to Article 37 of the Treaty, Member States are required to submit to the Commission 'general data' relating to any plan for the disposal of radioactive waste to determine the implementation of such plan in a Member State.[51] However, there is no definition of 'general data'. The Commission assesses whether the planned installations are liable to lead to an exposure, significant from the point of view of the health of the population of another Member State, or to significant contamination of the water, soil or airspace of another Member State.

The Commission may send inspectors into the territories of Member States. These inspectors have access at all times to all places and data, and to all persons who, by reason of their occupation, deal with materials, equipment or installations

47 Article 1 of the Council Directive 2013/59/EURATOM.
48 Article 2 of the Directive.
49 Article 5 of the Directive.
50 Article 35 of the Treaty.
51 Molodtsova (n 17) 280–281.

subject to the safeguards. The EURATOM safeguards are applied in conjunction with those of the IAEA under tripartite agreements concluded between the Member States, the Community and the IAEA.

In the event of infringement of these obligations, the Commission may impose sanctions on the persons or undertakings responsible. These sanctions can range from a simple warning to the total or partial withdrawal of source materials or special fissile materials, and can also include the withdrawal of special benefits (such as financial or technical assistance) or the placing of the undertaking under the administration of a person or a board.[52]

International Commission on Radiological Protection (ICRP)

The ICRP, a non-governmental body of experts, makes recommendations for the protection of people from the harmful effects of ionizing radiation. It was originally established in 1928 as the International X-ray and Radium Protection Committee and renamed in 1950. The primary aim of radiological protection, as stated by the ICRP, is to provide an appropriate standard of protection for mankind from exposure to radiation. The standards and recommendations of the ICRP are based on a precautionary approach limiting by all reasonable means the risk of health effects, but not on eliminating that risk entirely. The ICRP plays a central role in formulating the radiation protection standards and its recommendations directly influence the radiation protection laws and the regulations of most states, as well as international standards on radiation protection.[53] The International System of Radiological Protection developed by ICRP is based on (i) the current understanding of the science of radiation exposure its and effects, and (ii) value judgements. These value judgements take into account societal expectations, ethics, and experience gained in application of the system.[54] The 1990 Recommendations of the ICRP identify three types of exposure: exposure at work, medical exposure as part of diagnosis or treatment, and public exposure and recommended limits on the effective dose for occupational and public exposure.[55]

Conclusion

The IAEA has made a profound contribution in setting international standards on the use of nuclear energy, developing a liability regime, establishing safety and security norms for nuclear installations, and developing oversight mechanism for

52 See http://eur-lex.europa.eu/legal-content/EN/TXT/?uri=uriserv%3Axy0024, accessed 16 July 2018.

53 Molodstova (n 17) 192.

54 See http://www.icrp.org/, accessed 16 July 2018.

55 Stephen Tromans and James Fitzgerald, *The Law of Nuclear Installations and Radioactive Substances* (London, Sweet and Maxwell 1997) 38.

ensuring peaceful use of nuclear energy. While regulation of nuclear safety and security rests on individual states, IAEA is playing an important role in helping Member States to implement their nuclear energy programmes in a safe, secure and environmentally sustainable manner. The IAEA has law-making power which is used in the adoption of treaties (hard law) and recommendatory power which is exercised in formulating standards, codes and guidelines (soft law). The Agency's role in developing nuclear law – both in the form of soft law and hard law – is tremendous and has created many new norms under international law. However, not all nuclear states have fully implemented the treaties or soft law norms in their national regulatory framework.

After the Fukushima accident, it was realised that the current international nuclear regulatory system should be more effective and that the IAEA should be strengthened to enforce the international legal rules. Its ability in terms of oversight and monitoring of nuclear installations should be increased in view of the increasing number of states using nuclear energy. While the states are and should remain the current major players in the international system, the IAEA's role as global regulator needs to be further expanded.[56] It should be given greater leeway to conduct inspections. Currently this power is limited to agency projects and requests by members, but independent inspections could contribute to higher levels of safety.[57] These inspections would review not only the equipment, management and safety culture of the plants, but also the compliance with the regulatory schemes and international standards, avoiding the pitfalls of vague self-reports.[58]

The mandate of the IAEA is different from that of the NEA. While the NEA focuses on selected areas where the member countries seek such authoritative assessments and the development of common understandings, the mission of the IAEA is to accelerate and enlarge the contribution of atomic energy to peace, health and prosperity throughout the world. The IAEA mission encompasses all areas of nuclear technology and non-proliferation of nuclear weapons around the world. But the NEA does no work in most of the areas in which the IAEA operates. While the NEA believes non-proliferation is important, it does not engage in any work on non-proliferation policies or international agreements, and does not participate in inspections to assure compliance with non-proliferation treaties. The NEA also has no involvement in providing technical assistance to the developing world, which is a major focus for the IAEA. However, there are technological areas of common interest to both organizations. Both organizations are interested in the safe operation of reactors, waste disposal, protection

56 Gregory L. Schulte, 'Strengthening the IAEA: How the Nuclear Watchdog Can Regain Its Bark' (2010) 4 *Strategic Forum* 253; Emily Benz, 'Lessons from Fukushima: Strengthening the International Regulation of Nuclear Energy' (2013) 37 *William and Mary Environmental Law and Policy Review* 845, 880.

57 Benz (n 56) 881.

58 Karen McMillan, 'Strengthening the International Legal Framework for Nuclear Energy' (2001) 13 *Georgetown International Environmental Law Review* 983, 990.

of the public from radioactive exposure, and carrying on research and studies.[59] Two prominent examples of mutual effort are the IAEA/NEA Incident Reporting System (IRS) and the International Nuclear Event Scale (INES). The IRS addresses events at all types of nuclear installation as well as occurrences associated with the transportation of radioactive materials and the use of radioactive sources. The NEA has continued to work with the IAEA on both these systems, jointly managing the IRS and as a member of the Advisory Committee for INES. Thus, the development and implementation of these systems has followed a symbiotic, mutually beneficial path.[60]

EURATOM has greatly contributed to the development of Europe's nuclear industries, ensuring security of supply, and guaranteeing high safety standards for the public. It also aims at preventing nuclear materials intended principally for civilian use from being diverted to military use. The EURATOM Treaty introduces an extremely comprehensive and strict system of safeguards to ensure that civil nuclear materials are not diverted from the civil use declared by the Member States.

59 G.H. Marcus, 'The NEA and the IAEA: partnering for progress,' *NEA News* 2005 23(2).
60 Ibid.

10 Legislative trends on nuclear energy in selected countries

Introduction

Comprehensive nuclear legislation comprising safety, security, liability and licensing requirements is needed for the effective operation of nuclear installations. An adequate and transparent regulatory framework is essential for controlling the activities and all types of nuclear installation. Many states having commercial nuclear programmes have ratified nuclear treaties and have developed their own legislative schemes to implement the obligations under those treaties. This domestic legal framework consists of a liability regime, nuclear waste management, nuclear safety and decommissioning. Many national legal frameworks implement the principles of the third-party liability Conventions', and impose financial security requirements which vary from state to state.[1] In those states where the nuclear power plants are state-owned, separation between regulation and operation of nuclear power plants is maintained. Generally, the power of control of licensing and regulating nuclear operation is vested in the state or government agency while responsibility for the operational functions is entrusted to operators. Different states have quite different arrangements for the implementation and enforcement of the law. In many states, a single piece of legislation covers all aspects of the operation of nuclear installations, nuclear safety and security and management of radioactive waste.

An appropriate licensing regime should enable the licensee to know exactly what its responsibilities and duties are, and how to accomplish them while minimizing potential injuries to third parties resulting from such nuclear activities. In general, nuclear law should clearly identify and define the rights and obligations of regulatory bodies and operators in order to avoid duplication of regulation. Nuclear liability legislation must be applied without discrimination based on nationality, domicile or residence.[2]

1 'Liability for Nuclear Damage', World Nuclear Association, available at http://www.world-nuclear.org/information-library/safety-and-security/safety-of-plants/liability-for-nuclear-damage.aspx, accessed 16 July 2018.

2 Carlton Stoiber et al., *Handbook on Nuclear Law* (Vienna, International Atomic Energy Agency 2003) 115.

The following sections discuss the national regulatory framework of the USA, UK, India and Bangladesh on nuclear energy for peaceful purposes.

National legal framework on nuclear energy

USA

The USA is the world's largest producer of nuclear power with 99 nuclear power plants which account more than 30 per cent of worldwide nuclear generation of electricity.[3] In the 1950s, the US Government, realizing that nuclear energy could provide a cost-efficient and abundant source of electricity, adopted the Atomic Energy Act of 1954 to develop and encourage its civilian nuclear industry. This Act permitted for the first time the wide use of atomic energy for peaceful purposes.

The Atomic Energy Act of 1954 established the Atomic Energy Commission (AEC) and US Department of Energy (DOE) with sole federal responsibility to regulate the commercial use of nuclear materials, by-products and sources including the regulation of civilian nuclear reactors. Subsequently, the Energy Reorganization Act 1974 established two specialized organizations – the Nuclear Regulatory Commission (NRC) and the Energy Research and Development Administration (ERDA) – and abolished the Atomic Energy Commission. The NRC licenses all commercial nuclear power reactors in the United States. It also has statutory responsibility for the protection of public health and safety and the environment related to the possession and use of source, by-product and special nuclear material under the Atomic Energy Act. The National Environmental Policy Act (NEPA) of 1969 requires federal agencies to consider environmental values and factors in agency planning and decision-making. The Atomic Energy Act directed the AEC to encourage widespread participation in the development and utilization of atomic energy for peaceful purposes. At the same time, it instructed the AEC to prepare regulations that would protect public health and safety from radiation hazards. Thus, the 1954 Act assigned the AEC three major roles: to continue its weapons programme, to promote the private use of atomic energy for peaceful applications, and to protect public health and safety from the hazards of commercial nuclear power.

Third-party liability

Initially, when the first nuclear power plants were operated exclusively by a US state, the rule in the USA was that only the operator was liable in the case of a nuclear accident. Logically, the US suppliers and designers asked for contractual 'hold harmless' clauses in their contracts to channel liability to the state because,

3 'Nuclear Power in the USA', available at http://www.world-nuclear.org/information-library/country-profiles/countries-t-z/usa-nuclear-power.aspx, accessed 19 July 2018.

at the time, no insurance was available for nuclear activities. It should be noted that these clauses did not prevent victims from initiating lawsuits against US companies in the nuclear business. Indeed, these clauses contractually guaranteed that the state would fully bear the financial burden of any arising liability. In order to overcome the risk of third-party liability, which was hampering private sector participation in nuclear activities, the US Congress enacted the Price-Anderson Nuclear Industries Indemnity Act (commonly called the Price-Anderson Act) in 1957. This federal legislation has three purposes: first, it establishes public liability rules to provide compensation to the public who may be injured as a result of a nuclear accident at a commercial nuclear power plant or a facility of the US operated by a contractor. Second, the Act was intended to facilitate private sector participation in the nuclear industry. Third, it provided a ready source of funds to compensate injured victims of a nuclear accident. The concept of a 'nuclear incident' under the Price-Anderson Act is broad and applies to nuclear incidents within the United States causing damage within and outside the United States, and thus the Act covers transboundary damage. Originally the Act required that a total of at least $560 million in insurance or government indemnity be available to cover public liability claims arising out of an accident at a nuclear power plant or a nuclear facility. In the case of government-owned facilities, this amount was $500 million under the original Act. Each operator is required to maintain 'financial protection' (liability insurance) of such type and amount as the Nuclear Regulatory Commission shall require to cover public liability claims.

Historically, the USA followed 'economic channelling' of nuclear liability as opposed to the system of legal channelling of liability to the plant operator. For this reason, the USA never became a party to the Paris Convention and the Vienna Convention on Third Party Liability. On the other hand, the USA is a party to the Convention on Supplementary Compensation for Nuclear Damage, which recognizes that the American system provides protection equivalent to the Vienna and the Paris Conventions. The 1957 Price-Anderson Act provides for the principle of economic channelling of liability by which suppliers and designers can be held liable in the case of nuclear accident. It covers 'anyone liable' for a nuclear incident. Moreover, the Price-Anderson Act channels to one source of funds (that is, indemnification by the Department of Energy (DOE)) the payment of all claims arising from the legal liability of any person for a nuclear incident. This 'economic channelling' eliminates the need to sue all potential defendants or to allocate legal liability among multiple potential defendants. In enacting the Price-Anderson Act in 1957, the United States created the world's first national nuclear liability regime. Under the Act, each power plant operator now provides nuclear hazards coverage for anyone liable through a combination of private insurance from the American nuclear insurance pools and a retrospective assessment. Payments are guaranteed by the US Government and there is an inflation adjustment every five years. The Price-Anderson Act requires Nuclear Regulatory Commission licensees and the Department of Energy contractors to enter into agreements of indemnification to cover personal injury and property damage to those harmed by a nuclear or radiological incident, including the costs of incident response or precautionary evacuation and the costs of investigating and defending claims and settling suits for such damages.[4] The provisions of the Price-Anderson Act were first applied after the Three Mile Island Accident to pay compensation to the victims. The Price-Anderson Act is treated as a consumer-oriented legislation as it provides a substantial amount of insurance protection paid by the commercial sector at no cost to the public or the Government. It provides for a single federal court with jurisdiction over all claims of nuclear accident and contains numerous provisions to minimize protracted litigation and, in particular, eliminates the need to prove the fault of any of the various potential defendants.[5]

The Price-Anderson Act has been revised several times. In 1966, the US Congress amended the Price-Anderson Act for the purpose of further assuring prompt compensation to the public for nuclear incidents in the case of an extraordinary nuclear occurrence (that is, any nuclear incident that causes substantial off-site damage). In such cases, the Price-Anderson Act imposes strict liability by requiring the waiver of any defences related to the conduct of the claimant or fault of any person indemnified. This amendment maximizes protection of the public by eliminating legal barriers to claims that varied among the states.[6] The main reason for introducing the 'concept of extraordinary nuclear occurrence' and waiver of defence was to remove obstacles to a claimant's recovery for injury or damages arising out of a nuclear accident, i.e. the need to prove negligence or other tort.[7] The second major change to the Price-Anderson Act occurred in 1975 when the requirement for a 'secondary financial protection' layer was added in order to phase out the need for Government indemnity guarantees. The secondary lawyer is financed by a retrospective premium of up to $5 million per incident levied against each reactor licensee.[8] The 1988 Amendments to this Act significantly increased the amount of the DOE indemnification for a nuclear incident in the United States from $500 million to $9.43 billion, and made inclusion of DOE indemnification mandatory in all DOE contracts involving the risk of a nuclear incident.[9] Thus, the Act currently aims to ensure the availability of a pool of funds of about $10 billion, which is the highest amount of nuclear liability coverage in the world.

4 The Price-Anderson Act: Background Information, available at http://cdn.ans.org/pi/ps/docs/ps54-bi.pdf, accessed 16 July 2018.

5 Report to Congress on the Price-Anderson Act, US Department of Energy, available at https://www.energy.gov/sites/prod/files/gcprod/documents/paa-rep.pdf, accessed 16 July 2018.

6 Omer F. Brown II, 'Recent Developments from the Perspective of the United States', in Nathalie L.J.T. Horbach (ed.), *Contemporary Developments in Nuclear Energy Law: Harmonising Legislation in CEEC/NIS* (The Hague, Kluwer Law International 1999) 480–481.

7 Guy H. Cunninham, 'United States Extension of Indemnification to Utilities and Contractors', in Peter Cameron, Leigh Hancher, Wolfgang Kuhn, *Nuclear Energy Law after Chernobyl* (London, Graham and Trotman and International Bar Association) 143.

8 Ibid.

9 Report to Congress on the Price-Anderson Act (n 4) 5.

In order to strengthen the nuclear compensation system, the Radiation Exposure Compensation Act (RECA) of 15 October 1990 was amended in 2000 by Public Law No. 106–245 to provide for payment of compensation to individuals who contracted certain diseases due to unintended exposure to radiation resulting from the United States nuclear weapons testing programme. The Act sets out a list of conditions to be met for compensation. The 2000 Amendment to RECA expands the eligibility requirements for getting such compensation.

Nuclear waste management

The national policy on regulatory control of radioactive waste management in the USA has evolved through a series of laws that established the federal governmental agencies responsible for the safety of radioactive materials. The US legislation established a role for the following three federal agencies regarding the geologic disposal of HLW from civilian nuclear power plants. The DOE is responsible for developing general guidelines for the siting of a repository in a geologic formation, as well as for designing, building and operating this geologic repository. The EPA is responsible for promulgating generally applicable standards necessary to protect the public from releases of radioactive material from the geologic repository. The NRC is responsible the development of technical criteria and requirements for licensing any potential geologic repository, including repository construction, operations and closure. The NRC is an independent regulatory agency established under the Energy Re-organization Act of 1974 to ensure adequate protection of public health and safety, common defence and security, and the environment in the civilian use of nuclear materials in the US. The NRC's scope of responsibility includes regulation of: (i) commercial nuclear power; non-power research, test and training reactors; (ii) fuel cycle facilities; medical, academic, and industrial uses of nuclear materials; and (iii) the transport, storage, and disposal of nuclear materials and waste.

To fulfil its objectives, the NRC has established licensing procedures for regulating the use of by-product, source and special nuclear materials. Specifically, the NRC goals for radioactive waste management are: to ensure treatment, storage and disposal of waste produced by civilian use of nuclear materials in ways that do not adversely affect future generations, and to protect the environment. The NRC's research programme in nuclear waste safety focuses on improving the regulatory framework and reducing the burden on the licensees of assessing the performance of waste disposal, contaminated site clean-up, clearance and decommissioning activities. An important aspect of the NRC's regulatory programme is its inspection and enforcement activities. The US Nuclear Waste Technical Review Board (NWTRB) provides independent scientific and technical oversight of the DOE programme.

The Environmental Protection Agency (EPA) established under the National Environmental Policy Act (NEPA) 1969 has responsibility for setting generally applicable standards for radioactivity in the environment and accordingly the EPA has established standards for the clean-up of uranium mill-tailing sites, environmental standards for the uranium fuel cycle, and environmental radiation protection standards for the management and disposal of spent nuclear fuel (SNF), high level radioactive waste (HLW) and transuranic waste (TRU).

The Low-Level Radioactive Waste Policy Act of 1980 deals with disposal of low-level radioactive waste. This Act was amended in 1985 to make states responsible for providing for the disposal of commercial LLW generated within their borders. The Act encouraged states to enter into compacts that would allow several states to dispose of waste at a regional disposal facility. Most of the states have entered into such compacts. The NRC has no direct licensing responsibilities for LLW disposal facilities at this time. The Low-Level Radioactive Waste Policy Act of 1980 (LLWPA) and the Low-Level Radioactive Waste Policy Amendments Act of 1985 assigned to the states, rather than to the federal government, responsibility for providing disposal capacity for commercial LLW. With regard to HLW, the Nuclear Waste Policy Act of 1982 and the Nuclear Waste Policy Amendments Act of 1987 (NWPAA) contain detailed provisions for the disposal of HLW with the DOE having operational responsibility for the HLW repository, the NRC having regulatory responsibility for the transportation, storage and geologic disposal of the waste and the US Nuclear Waste Technical Review Board (NWTRB) having responsibility to evaluate the technical and scientific validity of activities undertaken by the DOE.

Wastes from uranium mill tailing in the USA is regulated by the Uranium Mill Tailings Radiation Control Act of 1978 which aims at (i) oversight and programmatic direction for the uranium recovery programme; (ii) implementation of policies and programmes; and (iii) review of uranium recovery licensing and inspection programmes for technical adequacy and consistency. This Act vested the EPA with overall responsibility for establishing environmental standards for the decommissioning of uranium production facilities, the NRC with responsibility for licensing and regulating uranium production and related activities, including decommissioning, and DOE with responsibility for long-term monitoring of the decommissioned sites.

HLW disposal has become a major subject of public concern in the USA. The US Department of Energy has by statute ultimate responsibility for the disposal of high-level radioactive waste. In its Strategic Plan, the NRC set the following as its goal in nuclear waste safety: 'Ensure treatment, storage, and disposal of waste produced by civilian uses of nuclear material in ways that do not adversely affect this or future generations.'

Most spent fuels are now in temporary storage at the reactors where they were produced or in intermediate storage either at the reactors or alternative sites. The Energy Policy Act 1992 mandated a new and different process for developing the HLW disposal regulations for the proposed repository at Yucca Mountain, Nevada. The Energy Policy Act 1992 directs the EPA to issue environmental standards associated with such sites to protect public health and safety.[10] DOE

10 EPA, Radioactive Waste Disposal: An Environmental Perspective, see https://www.epa.gov/radiation/radioactive-waste-disposal-environmental-perspective, accessed 16 July 2018.

issued its final repository siting guidelines for Nuclear Waste Repositories in Yucca Mountain Site in 2001. In June 2008, the Department of Energy submitted a licence application to the Nuclear Regulatory Commission for authorization to begin construction of a repository at Yucca Mountain site. However, owing to public opposition, legal challenge and disapproval from the Nevada government, fear of leakage and other environmental uncertainties, the plan to use Yucca Mountain in Nevada, which is the only designated long-term waste disposal site, was suspended in 2009. Therefore, there is currently no facility for permanent disposal of high-level waste in the USA.[11]

Decommissioning

In the United States, private sector contractors have been engaged by the DOE to conduct decommissioning and clean-up operations on government-owned sites on a cost-reimbursement basis. However, the NRC has overall responsibility for assuring the safe and timely decommissioning of nuclear facilities which it licenses. In the licence the NRC specifies decommissioning requirements, and provides guidance to licensees on how to plan for and prepare their sites for decommissioning.[12] For the NRC, decommissioning means to remove nuclear facilities safely from service and to reduce residual radioactivity to a level that permits release of the property for unrestricted use or for use under restricted conditions and termination of the licence.[13] Decommissioning activities do not include the removal and disposal of spent fuel, or the removal and disposal of non-radioactive structures and materials beyond that necessary to terminate the NRC licence.[14] This action is taken by a licensee before termination of the licence. In other cases, non-licensed facilities may also be required to decontaminate and decommission the site in order to meet NRC release limits.

The UK

Commercial use of nuclear energy in the UK began in 1956 and there are currently 23 nuclear power plants generating about 18 per cent of its electricity; all but one of these is scheduled to retire by 2030. The UK Government is planning to build new nuclear power stations. The country has full fuel cycle facilities, including major reprocessing plants. The first UK legislation on nuclear energy was the Atomic Energy Authority Act 1954, which established the UK Atomic Energy Authority. The main purposes of the Authority was to produce, use and dispose of atomic energy and to carry out research into atomic energy. The Nuclear Installation (Licensing and Insurance) Act 1965 deals with the

11 Radioactive Waste, see https://www.nrc.gov/reading-rm/doc-collections/fact-sheets/radwaste.pdf, accessed 16 July 2018.

12 'Nuclear Legislation in OECD and NEA Countries: USA', OECD, 2016, 12.

13 Ibid.

14 Ibid.

requirements for the licensing of nuclear reactors and other installations in the UK.[15] According to this Act, activities relating to the management and handling of nuclear installations and materials ranging from installing and operating a nuclear reactor to conducting ancillary activities such as storage, processing or disposal of radioactive material require a nuclear site licence.[16] The UK Government's policy on nuclear energy was stated in a 2008 White paper titled 'Meeting the Energy Challenge: a White Paper on Nuclear Power' and focuses on goals of nuclear energy towards low-carbon energy to meet the challenges of climate change and to ensure security of supply.

Third party liability regime

The nuclear liability regime in the UK is based on the Paris and Brussels Conventions. The third party nuclear liability in the UK is governed by the Nuclear Installation Act 1965, under which primary liability for a nuclear incident attaches to the holder of a nuclear site licence. This Act provides that the operator of a nuclear installation is strictly liable for nuclear damage to third parties caused by radioactive emissions from the installation. The operator's liability for personal injury and property damage for any one incident is capped and limited in time. Operators must have insurance or other financial security in place covering their potential liability. Operators also bear prime responsibility for safety and environmental protection relating to activities carried out on their sites. The Office for Nuclear Regulation (ONR) requires the licensee to have an adequate management structure, capability and resources to do this before granting a nuclear site licence.[17] The Nuclear Installations (Liability for Damage) Order (NIO) 2016, which amends the Nuclear Installations Act 1965, aims to implement the 2004 Amending Protocol to the Paris Convention on Nuclear Third Party Liability and the Brussels Supplementary Convention. Under section 3 of the NIO, it is the duty of the licensee to ensure that no occurrence involving the emission of ionizing radiations causes (a) injury to any person, (b) damage to any property, or (c) significant impairment of the environment. This amending Order has brought major changes to the existing nuclear liability regime in the UK. It means that in the event of a nuclear incident an increased amount of compensation will be available, in respect of a broader range of damage, to a wider category of claimants. Furthermore, the cap on operator liability will be raised, geographic scope will be widened, limitation periods will be extended, and the way in which jurisdiction is decided will be altered. Finally, victims will have greater potential for recourse than under the existing regime. The key provisions

15 For detailed discussion, see Stephen Tromans, and James Fitzgerald, *The Law of Nuclear Installations and Radioactive Substances* (London, Sweet and Maxwell 1997) 55–70.

16 Sections 3–5 of the Act.

17 Richard M. Temple, Christina Penny, and Mary Anne Sullivan, 'Liability for Nuclear Incidents: Should the UK now Follow the US Approach?' (2006) 18(3) *Journal of Environmental Law* 443–457.

of the 2016 Order will come into force when the 2004 Protocol comes into force in respect of the UK.

The main changes made to the liability regime by the NIO are as follows:

Introduction of three new categories of compensable damage

The existing regime applies only to personal injury and property damage. The NIO introduces three new categories of damage: costs of measures of reinstatement of the impaired environment; loss of income deriving from any use of the environment; and costs of preventative measures for an actual or a 'grave or imminent threat' of a nuclear incident.[18]

Rise in cap on operator liability and funds available for compensation

Under the existing regime, there is a £140m cap on liability for operators for any one incident; that will rise to €1.2bn under the new regime. Thus, operators must put in place insurance or other financial security to cover their potential liability.[19]

Wider geographical scope

The new liability regime will broaden the geographical scope to include non-Paris Convention states. Under the previous regime, claimants from non-Paris Convention states could not seek compensation. The geographical scope of the Paris Convention will now be increased to include all 'qualifying territories', which is broader than the previous 'relevant territories'.[20] Qualifying territories includes all 'relevant territories' that were previously within its scope, and also includes non-nuclear states and those states that have equivalent and reciprocal liability arrangements.[21] This means that people of a state which is a non-nuclear and not party to the Paris Convention, suffering from nuclear damage because of a nuclear incident in the UK, can now make a claim in the UK under the new nuclear liability regime. They can now seek compensation in the UK under the new regime, although it does not bar them from bringing claims in their own national courts.[22]

18 'Nuclear Changes to the UK Nuclear Liability Regime', see http://knowledge.freshfields.com/m/Global/r/1545/nuclear_liability_regime__major_changes_for_the_uk_regime, accessed 17 July 2018.

19 'Nuclear Liability Regime: Major Changes for the UK Regime Finalised – In Force Soon', see http://knowledge.freshfields.com/m/Global/r/1545/nuclear_liability_regime__major_changes_for_the_uk_regime, accessed 17 July 2018

20 Ibid.

21 Ibid.

22 Ibid.

Extended limitation period

The current Paris Convention limits the right to claim compensation to 10 years from the date of a nuclear incident. This has been extended by the Amending Protocol to 30 years for personal injury claims. For all other claims the 10-year limitation continues to apply. Under the NIO, the right to claim compensation will be extended from 10 years to 30 years for personal injury claims.

Changes in the insurance market

Under the Paris Convention, operators are required to maintain insurance or other financial security to cover potential nuclear liability to third parties. One of the consequences of the new liability regime is that operators must increase their existing form of security to cover this additional level and scope of liability. The increased level of liability will make operators' insurance obligations more onerous and more expensive since it will require many nuclear operators to have insurance in place for a much greater amount. Realizing the difficulties for operators obtaining insurance to cover the full extent of their increased liability for the 30-year period for personal injury claims, and the increased liability cap, the 2016 NIO empowers the UK Government to provide insurance itself on commercial terms in order to fill the gap if the insurance market is unable to meet this demand.

Jurisdiction

Under the NIO, the courts of only one Paris Convention state where a nuclear incident has occurred will deal with claims arising from an incident. The Exclusive Economic Zones under international law and other types of maritime zone are now covered when it comes to allocation of jurisdiction.[23]

Interaction between existing and future nuclear power plants

Many of the new nuclear power stations which are planned for the UK will be built adjacent to an existing nuclear licensed site. There is potential for activity on the new nuclear site to interfere with radioactive materials previously discharged by the neighbouring legacy nuclear site. This may create uncertainty in determining liability around the interaction between new-build nuclear sites and legacy nuclear sites. The 2016 NIO seeks to clarify the interaction of potential liability in such sites. Under the 2016 NIO, the mere presence of nuclear matter in a place as a result of a previous occurrence is not to be treated as a separate 'occurrence'.[24]

23 Ibid.

24 'Changes to UK Nuclear Liability Regime', see http://www.world-nuclear-news.org/V-Changes-to-UK-nuclear-liability-regime-07031701.html, accessed 17 July 2018.

Thus, no new occurrence will arise if the nuclear site licensee of the new-build site disturbs a previous discharge by a legacy nuclear site.

Nuclear waste management

The UK is party to the Joint Convention on the Safety of Radioactive Waste and Spent Fuel Management 1997. As in other states, nuclear wastes in the United Kingdom originating from the nuclear power industry include waste from the manufacture of fuel, reactor operations, decommissioning, spent fuel reprocessing and related research and development activities. Waste also arises from the defence programme, of which the major components are nuclear weapons production and the nuclear submarine propulsion programme. In addition, many medical, industrial, educational and research establishments produce small quantities of radioactive waste. The UK Government policy on radioactive waste management is set out in a White Paper of July 1995 titled 'Review of radioactive waste management policy – final conclusions' which focuses on sustainable management of radioactive waste and maintains that radioactive wastes should be managed and disposed of in ways that protect the public, the workforce and the environment. The radiation protection principles and criteria adopted in the United Kingdom and applied by the regulatory bodies are designed to ensure that there is no unacceptable risk associated with radioactive waste management.[25]

The UK Government's current policy on radioactive management is based on the following fundamental principles: radioactive wastes are not created unnecessarily; such wastes as are created are safely and appropriately managed and treated; and they are then safely disposed of at appropriate times and in appropriate ways.[26] The fundamental aim of UK policy is to ensure that radioactive waste is managed in a way that protects the public, the workforce and the environment and safeguards the interests of existing and future generations and in a manner that commands public confidence and takes due account of costs.[27] The policy for the long-term disposal of higher activity wastes in England is to manage these through geological disposal, with safe and secure interim storage. Nuclear waste disposal in the UK is dealt with by the 1993 Radioactive Substances Act, under which no person may dispose of radioactive waste except in accordance with an authorization under the Act. Licensees must produce safety cases for all operations, including radioactive waste conditioning operations, which consider safety, radioactive waste management and environmental protection. The developer of a disposal facility for radioactive waste will be required to apply to the relevant Agency for authorisation of disposals on or from the site of the facility. Control

25 'The Regulatory Control of Radioactive Waste Management, Overview of 15 NEA Member Countries', OECD 2004, available at https://www.oecd-nea.org/rwm/docs/2004/rwm-rf2004-1.pdf, accessed 17 July 2018.

26 'Basic Principles of Radioactive Waste Management', available at http://www.onr.org.uk/wastemanage/basic-principles.pdf, accessed 17 July 2018.

27 Ibid.

under the Act is exercised in England and Wales by the Environment Agency and in Scotland by the Scottish Environment Protection Agency. In addition to these, the Nuclear Decommissioning Authority has established the Radioactive Waste Management Directorate to manage the delivery of geological disposal for higher activity wastes. In March 2010, the Nuclear Decommissioning Authority issued a report on the steps towards the establishment of a geological disposal for long-term management of high-level nuclear wastes.[28] However, this will be preceded by safe and secure interim storage until a disposal facility can receive waste.

In the UK, radioactive waste is classified under the following broad categories, according to its heat-generating capacity and activity content: 1. High-level (HLW); 2. Intermediate-level waste (ILW); 3. Low-level waste (LLW); and 4. Very-low-level waste (VLLW), which can be safely disposed of with ordinary refuse. Most of the LLW waste is currently disposed of to the LLW Repository – a shallow burial facility at Drigg in Cumbria. Solid LLW may be buried with special arrangements in municipal landfills. ILW and HLW are generally stored y where they arise. In the UK, the relevant costs and commercial risks in radioactive waste must be borne by the owner of the waste.

The Energy Act 2013 of the UK makes provision for reforming the electricity market for the purpose of encouraging low-carbon electricity generation or ensuring security of supply; and the establishment and functions of the Office for Nuclear Regulation (ONR). The Office for Nuclear Regulation has the following areas of regulation: nuclear safety, health and safety, the nuclear security and safeguards ,and the transportation of nuclear materials.[29] This Act also gives the ONR the responsibility for enforcing the relevant provisions of the Nuclear Installation Act 1965 and the Nuclear Industries Security Regulations 2003. The ONR independently regulates safety and security at 37 licensed nuclear sites in the UK. These include the existing fleet of operating reactors, fuel cycle facilities, waste management and decommissioning sites as well as the nuclear defence sector.[30] The ONR is the government agency responsible for licensing sites for nuclear installations on being satisfied that certain requirements are met. All nuclear installations must have a Site Licence before any nuclear related activities commence. The ONR Safety Assessment Principles (SAPs) set out the basic principles of radioactive waste management:

- A strategy should be produced and implemented for managing radioactive waste on a site which should be consistent with government policy and sustainable development.
- The generation of radioactive waste should be prevented, or where this is not reasonably practicable, minimized in terms of quantity and activity.

28 'Geological Disposal: Step Towards Implementation', National Decommissioning Authority, UK, available at file:///C:/Users/user/Downloads/Geological-Disposal-Steps-Towards-Implementation-March-2010.pdf, accessed 19 July 2018.
29 Sections 69, 70, 72 and 73 of the Act.
30 Ibid.

- The total quantity of radioactive waste accumulated on site should be minimized so far as is reasonably practicable.
- Radioactive waste should be characterized and segregated to facilitate subsequent safe and effective management.
- Radioactive waste should be stored in accordance with good engineering practice and in a safe condition.
- Radiological hazards should be reduced systemically and progressively.
- Information that might be needed for the current and future safe management of radioactive waste should be recorded and preserved.[31]

Safety of nuclear installations

The safety of operational nuclear facilities in the UK, including those for waste treatment and storage, is regulated by the Health and Safety Executive (HSE) according to the 1965 Nuclear Installations Act (NI Act). The NI Act requires organizations to obtain a nuclear site licence from the HSE before using a site for licensable activities. It also enables the HSE to attach to any licence granted conditions in the interests of safety and for handling nuclear matter. Such conditions include the requirement for licensees to justify the safety of operations, i.e., provide a safety case and make arrangements for the safe management of radioactive waste.

The regulatory objectives of the safety of long-lived waste repositories in the UK during their operational phase are: to deliver effective and efficient regulation of the nuclear industry; to maintain and improve standards of protection of people and the environment from the potential hazards from ionizing radiations; and to ensure that radioactive waste is appropriately managed in both the short and long term, in accordance with legislation, UK Government policy, and international obligations.

The Radiological Protection Act 1970 is the main piece of legislation to deal with radiological protection. This Act created the National Radiological Protection Board, which the agency responsible for advancing the acquisition of knowledge about protection from radiological hazards and for providing information to persons and government departments about such protection. The Health and Safety at Work etc Act 1974 is the main piece of legislation covering occupational health and safety in the UK.[32] The HSE, together with local authorities, is responsible for enforcing the Act and a number of other Acts and Statutory Instruments relevant to the working environment. This Act imposes duties on all employers, including those in the nuclear industry, to look after the health and safety of both their employees and the public. The Ionising Radiations Regulations 1985 made under this Act of 1974 constitute the main regulations dealing

31 ONR, Safety Assessment Principles for Nuclear Facilities, 2014 edn, available at http://www.onr.org.uk/saps/, accessed 17 July 2018.

32 The Act is available at http://www.legislation.gov.uk/ukpga/1974/37/pdfs/ukpga_1974 0037_en.pdf, accessed 17 July 2018.

with radiological protection and implementing in part in the UK the EURATOM Basic Safety Standard Directive. The other specific regulations under the Health and Safety at Work etc Act are the Ionising Radiations Regulations 1999 and Radiation (Emergency Preparedness and Public Information) Regulations 2001.

Another piece of relevant legislation on nuclear energy is the Energy Act 2013. Because of the particular hazards associated with the nuclear industry, there are special provisions for nuclear safety under the Energy Act 2013. The UK's approach regarding safety is that nuclear licensees are required to build, operate and decommission nuclear sites in a way that ensures that risks are kept as low as reasonably practicable, which is referred to as the ALARP principle.[33]

The Nuclear Industries Security Regulations 2003 deal with security of nuclear installations, placing significant obligations on the operators of civil licensed nuclear sites with regard to physical security measures for facilities, nuclear material and the security of Sensitive Nuclear Information (SNI).[34]

The Nuclear Safeguards Act 2000 implements the 1998 Additional Protocol to the 1968 Treaty on the Non-Proliferation of Nuclear Weapons. Under the Act, the Secretary of State may serve notice on any person requiring him/her to provide information for the purposes of the Additional Protocol. The Act also secures the exercise of the IAEA's rights, in particular of the Agency Inspector, under the Additional Protocol.

Decommissioning

The Environmental Impact Assessment for Decommissioning Regulations (EIADR) 1999 is a legal instrument requiring the environmental impact of decommissioning nuclear power stations and other nuclear reactors to be considered in detail before consent for the decommissioning work to begin.[35] In addition, EIADR also applies to projects serving national defence purposes, in particular the decommissioning of reactors in nuclear submarines. The decommissioning of nuclear power stations and other nuclear reactors within the scope of EIADR may only proceed with consent from the HSE. In order to obtain consent, a detailed environmental impact assessment must be submitted for the proposed decommissioning project and the mitigation measures to be used to avoid or minimize any significant adverse impacts on the environment. This is considered by HSE in extensive consultation with the relevant regulatory authorities, such as the appropriate environmental agency and local highway and planning authorities, together with the public and any other interested parties.[36]

The Energy Act 2004 of the UK is designed to pave the way for extensive private sector participation at a number of levels in a long-term decommissioning

33 A Guide to Nuclear Regulation in the UK, available at http://www.onr.org.uk/documents/a-guide-to-nuclear-regulation-in-the-uk.pdf, accessed 17 July 2018.

34 Ibid.

35 Nuclear Reactors (Environmental Impact Assessment for Decommissioning) Regulations, available at http://www.onr.org.uk/eiadr.htm, accessed 17 July 2018.

36 Ibid.

and clean-up programme of existing nuclear sites in the UK. A new Government regulatory board, the Nuclear Decommissioning Authority (NDA), was created in 2005 under the Energy Act 2004 to oversee the development and implementation of the decommissioning programme. The Nuclear Decommissioning Authority (NDA) is responsible for the decommissioning and clean-up of all civil public-sector nuclear sites in the UK.

India

India has a long history of civilian nuclear industry. However, it has ratified only a small number of nuclear treaties. India is not a member of the NPT or the CTBT. But it has signed nuclear cooperation agreements with several countries including the USA. Currently, there are 20 operating Nuclear Power Plants in India for civilian purposes. The Atomic Energy Act 1962 empowers the Government to produce, develop, use and dispose of atomic energy either by itself or through any authority or Corporation established by it or a government company. India is not party to the Vienna or Paris Conventions on third party liability. The Atomic Energy Regulatory Board (AERB) is the national authority for ensuring that the use of ionizing radiation and nuclear energy does not cause any undue risk to the health of workers, members of the public or to the environment. It is responsible for the stipulation and enforcement of rules and regulations pertaining to nuclear and radiological safety, and has powers to execute various functions to carry out its responsibilities. These include the development of Safety Codes, Guides and Standards stipulating requirements applicable for siting, design, construction, commissioning, operation and decommissioning of nuclear and radiation facilities and for the conduct of regulatory and safety functions; carrying out safety reviews of nuclear and radiation facilities under design, construction and operation; ensuring compliance by nuclear and radiation facilities with the stipulated safety requirements; issuing regulatory consents for siting, construction, commissioning, operation and decommissioning of nuclear and radiation installations; organizing and conducting regulatory inspections and enforcing corrective actions as necessary, at the facilities being regulated; assessment of radiological safety status with regard to personnel exposures and environmental radioactivity releases in nuclear and radiation facilities.

Third party liability

The (Indian) Civil Liability for Nuclear Damage Act 2010 (CLND Act) channels all legal liability for nuclear damage exclusively to the operator. Section 17 of the CLND Act creates supplier liability by providing a right of recourse for the operator of a nuclear establishment. This provision marks India's partial shift from legal channelling to economic channelling of liability.[37] Section 17 of the Act provides

37 Ayushi Sutaria, 'Placing the Indian Civil Nuclear Liability Regime in Context: The Extent of Supplier's Liability' (2014) 17(1) *Journal of Risk Research* 97–113.

that the operator of the nuclear installation, after paying the compensation for nuclear damage, shall have the right to recourse where:

- a Such right is expressly provided for in a contract in writing;
- b The nuclear incident has resulted as a consequence of an act of supplier or his employee, which includes supply of equipment or material with patent or latent defects or sub-standard services;
- c The nuclear incident has resulted from the act of commission or omission of an individual done with the intent to cause nuclear damage.

The situations identified in section 17(b) relate to actions and matters such as product liability stipulations or conditions or service contracts. Section 2(1)(m) of the Act defines 'operator' as the Central Government or any authority or corporation established by it or a government company that has been granted a licence pursuant to the Atomic Energy Act 1962 for the operation of the installation. Currently, all nuclear power plants are owned by the Government or government-owned entities. However, the prevailing law permits joint ventures between private and government companies if the Government holds the majority stake.

While the CLND Act allows a one-stop shop for victims, who can limit their legal actions to suing the operator, it also allows the operator to turn to more pockets and sue nuclear equipment suppliers and designers, typically huge multinational corporations with a solid financial structure. In this way, the nuclear liability package provided for in the laws of the USA and India is a gateway to justice in the case of a nuclear accident which may be caused by a combination of design defects and operator errors.[38]

Exclusive operator liability in the case of a nuclear accident has consistently been justified by a need to protect victims, who will not need to sue various parties, but only the operator. The novel approach of the Indian law is that while it retains the principle of exclusive liability of the operator, it allows the operator to sue the suppliers and designers. It also implies that suppliers and designers may need to take out insurance when supplying and designing nuclear material.[39]

India has a nuclear insurance pool which covers risks pertaining to the liability of the nuclear operator under section 6(2) of the CLND Act, as well as the liability of the suppliers under section 17. The CLND Act prescribes that the maximum amount of liability in respect of each nuclear incident shall be the rupee equivalent of 300m Special Drawing Rights (SDRs).[40] The Act lays down that the operator's maximum liability shall be Rs15 billion. Should the total liability

38 Evelyne M. Ameye, 'United States and India: Two Nuclear States with Legislation that Truly Holds Responsible Parties Liable in Case of a Nuclear Accident' (2015) 18(8) *Journal of Risk Research* 1070–1082.

39 Ibid.

40 Section 6(1) of the Act.

exceed Rs15 billion, this gap will be covered by Central Government.[41] Although Indian law provides for establishment of a 'Nuclear Liability Fund' by charging the operators a levy, the Fund is yet to be established.

Nuclear waste management

The Atomic Energy (safe disposal of radioactive wastes) Rules 1987 deal with nuclear waste management in India. Prior authorization from a competent authority is required for disposal of radioactive waste.[42] An application for authorization should detail (a) the process, materials and equipment generating radioactive wastes in the installation; (b) the equipment and systems to monitor and control the radioactive wastes and to reduce environmental releases; (c) the environment around the installation; (d) the processes and equipment in the installation for conditioning, treatment and disposal of radioactive waste and the staff employed for the purpose; (e) safety devices incorporated in the waste disposal installation to contain the radioactive effluents and control their release and to keep these releases as low as reasonably achievable (ALARA); (f) an estimate of the amounts of annual releases, and an analysis of their anticipated environmental impact; (g) an analysis of the potential accidents which may occur in the installation; (h) procedures to be followed for safe collection of radioactive wastes arising from such accidents; and (i) design features of surveillance equipment to monitor the normal releases of activity.[43] Any authorized person may inspect any radioactive disposal installation; inspect any therein; and make tests and or measurements for evaluating radiation hazards.[44] In the event of accidental release of any radioactive material resulting in personnel, surface or environmental contamination, the Radiological Safety Officer shall take steps for the immediate decontamination of the affected personnel and areas and take other remedial measures.[45] Non-compliance with the conditions of authorization may result in cancellation or suspension of such authorization.[46]

Decommissioning

In India, the AERB has issued a Safety Manual on Decommissioning of Nuclear Facilities which outlines the requirements for decommissioning including: the criteria for occupational exposures, discharge of radionuclides to the environment, criteria for long-term waste disposal and clearance levels. It also prescribes requirements with regard to advance planning for decommissioning of nuclear facilities and quality assurance during decommissioning. The criteria for

41 Section 7(1)(a) of the CLND Act.
42 Rule 3.
43 Rule 4.
44 Rule 10.
45 Rule 14.
46 Rule 18.

categorization of wastes and their mode of disposal is also prescribed. In India, full-scale decommissioning of a major nuclear facility under regulatory control has not yet been necessary. The principal safety objectives of decommissioning are decontamination and disassembly of a facility for clean-up of the site; protection of the workers, the public and the environment from the radiological and non-radiological hazards resulting from decommissioning; compliance with the prescribed limits to ensure that all radiation exposures are kept below the set limits and as low as reasonably achievable (ALARA); minimization of the burden on future generations taking into account social and economic factors in general and selection of the decontamination process for safe and effective management of radioactive waste.[47]

Nuclear safety

The AERB, established in 1983, is tasked with regulating the safety and security aspects of the country's civilian nuclear facilities. However, it is not an autonomous body as it depends on the Department of Atomic Energy (DAE) for all practical purposes, hence it has been unable to perform its regulatory functions effectively. The Atomic Energy (Radiation Protection) Rules 2004 provide for the issuance of a licence by the AERB for handling of radioactive substances. These Rules require a licence to establish a radiation installation for siting, design, construction, commissioning and operation; and to decommission a radiation installation. AERB formulates safety requirements for nuclear and radiation facilities in the country and has issued safety codes for regulation, siting, design, operation and quality assurance. AERB also issues safety codes and safety standards prescribing the requirements for radiation installation and transport of radioactive material, and the licensee shall ensure compliance with these.[48]

Bangladesh

Bangladesh is constructing its first nuclear power plants to meet rapidly-increasing demand and reduce dependence on natural gas. The Bangladesh Atomic Energy Commission (BAEC), the nuclear regulatory body, was established in 1973 to carry out nuclear research. In 2001 it adopted the Nuclear Power Action Plan. Bangladesh currently operates a research reactor. In May 2010, Bangladesh entered into an agreement with the Russian Federation for building two reactors at Rooppur for a civilian nuclear power plant. The agreement provides for nuclear cooperation in areas such as siting, design, construction and operation of power and research nuclear reactors, water desalination plants, and elementary particle accelerators. Other areas covered included fuel supply and wastes. Under this

47 S.A.H. Ashraf, S.K. Chande, 'Decommissioning of Nuclear Activities: Indian Perspective', available at http://www.iaea.org/inis/collection/NCLCollectionStore/_Public/33/052/33052267.pdf, accessed 17 July 2018.

48 Rule 16.

arrangement, Russia will manage wastes and decommissioning. It also has framework agreements for peaceful nuclear energy applications with the US, France and China. The IAEA approved a Technical Assistance Project for the Rooppur Nuclear Power Plant to be initiated between 2009 and 2011. Construction of the first Rooppur unit began in November 2017, with commercial operation due in 2023. Rosatom, the Russian Atomic Energy Corporation, will maintain the plant for the first year of operation before handing over to the BAEC. In March 2018, Bangladesh, India and Russia signed a Memorandum of Understanding on cooperation on implementing the Rooppur nuclear power plant. Under the deal, Indian companies can be involved in construction and installation works, supply of materials and equipment of a non-critical category in the interests of the project.

The Nuclear Power Plant Act 2015 set up the Nuclear Power Company of Bangladesh (NPCB) to run the plant, though ownership remains with the BAEC.

On 19 June 2012 the Government enacted the Bangladesh Atomic Energy Regulatory Act (BAER Act), establishing an independent regulatory body. The Act covers nuclear safety, security and safeguard of nuclear as well as radioactive materials and also ensures civil liability for nuclear damage in the event of an accident. It also deals with radiation safety; licensing of activities in the field of peaceful use of atomic energy; oversight and control activity including the development and implementation of inspection programmes; management of radioactive waste and spent nuclear fuel, including their transportation and safe storage; physical protection of nuclear installations, radiation sources, storage facilities, nuclear materials and radioactive substances, control of nuclear materials; quality assurance of equipment for nuclear power plants; and emergency preparedness and emergency response; and training of nuclear regulatory body personnel. The BAER Act 2012 also aims to develop the capacity of the nuclear regulatory body. On 12 February 2013, a separate regulatory organization, the Bangladesh Atomic Energy Regulatory Authority (BAERA), was established in order to attain the required transparency in nuclear safety and radiation control especially in all stages of licensing and inspection of nuclear facilities and radiation sources. This authority is responsible for the regulation of the use of atomic energy, radiological practices and relevant activities under the provision of the Nuclear Safety and Radiation Control Act 1993 and the NSRC Regulations 1997.

Safety of nuclear installations

Safety of nuclear installations is regulated by the Law on Nuclear Safety and Radiation Control Act 1993. Under this Act the BAEC was empowered to work as the nuclear regulatory body. The Nuclear Safety and Radiation Control Rules were formulated for that purpose in 1997.

Nuclear safety, security and protection are comprehensively regulated by the BAER Act 2012. Under this Act, the authorization holder has the power of regulatory control over the nuclear installation and he/she shall be responsible for determination of the location of a nuclear installation, security and safety of the nuclear installation, management of radioactive wastes, physical protection of the nuclear installation, and emergency preparedness measures.[49] An authorization holder is a person who has been given permission to exercise certain functions by the regulatory authority or the Nuclear Authority.[50] It prescribes that the authorization holder will be responsible for safety and security of radioactive materials and shall ensure adequate human resources for this purpose.[51] The authorization holder shall take the necessary steps for safety and security of nuclear material, ensure necessary funds and technical support for nuclear safety; and also formulate strategies for administering the nuclear installation, and for decommissioning.[52] The regulatory body shall also be responsible for safety of radiation, physical protection of nuclear material, prevention of trafficking of nuclear material and shall implement the safeguard agreement between the Government of Bangladesh and the IAEA in order to prevent proliferation of nuclear weapons.[53]

Third party liability

Under the BAER Act, the operator or foreign operator is liable to pay compensation for any harm caused by nuclear incident. The operator or foreign operator is also liable for theft or loss of nuclear material from nuclear installation. The third party liability will be applied in the place where the nuclear harm is caused.[54] The operator or foreign operator is also liable for harm caused during transportation of nuclear material within or beyond the territory of Bangladesh.[55] The highest amount of liability is 300 million BDT or such amount as declared by the Government of Bangladesh for each nuclear incident and the operator must have insurance or other financial security to cover the amount of liability.[56] If the stated amount of liability for compensation for nuclear harm is considered inadequate, the Government of Bangladesh must ensure the rest of the amount for payment of compensation, which must not exceed 300 million BDT.[57] If claims for compensation exceed the liability amount stated in this Act, the compensation for loss of life or individual harm shall be met on the basis of priority.[58] The claim for compensation can cover a nuclear incident committed in the territory or Exclusive Economic Zone (EEZ) of Bangladesh.[59] The grounds for exemption from liability include grave natural disaster, war, conflict

49 Article 23 of the Act.
50 Section 2(1) of the Act.
51 Section 29 of the Act.
52 Section 30 of the Act.
53 Sections 31, 33, 37 of the Act.
54 Section 43 of the Act.
55 Section 44 of the Act.
56 Sections 45 and 46 of the Act.
57 Section 46(3) of the Act.
58 Section 48 of the Act.
59 Section 49 of the Act.

or civil strife. The operator will be exempted from liability if it is proved that such damage is due to negligence or the intentional act of the affected parties.[60]

Radioactive waste management

The operator shall be responsible for the safe management and safety of radioactive wastes. For proper management of radioactive wastes, the authorization holder shall ensure an adequate trained human and financial resources for the safety and security of nuclear facility during its operation and decommissioning. The financial resources must be adequate to meet the expenses of institutional control and monitoring of radioactive wastes even after closure of the disposal facility.[61] The management of radioactive wastes shall be carried out by maintaining subcriticality, ensuring removal of residual heat, and reducing the impact of radiation on workers, the public and the environment.[62]

Emergency preparedness and preventative measures

The authorized person and the operator of nuclear power plant must have emergency preparedness, a plan for prevention, and remedial measures for a negative impact on public health, environment and property due to a possible nuclear or radiological accident or incident. The emergency plan includes preliminary on-site emergency provisions, an off-site emergency plan, guidelines for emergency transportation, and an emergency planning zone.[63]

Decommissioning

There is no detailed provision on decommissioning under the Act. However, the licence for decommissioning will be given by BAERA.[64] The regulatory authority is required to establish a Decommissioning Fund to meet the expenses of decommissioning.[65] The detailed provisions are needed to address the regulatory challenges in decommissioning activities.

Bangladesh needs to arrange sufficient funds for liability to meet potential compensation demands in case of an accident. Owing to cost constraints, it is difficult for Bangladesh to establish a complete fuel preparation and reprocessing capability for generating nuclear energy. Bangladesh is therefore currently reliant on foreign technology and expertise, including safety oversight for development and operation of its nuclear power plant.

60 Section 50 of the Act.
61 Section 39 of the Act.
62 Section 39 of the Act.
63 Section 40 of the Act.
64 Section 18 of the Act.
65 Section 22 of the Act.

Conclusion

From the above it is clear that while the UK and Bangladesh follow the legal channelling of liability, the USA and India follow the economic channel of liability so that suppliers and designers of defective reactors can be held liable in the case of a nuclear accident. India's recent shift is premised on the fact the supplier company should take all the required care and responsibility in building the nuclear reactor and it can adequately protect victims in case of a nuclear accident. In addition, an exposure of suppliers and designers to liability can only increase their incentive to deliver safe material, enhance prevention and efficiently internalize risk costs. However, there is a difference of approach between the USA and India in adopting the economic channelling of liability. In the USA, this is achieved through economic channelling with umbrella insurances covering the liability of operators, suppliers and designers, whereas Indian law provides for a right of recourse by the operator against the suppliers and designers where a nuclear accident is due to deficiencies in supply or design.

11 Review of regulatory responses to the Fukushima accident

Introduction

Every nuclear disaster has created opportunities for change and re-evaluating existing regulatory framework and as such, every incident has been responded by global community with regulatory change for strengthening safety and security of nuclear installation and measures for protection of people and environment from radiation. Thus, nuclear energy disasters hold a tenuous relationship with energy policymaking.[1]

Several factors, including management failure, defective design of the nuclear plant and opaque operation of the plant contributed to the overall severity of the Fukushima accident. After the accident, public distrust of nuclear power in Japan and other countries increased, as demonstrated by their opposition to the construction of new nuclear power plants. Existing laws and regulations on nuclear energy have been reviewed and reformed in some countries in response to public outcry. While in most countries the nuclear plans are unaffected, some have delayed their nuclear energy plans. For example, Thailand has delayed three years, citing IAEA recommendations. Japan also led the Integrated Support Centre for Nuclear Non-Proliferation and Nuclear Security.

After the Fukushima accident, some countries reviewed their energy options. For example, Germany plans to shut down all of its nuclear reactors by 2022, ending its reliance on nuclear energy in favour of safer energy from wind, solar and hydroelectric power. Italy is the only country that has permanently closed all of its functioning nuclear plants, after voting overwhelmingly against nuclear power. Switzerland and Spain have banned the construction of new reactors. Switzerland is phasing out nuclear power. On the other hand, although France passed a law after Fukushima which aims to reduce the share of nuclear power in the national electricity mix, the country's nuclear industry remains unaffected as no nuclear reactor has been shut down.[2] Similarly, the UK Government did not change its decision to increase nuclear power generation after the Fukushima

1 Lincoln L. Davie, 'Beyond Fukushima: Disasters, Nuclear Energy, and Energy Law' (2011) 6 *Brigham Young University Law Review* 1937.

2 Christina Stuart, 'The French Exception: The French Nuclear Power Industry and Its Influence on Political Plans to Transition to a New Energy System', in Peter Van Ness and Mel Gurtov (eds.), *Learning from Fukushima: Nuclear Power in East Asia* (ANU Press 2014) 27.

accident. The policy response to Fukushima reflects a shift in the use of nuclear energy that puts greater emphasis on sustainability.[3] After the Fukushima accident, nuclear regulatory authorities in many countries have undertaken a number of measures focusing on the potential impact of external hazards, on plant improvements, and enhancements in the robustness of safety functions. The areas of such measures include a re-examination of external hazards; improvement of the robustness of the electrical systems; protection of the reactor containment system; protection of spent fuel in storage pools; reinforcement of safety culture, including human and organizational factors in decision-making during emergencies; and continued safety research.[4] In brief, the Fukushima accident led to the safety reassessment of nuclear fuel cycle facilities, changes to regulations and international good practice; reassessment of the design of the facility against flooding; assessment of capability of emergency response from external sources, owing to the widespread effects of some natural disasters; and reviewing of emergency arrangements, accident management and communication of information.[5]

The Fukushima accident also led to the necessity to update the design and operating documentation, including that related to maintenance, periodic testing and inspection programmes, and updating operating procedures; and revising the training and qualification programme for facility operating personnel.[6]

Regulatory responses in Japan

After the Fukushima incident, Japan created three organizations: the Council on Energy and Environment, the Nuclear Regulation Agency and the Fundamental Policies Committee.. In 2012 Japan established a new safety regulatory body, the Nuclear Safety and Security Agency, on the basis of the principle of 'separating regulation from utilization'. Previously, the nuclear safety regulatory body, the Nuclear and Industrial Safety Agency (NISA) was part of the Ministry of Economy, Trade and Industry. The new separate regulatory body was established as an external agency of the Ministry of Environment by integrating into it the functions of the Nuclear Safety Commission (NSC). Japan is planning to phase out its nuclear energy by 2040.

The Fukushima accident has generated the following implications for reforming nuclear energy industry:

Change in the liability regime

The Fukushima accident also brought the issue of supplier liability into the forefront and demand for a change in the economic channelling of liability became a

3 Lincoln L. Davie (n 1).

4 'Five Years after the Fukushima Daiichi Accident: Nuclear Safety Improvements and Lessons Learnt' NEA, OECD 2016, 21.

5 'Safety Reassessment for Nuclear Fuel Cycle Facilities in light of the Accident at the Fukushima Daiichi Nuclear Power Plant', Safety Reports Series No. 90 (Vienna, IAEA 2016) 2.

6 Ibid, 5.

focal point. According to the Japanese Act on compensation, only the operator of the nuclear power plant can be held liable, thus excluding liability of other potential partners that contributed to the risk. After the accident, many experts and environmental organizations argued that Japan should adopt supplier liability, especially in light of the fact that much of the compensation paid out for the Fukushima disaster was taxpayer-funded. In January 2014, about 1400 plaintiffs filed a lawsuit against the three companies that supplied the reactors at the Fukushima nuclear power plant, namely Toshiba, General Electric and Hitachi. This lawsuit, filed at the Tokyo District Court, challenges current regulations that provide supplier immunity from liability in nuclear accidents and that place the liability solely on the operator, in this case, the Tokyo Electric Power Company (TEPCO). The plaintiffs have argued that the three suppliers failed to implement safety improvements to the four-decade-old boiling water reactors at the nuclear power plant, and are seeking a symbolic compensation to raise awareness of the issue of supplier immunity from nuclear liability.

Another important issue raised in the aftermath of the Fukushima accident is the effectiveness of nuclear liability provided for in the various international Conventions and domestic laws as well as the sufficiency of funds to meet compensation demands. A consistent criticism is that none of the legal frameworks pertaining to nuclear liability provides for adequate compensation structures from the operator, and most of the compensation in the event of a nuclear incident would actually be funded by taxpayers. Considering this inadequacy in compensation and loopholes in the existing liability system, some countries, including India, have introduced an expanded concept of supplier liability. In the wake of Fukushima there are renewed efforts to reform the current liability regime and to reduce the uncertainty around nuclear liability regime, which is evident in the IAEA's Action Plan on Nuclear Safety.[7]

Improving safety standards

The Fukushima accident led to the reassessment of the siting, design and nuclear fuel cycle facility, and emergency preparedness and response in many states. Many states reviewed the safety standards of nuclear reactors after the Fukushima incident and undertook safety assessment of the nuclear power plants (NPPs). For example, the Chinese Government immediately took a decision to assess the safety status of all NPPs, both in operation and in construction, and to suspend temporarily all applications for constructing new nuclear power plants. The following major actions have been implemented by the Chinese Government: (1) an expert group has been assigned to complete specified nuclear safety inspections to all NPPs in operation to evaluate their safety status; (2) all NPPs under constructions have been inspected by the expert task force to ensure new NPP construction fulfils safety requirements and high quality standards; (3) all NPPs

7 See Raphael J. Heffron, Stephen F. Ashley and William J. Nuttall, 'The Global Nuclear Liability Regime post Fukushima Daiichi' (2016) 90 *Progress in Nuclear Energy* 4.

planned for construction must adopt advanced safety standards; (4) all applications for new NPP projects have been temporarily suspended until the new nuclear safety plan be approved. Although the policy to develop nuclear energy was not changed, 'safety first', and 'quality assurance' became the main policy for future NPP projects.[8]

After Fukushima, the NRC of the USA tightened up its guidelines, adding safeguards and measurement devices for spent fuel pools, ordering hardened, more reliable vents from containment buildings and requiring greater emergency communications, all areas that failed at Fukushima, whilst utilities added new back-up generators at or near reactor sites to make sure power to plants cannot fail as happened in Fukushima. Similarly, after the Fukushima accident, the EU launched voluntary 'stress tests' for all of its 143 nuclear power plants based on a set of common criteria in an effort to enhance safety and security. On the basis of nuclear stress tests carried out in 2011 and 2012, and the lessons learned from Fukushima, the EU amended its Nuclear Safety Directive in 2014. The amended Directive requires EU Member States to give the highest priority to nuclear safety at all stages of the lifecycle of a nuclear power plant. This includes carrying out safety assessments before the construction of new nuclear power plants and ensuring significant safety enhancements for old reactors. Specifically, the Directive calls for the role of national regulatory authorities to be strengthened by ensuring their independence from national governments. According to the Directives, EU countries must provide the regulators with sufficient legal powers, staff and financial resources to create a system of peer reviews. The EU Directive requires a safety re-evaluation for all nuclear power plants to be conducted at least once every 10 years.[9]

Improving emergency preparedness

The existing emergency plan and associated procedures and arrangements need to be reviewed to ensure that they are adequate and realistic, particularly for conditions more severe than design-based accidents initiated by an extreme external event affecting several facilities simultaneously.[10]

It should include information on the timing and consequences of accident conditions and sequences, including events that involve the total loss of all safety measures; identification of new actions that are facility specific, site-wide, or off-site and that could be taken to mitigate the effects of accident conditions; a clearly defined command and control system that is well understood by all involved is in place to effectively manage the response to an emergency; decide

8 Zhiwei Zhou, 'Challenges of Nuclear Safety to Sustainable Development of Chinese Nuclear Energy in Post-Fukushima Era' in Yao (ed.), *Zero-Carbon Energy Kyoto 2012, Green Energy and Technology* (Springer 2013).

9 See https://ec.europa.eu/energy/en/topics/nuclear-energy/nuclear-safety, 17 July 2018.

10 'Safety Reassessment for Nuclear Fuel Cycle Facilities in light of the Accident at the Fukushima Daiichi Nuclear Power Plant' (n 5) 28.

promptly on protective actions and other response actions to be taken; the existence of adequate procedures and means for effective communication during an emergency.[11] Pre-established communication procedures need to be in place to ensure effective communication between on-site response personnel at different locations on the site and off-site response organizations, and effective communication to the public.[12] Communication needs to be carried out in a coordinated manner so that consistent messages are given to the public.[13]

For example, in India, after the Fukushima accident, AERB carried out special regulatory inspections to assess the capabilities of all NPPs and their preparedness to deal with the situations arising out of extreme natural events resulting from flood, tsunami, earthquake, etc. The approach of the review and assessment focused on confirmation of capability to withstand currently defined site-specific external events; and review of the severe accident management programme. Based on the above reviews, the measures identified for implementation of the recommendations for further improving the safety margins in NPPs for external events were identified. Post-Fukushima reviews have identified the need for the creation of an emergency facility at each NPP site which will remain functional under such conditions. The facility will have adequate radiation shielding and will be seismically qualified. As a part of the existing licensing requirement, every NPP has to establish emergency preparedness and response plans. These plans should ensure that there exist sufficient means to cope with an emergency and meet the regulatory requirements. Subsequent to the Fukushima accident, the National Disaster Management Authority (NDMA), NPCIL and AERB took up review of existing Emergency Preparedness and Response plans at all NPPs to ascertain and evaluate the response and coordination among different agencies during an offsite nuclear emergency.[14] The accident exposed the ineffectiveness of the Convention's preventative monitoring mechanisms; a stronger monitoring regime would seem indispensable in preventing another Fukushima. This could be rectified by the introduction of expert peer review, or by amending the NSC provisions.[15] At the 2nd Extraordinary Meeting of the Contracting Parties to the NSC 214, the Contracting Parties made several suggestions which demonstrated their willingness to improve the effectiveness of the Convention. These included introducing external expert review, and the assessment and verification of safety in accordance with state-of-the-art science and technology, further developing the IAEA standards and using them in assessing compliance with the NSC.[16] The Fifth Review Meeting of the NSC was also convened in Vienna, Austria, from 4

11 Ibid.

12 Ibid.

13 Ibid.

14 S.S. Bajaj, 'Regulatory Practices for Nuclear Power Plants in India (2013) 38(5) *Sadhan* 1027–1050, 1043.

15 Menno Kamminga, 'The IAEA Convention on Nuclear Safety' (1995) 44 *International and Comparative Law Quarterly* 872, 875.

16 Ibid, 391.

to 14 April 2011 to discuss safety issues and draw lessons from the Fukushima accident. At this meeting the parties also reiterated the need to:

> Reaffirm their commitment to the objectives of the NSC: to achieve and maintain a high level of nuclear safety worldwide through enhancement of national measures and international cooperation; to establish and maintain effective defences in nuclear installations against potential radiological hazards and to prevent accidents with radiological consequences and to mitigate such consequences should they occur.[17]

The Fukushima nuclear accident raised questions about the implementation of the Convention by the Japanese Government and identified the need to reassess the obligation of each Contracting Party deriving from the NSC provisions in the light of lessons learned from the accident. Several major deficiencies, such as the lack of independence of the regulatory body from the body entrusted with the promotion of nuclear energy and its ineffectiveness in dealing with severe accidents, may demonstrate the failure of the Japanese Government in exercising the obligation of due diligence. Moreover, serious oversight in evaluating all relevant site- and design-related factors, the design and construction of the installation, and effectively responding to the emergency additionally validate the argument about the lack of due diligence. This obligation involves the responsibility of a state to ensure the safe operation of all nuclear installations in the country through licensing, assessment and verification of safety, quality assurance, and the development of emergency plans and procedures, regardless of the fact that the plant was operated by a private company.[18]

However, as a result of the accident at the Fukushima Daiichi nuclear power plant, Member States have undertaken specific actions to address the lessons learned. These actions have resulted in the significant improvement of the safety of nuclear power plants against severe accidents. In particular, 'stress tests' were performed by all countries with nuclear power plants, which led to the findings that while there was no need for the immediate shutdown of nuclear installations, there was a need to increase facility robustness to withstand extreme situations beyond existing safety margins.[19] The Fukushima Daiichi accident also highlighted the need to strengthen and harmonize approaches to emergency preparedness and response in the event of an accident, where a radioactive release could affect neighbouring countries.

17 'Summary Report of the 5th Review Meeting of the Contracting Parties to the Convention on Nuclear Safety' (14 April 2011), IAEA, available at http://www-ns.iaea.orgS at 3, accessed 17 July 2018.

18 Aleksandra Čavoški, 'Revisiting the Convention on Nuclear Safety: Lessons Learned from the Fukushima Accident' (2013) 3(2) *Asian Journal of International Law* 365–391.

19 See 'Five Years after the Fukushima Daiichi Accident: Nuclear Safety Improvements and Lessons Learnt', NEA Report OECD 2016, available at https://www.oecd-nea.org/nsd/pubs/2016/7284-five-years-fukushima.pdf, accessed 17 July 2018.

Strengthening regulatory bodies

The Fukushima accident was partly blamed on regulatory failures as it was evident that there was a severe delay in implementing tsunami counter-measures. There was a communication gap between the expert community on nuclear reactor safety, which consisted mainly of those in the engineering field, and that of earthquake resistance, which was made up of those in the scientific field.[20] Assessments of the Japanese nuclear regulatory system following the Fukushima Daiichi accident revealed that regulatory agencies were not independent. The post-Fukushima incident also emphasized the importance of independence and strengthening regulatory bodies for maintenance, periodic testing and inspection of nuclear installation. Independence of regulatory agencies suggests that there should be an effective separation between the functions of the regulatory body and the functions of organizations promoting use of nuclear energy. In its preliminary report prepared after the Fukushima accident of 11 March 2011, some of the findings of the IAEA were that:

> 'The tsunami hazard for several sites was underestimated. Nuclear regulatory systems should address extreme external events adequately, including their periodic review, and should ensure that regulatory independence and clarity of roles are preserved in all circumstances in line with IAEA Safety Standards.'[21]

The IAEA also found that, notwithstanding the fact that the catastrophe was caused by a natural disaster, there were, inter alia, serious deficiencies in the siting and design of the plant and the emergency readiness of the country, as well as an incomplete and imprecise legislative and regulatory framework.

As was recognized in the early stages of the Fukushima Daiichi accident, the effective involvement of the regulatory body is essential not only during normal operating conditions but also in accident conditions. Therefore, appropriate attention needs to be given to the regulatory body's ability to perform safety reviews and assessments in the case of extreme events.[22] According to the IAEA, the regulatory body should ensure the availability and adequacy of the human and financial resources necessary to perform existing, expanded or new regulatory

20 See Hideaki Shiroyama, 'Nuclear Safety Regulation in Japan and Impacts of the Fukushima Daiichi Accident' in Joonhong Ahn, Cathryn Carson, Mikael Jensen, Kohta Juraku, Shinya Nagasaki, Satoru Tanaka (eds), *Reflections on the Fukushima Daiichi Nuclear Accident: Toward Social-Scientific Literacy and Engineering Resilience* (Springer, 2015) 283–296.

21 International Atomic Energy Agency, 'IAEA International Fact Finding Expert Mission of the Nuclear Accident Following the Great East Japan Earthquake and Tsunami: Preliminary Summary' (1 June 2011), available at https://www-pub.iaea.org/MTCD/meetings/PDFplus/2011/cn200/documentation/cn200_Final-Fukushima-Mission_Report.pdf, accessed 17 July 2018.

22 'Safety Reassessment for Nuclear Fuel Cycle Facilities in Light of the Accident at the Fukushima Daiichi Nuclear Power Plant' (n 5) 5.

functions during an extreme event; verify compliance by the operating organization with new safety requirements; develop and establish processes for improved dissemination and use of operating experience; ensure that regulatory roles and responsibilities for data-gathering and use during and after an emergency are clearly specified.[23]

Public participation in nuclear decision-making process

After the Fukushima accident, the nuclear industry also witnessed an increasing demand for disclosure of and access to information and stakeholder involvement in regulatory decision-making due to the deep public fears of nuclear radiation. There was increasing demand for better information for nuclear radiation and its risks.[24] It is important for the public to be involved throughout the entirety of the process from licensing to the creation and implementation of the emergency plan. Fukushima also demonstrated the necessity of the involvement of stakeholders, including local authorities, industry, non-governmental organizations, government officials and the public in decision-making to enhance the credibility, legitimacy, sustainability and final quality of regulatory and off-site emergency management decisions.[25] Experience during the accident also highlighted the necessity of sharing information between regulators stakeholders to ensure that all aspects of safety in relation to nuclear facilities are understood.[26]

Enhancing transparency

Concern for transparency is not new in the nuclear industry. In 2004 a case was filed in the Indian Supreme Court seeking disclosure of information about safety violations and defects in various nuclear installations and power plants across the country. The information was sought on the basis of a Report prepared by the Atomic Energy Regulatory Board (AERB) in November 1995 documenting safety defects and weaknesses of the nuclear installations, citing 130 instances which are said to be matters of concern.[27] Although the Court dismissed the case on the ground that disclosure was held not to be in the interest of national security, this case highlighted the widespread view that the Indian industry operated under a veil of secrecy.[28]

23 Ibid (n 5) 28.

24 Sidney D. Drell, George P. Shultz, and Steven P. Andreasen, 'Reducing the Global Nuclear Risk', October–November 2012 *Policy Review* 17.

25 'Five Years after the Fukushima Daiichi Accident: Nuclear Safety Improvements and Lessons Learnt' (n 19) 17.

26 Ibid.

27 *Peoples Union for Civil Liberties v Union of India* 2 SC 476

28 Yash Thomas Mannully, 'Law Relating to Nuclear Liability and Compensation in India' (2010) 3 *International Journal of Nuclear Law* 112.

The Fukushima accident renewed the call for transparency regarding safety in the nuclear energy industry, management of spent fuel and regulatory matters. The disaster revealed Japan's rather bleak nuclear record which made clear that increased transparency can go a long way to reducing the severity and frequency of nuclear incidents, as well as to promoting public knowledge and support for the industry.[29] In order to enhance transparency, the EU Directive of 2014 requires operators of nuclear power plants to release information to the public, both in times of normal operation and in the event of incidents.[30] Transparency measures offer potential ways to address these concerns, by sharing the information relevant to nuclear energy and showing a willingness to ensure that the increase in nuclear energy does not risk operational safety, the environment or nuclear proliferation.[31] Transparency includes not only access to information but requires effective interactions between public and regulatory bodies. Clarity and transparency in communication between the regulatory body and the operating organization need to be ensured and the reporting of results of the safety assessment and reassessment shall be made public.[32] After Fukushima, many OECD countries have further developed their policies on transparency in nuclear energy activities and some countries have established national information systems providing online data on the current radiological situation around their nuclear power plants, as well as increasingly making publicly available their peer review results, annual reports, regulatory decisions and the rationale and basis for these decisions.[33]

IAEA response after the Fukushima accident

After the Fukushima accident, the IAEA became actively involved in effectively responding to it and, at the same time, to restoring institutional and public confidence in nuclear safety. In September 2011, in the wake of the accident, the IAEA adopted an Action Plan on Nuclear Safety to strengthen the global nuclear safety framework. The IAEA Action Plan calls upon Member States 'to work towards establishing a global nuclear liability regime that addresses the concerns of all states that might be affected by a nuclear accident with a view to providing appropriate compensation for nuclear damage', and 'to give due consideration to the possibility of joining the international nuclear liability instruments as a step

29 Emily Benz, 'Lessons from Fukushima: Strengthening the International Regulation of Nuclear Energy' (2013) 37 *William and Mary Environmental Law and Policy Review* 845, 869.

30 See https://ec.europa.eu/energy/en/topics/nuclear-energy/nuclear-safety, accessed 17 July 2018.

31 Kazuko Hamada, 'Transparency and Nonproliferation in the Asia-Pacific Region: Enhancing Transparency, Strengthening the Nonproliferation Regime' (2008) 50 *Progress in Nuclear Energy* 660.

32 'Safety Reassessment for Nuclear Fuel Cycle Facilities in light of the Accident at the Fukushima Daiichi Nuclear Power Plant' (n 5) 4.

33 'Five Years after the Fukushima Daiichi Accident: Nuclear Safety Improvements and Lessons Learnt' (n 19) 31.

towards achieving such a global regime'.[34] The Action Plan focuses, in particular, on protection of people and the environment from ionizing radiation. Thus, the Fukushima accident reflects a renewed commitment of the international community to improve the nuclear safety and liability regime. Also, there are increasing demands for international harmonisation of safety standards. After the incidents, the following suggestions were put forward by IAEA:[35]

- nuclear power plant design against external events;
- offsite response to emergency situations (for example, station blackout);
- emergency management and preparedness following worst case accident scenarios;
- safety consideration for operation of multi-units at the same nuclear power plant site;
- cooling of spent fuel storage in severe accident scenarios;
- training of nuclear power plant operators for severe accident scenarios;
- radiological monitoring following nuclear power plant accidents involving radiological release; and
- communications in emergency situations.

The IAEA also activated its 'Incident and Emergency Centre' and sent specialized expert missions to fully understand the accident and to provide assistance and expertise to Japan. The IAEA also called upon its Member States: to systematically and regularly review the safety of all nuclear power plants; to ensure that their regulatory bodies are as effective as possible and regulators must be genuinely independent, adequately funded, and staffed by well-trained personnel; and strengthen the global emergency preparedness and response system.

In order to address the shortcomings of the Convention on Nuclear Safety (CNS), the Vienna Declaration on Nuclear Safety has been adopted by the Contracting Parties. The Declaration contains principles for the implementation of the objective of the CNS to prevent accidents and mitigate radiological consequences. The Declaration is part of an ongoing international effort to strengthen nuclear safety in the wake of the Fukushima-Daiichi accident in Japan. The Declaration addressed the weaknesses of Article 18 of the CNS related to the design and construction of nuclear installations. The Declaration provides that new nuclear power plants are to be designed, sited and constructed consistent with the objective of preventing accidents in the commissioning and operation; and comprehensive and systematic safety assessments are to be carried out periodically and regularly for existing installations throughout their lifetime in order to

34 IAEA Action Plan on Nuclear Safety, available at https://www.iaea.org/newscenter/focus/nuclear-safety-action-plan 17 July 2018

35 Summary report of the Fifth Review Meeting of the Contracting Parties to the Convention on Nuclear Safety, 4–14 April 2011, Vienna, available at http://www-ns.iaea.org/downloads/ni/safety_convention/cns-summaryreport0411.pdf, accessed 17 July 2018.

identify safety improvements.[36] Under the Declaration, the Contracting Parties to the CNS further decided that these principles should be reflected in their actions with immediate effect, in particular when preparing their reports on the implementation of the CNS. Each national report should include inter alia an overview of implementation measures, planned programmes and measures for the safety improvements identified for existing nuclear installations.[37]

Conclusion

The Fukushima accident resulted in a major crisis of global public confidence in the safety of nuclear power plants. The main lessons to be learned from the accident include the need to address the uncertainty and the magnitude of the consequences of extreme natural hazards in order to maintain the safety of nuclear installations; improve the safety of existing installations as far as reasonably practicable, and improve emergency preparedness and response capabilities to deal with the consequences of a severe accident anywhere in the world.[38] The experience of Fukushima also emphasized the upgrading of nuclear plant systems, operating procedures and operator training.[39] In particular, strengthening capabilities of personnel for identifying, evaluating and managing the risks from beyond-design-basis events is critically important to withstand the risks of such an accident.[40] The Fukushima Daiichi accident also questioned the effectiveness of the international liability regime and highlighted the importance of introducing suppliers' liability, given the contributory risks of third parties in the Fukushima accident, and increasing the amount of compensation, as an accident within the nuclear sector will almost inevitably exceed the amount stated in the legal liability cap.

36 Vienna Declaration on Nuclear Safety, February 9, 2015, CNS/DC/2015/2/Rev.1.

37 Ibid.

38 'International Conference on Effective Nuclear Regulatory Systems: Sustaining Improvements Globally', Proceedings of an International Conference organized by the IAEA and held in Vienna, 11–15 April 2016, IAEA, 2017, 10–11.

39 'Lessons Learned from the Fukushima Nuclear Accident for Improving Safety of U.S. Nuclear Plants', Nuclear and Radiation Studies Board, July 2014, available at https://www.nap.edu/resource/18294/fukushima-brief05-PDFfromNAP-LoRes.pdf, accessed 17 July 2018.

40 Ibid.

12 Concluding remarks

An abundant, secure and inexpensive supply of energy, environmentally sustainable energy production and use, and avoidance of undue dependence on any single fuel or supplier have become the energy policy goals of many countries. In order to gain energy independence, many countries are producing energy from nuclear power as a means of strengthening energy supply security and diversifying beyond reliance on fossil fuels. Nuclear energy is now a significant and long-term energy source for both developed and developing countries in the context of rising concern about security of supply from fossil fuels. Concern over reducing greenhouse gas emissions and the threat of climate change are yet to be considered as main drivers of the planning and establishment of nuclear power. Although, in the OECD countries, nuclear power plants operating under independent and competent regulatory regimes, supported by robust legislation and standards, have achieved a good safety record, in many countries there are some concerns about the risks posed by nuclear energy. Despite the concerns about cost, environmental impact, safety and security implications in terms of weapons proliferation and terrorism, many countries are aspiring this energy source and are undertaking nuclear projects.

International nuclear law is now a well-developed body of norms, standards, procedures, recommendations, guidelines and directives adopted by global institutions such as the IEAEA and regional organizations such as EURATOM, the EU, NEA and ICRP. However, the implementation and enforcement of the growing corpus of nuclear law remain a big challenge for the international community. Any country undertaking nuclear projects will need to strengthen its legal and institutional frameworks and human resources capabilities.

At the international level, the existing liability regime should be properly implemented through legislative and administrative measures by the States Parties to the nuclear liability treaties. An effective global nuclear liability regime depends on greater adherence to the nuclear treaties. All states with nuclear installations, and other states that may be affected by a nuclear accident, should adhere to updated nuclear liability regimes. Fewer than half of the reactors in operation or under construction worldwide are currently subject to any of the international nuclear liability regimes in force.[1] The patchwork nature of the Conventions currently in force results in varying levels of liability amounts and financial security limits. A common and coherent liability regime that is accessible to victims should be in place.

At national level, the keys to an effective nuclear regime are: strengthening the role and independence of the national regulatory authorities; enhancing transparency in nuclear safety; strengthening existing nuclear safety arrangements, reinforcing monitoring; and ensuring emergency preparedness. National regulatory authorities and plant operators should develop a public information strategy, not only in the event of an accident but also in times of normal operation of the plant. Confidentiality clauses in some treaties under which certain information cannot be disclosed run counter to transparency in nuclear information.

For effective implementation of nuclear treaties, it is important that compliance is monitored by the IAEA, which is the only treaty-monitoring body for a large number of such treaties. Unlike other treaty bodies, such as human rights and environmental treaties, the IAEA is an umbrella organization which monitors all the nuclear treaties. On the other hand, under human rights or environmental law each treaty has its specific treaty body which monitors its implementation. But states are still reluctant to cede authority to different international bodies or establish a separate treaty body under each nuclear treaty and to allow it to monitor implementation. This weak implementation mechanism is a key problem of international nuclear law.

Although the Chernobyl and Fukushima nuclear accidents have significantly changed public perception of nuclear power, it is expected that nuclear energy will continue to be treated as an important source of energy in the future to ensure security of supply. Safety and security of nuclear installations, management of nuclear wastes, increased liability, and the long-term nature of decommissioning will continue to dominate the regulatory regime of nuclear energy. However, concerns about transparency, enhanced access to information and public participation will shape social aspects of the nuclear energy in future.

Despite the fact that nuclear accidents have the potential for a catastrophic impact on the environment, the international regime on nuclear law has been inadequate in addressing the protection of the environment. Its current approach is still anthropocentric, as reflected by the focus of nuclear law on protecting people and property. According to one commentator, 'The influence of environmental law has not yet succeeded in ensuring that the environment is effectively protected by international nuclear law'.[2]

1 'Progress Towards a Global Nuclear Liability Regime', (2014) 93 *Nuclear Law Bulletin*, NEA No. 7181 Nuclear Energy Agency Organisation for Economic Co-operation and Development.

2 Sam Emmerechts, 'Environmental Protection under Nuclear Law: Still a Long Way to Go' in *International Nuclear Law: History, Evolution and Outlook*, OECD 155.

Many developing countries are making nuclear energy plans for security of supply. The main issues are security, safety and non-proliferation. The lessons learned from the three accidents demonstrate that ensuring safety is a continual process and the safety culture is still evolving with operating experience. In particular, the Fukushima accident underscores the need for robust understanding and enhanced knowledge of external hazards caused by natural events. The key challenges for the future of nuclear energy projects remain: credible environmental impact assessments; effective multi-stakeholder participation in the nuclear decision-making process; a transparent licensing process; a strong regulatory framework; permanent disposal of high-level radioactive wastes; and ensuring that safety standards are strictly adhered to.

Bibliography

Books

Adede, A. O., *The IAEA Notification and Assistance Conventions in Case of a Nuclear Accident* (London: Graham and Trotman/Martinus Nijhoff Publishers, 1987)

Ahn, Joonhong, Carson, Cathryn, Jensen, Mikael, Juraku, Kohta, Nagasaki, Shinya, and Tanaka, Satoru (eds), *Reflections on the Fukushima Daiichi Nuclear Accident: Toward Social-Scientific Literacy and Engineering Resilience* (London: Springer, 2015)

Alam, Shawkat, *Sustainable Development and Free Trade* (London: Routledge, 2008)

Axelrod, Regina S. and VanDeveer, Stacy D. (eds.), *The Global Environment: Institutions, Law and Policy* (4th edn, Washington, D.C.: Sage, 2015)

Benidickson, Jamie, Boer, Ben, Benjamin, Antonio Herman and Morrow, Karen (eds), *Environmental Law and Sustainability after Rio* (Cheltenham: Edward Elgar, 2011)

Bergkamp, Lucas, *Liability and Environment* (The Hague: Kluwer Law International, 2001)

Birnie, Patricia and Boyle, Alan, *International Law and the Environment* (2nd edn, New York: Oxford University Press, 2002)

Boyle, A. and Freestone D. (eds), *International Law and Sustainable Development* (Oxford: Oxford University Press, 1999)

Brown Weiss, Edith, *In Fairness to Future Generations: International Law, Common Patrimony and Intergenerational Equity* (Dobbs Ferry, NY: Transnational Publishers, 1989)

Brown Weiss, Edith, Barstow Magrow, Daniel, McCaffrey, Stephen C. and Tarlock, A. Dan, *International Law for the Environment* (West Academic Publishing, 2016)

Cameron, Peter, Hancher, Leigh, Kuhn, Wolfgang, *Nuclear Energy Law after Chernobyl,* (London: Graham and Trotman and International Bar Association, 1988)

Campigio, Luigi et al. (eds), *The Environment After Rio: International Law and Economics* (Springer, 1994)

Fisher, Douglas (ed.), *Research Handbook on Fundamental Concepts of Environmental Law* (Cheltenham: Edward Elgar, 2016)

Hangin, Xue, *Transboundary Damage in International Law* (New York: Cambridge University Press, 2003)

Holder, Jane and Lee, Maria, *Environmental Protection, Law and Policy: Text and Materials* (2nd edn, Cambridge: Cambridge University Press, 2007)

Horbach, Nathalie L.J.T. (ed.), *Contemporary Developments in Nuclear Energy Law: Harmonising Legislation in CEEC/NIS* (The Hague: Kluwer Law International, 1999)

Kiss, Alexandre and Shelton, Dinah, *International Environmental Law* (3rd edn, Transnational Publishers, 2004)

Nanda, Ved P. and Pring, George, *International Environmental Law and Policy for the 21st Century* (New York: Transnational Publishers, 2003)

Ness, Peter Van and Gurtov, Mel (eds), *Learning from Fukushima: Nuclear Power in East Asia* (Acton: ANU Press, 2014)

Nocera, Fabrizio, *The Legal Regime of Nuclear Energy: A Comprehensive Guide to International and European Union Law* (Antwerp, Oxford: Intersentia, 2005)

Nollkemper, A., *The Legal Regime of Transboundary Water Pollution: Between Discretion and Constraint* (London: Martinus Nijhoff and Trotman, 1993)

Nucci, Maria Rosaria Di, Brunnengräber, Achim, Mez, Lutz and Schreurs, Miranda, *Comparative Perspectives on Nuclear Waste Governance: An International Comparison* (Springer, 2015)

Pilat, Joseph F. and Busch Nathan E. (eds), *Routledge Handbook of Nuclear Proliferation and Policy* (Abingdon: Routledge, 2018)

Sadeleer, Nicolas de, *Environmental Principles: From Political Slogans to Legal Rules* (Oxford: Oxford University Press, 2002)

Sands, Philippe and Peel, Jacqueline, *Principles of International Law* (3rd edn, Cambridge: Cambridge University Press, 2012)

Schachter, O., *International Law in Theory and Practice* (Dordrecht: Martinus Nijhoff, 1991)

Stoiber, Carlton, Baer Alec, Pelzer, Norbert, Tonhauser, Wolfram, *Handbook on Nuclear Law* (Vienna: International Atomic Energy Agency, 2003)

Takeshi, Yao (ed.), *Zero-Carbon Energy Kyoto 2012* (Tokyo: Springer, 2013)

Tromans, Stephen and Fitzgerald, James, *The Law of Nuclear Installations and Radioactive Substances* (London: Sweet and Maxwell, 1997)

Zillman, Donald N., Lucas, Alastair R. and Pring, George (Rock) (eds.), *Human Rights in Natural Resource Development* (Oxford: Oxford University Press, 2002)

Journals articles

Ahmed, J.U. Ahmed and Daw, H.T. Daw, 'Environmental Impacts of the Production and Use of Nuclear Energy: A Summary of the United Nations Environment Programme Study' (1980) 22 (2) *IAEA Bulletin* 27

Alvarez-Dardet, Carlos, 'Nuclear Waste as a Public Health Challenge' (2001) 55 *J. Epidemiology and Community Health* 449

Ameye, Evelyne and Arregui, Inigo Igartua, 'National Nuclear Third Party Insurance Pools Revisited from a European Union Competition Law Perspective' (2012) 30 *Journal of Energy and Natural Resources Law* 265, 266

Ameye, Evelyne M., 'United States and India: Two Nuclear States with Legislation that Truly Holds Responsible Parties Liable in Case of a Nuclear Accident' (2015) 18(8) *Journal of Risk Research* 1070–1082

Arnold, Adam, 'The Quest for Sustainable Energy Security: Germany's Nuclear Scrutiny vs. "All of the Above"' (2015) 15 *Sustainable Development Law and Policy* 26

Bajaj, S.S., 'Regulatory Practices for Nuclear Power Plants in India' (2013) 38(5) *Sadhana* 1027–1050, 1043

Baradi, Mohamed El, Nwogugu, Edwin and Rames, John, 'International Law and Nuclear Energy: Overview of the Legal Framework' (1995) 3 *IAEA Bulletin* 22

Bechhoefer, Bernhard G. and Stein, Eric, 'Atoms for Peace: The New International Atomic Energy Agency' (1957) 55(6) *Michigan Law Review* 747–798

Begum, Najnin and Nabi, Rakiba, 'Public Participation in Environmental Decision Making in Bangladesh: To What Extent is the Existing Regulatory Framework Effective' (2011) 51 (1) *Indian Journal of International Law* 67–84

Beken, Tom Vander Nicholas Dornb, Stijn Van Daele, 'Security Risks in Nuclear Waste Management: Exceptionalism, Opaqueness, and Vulnerability' (2010) 91 *Journal of Environmental Management* 940–948

Benz, Emily, 'Lessons from Fukushima: Strengthening the International Regulation of Nuclear Energy' (2013) 37 *WM. and Mary Environmental Law and Policy Review* 845, 869

Bertel, Evelyne and Vate, Joop Van de, 'Nuclear Energy & the Environmental Debate: The Context of Choices' (1995) 4 *IAEA Bulletin*

Bourdon, P., 'The Growing Interrelationship Between Nuclear Law and Environmental Law' (2015) 33 (2) *NEA News* 15–18.

Čavoški, Aleksandra, 'Revisiting the Convention on Nuclear Safety: Lessons Learned from the Fukushima Accident' (2013) 3 *Asian Journal of International Law* 365–391

Cameron, Peter D., 'The Revival of Nuclear Power: An Analysis of the Legal Implications' (2007) 19(1) *Journal of Environmental Law* 71–87

Carole Klein-Chesivoir, 'Avoiding Environmental Injury: The Case for Widespread Use of Environmental Impact Assessments in International Development Projects' (1990) 30 *Virginia Journal of International Law* 517–518

Casey-Lefkowitz, Susan et al, 'The Evolving Role of Citizens in Environmental Enforcement' (1996) 11 *National Environmental Enforcement Journal* 40

Clapp, Richard W., 'Nuclear Power and Public Health' (2005) 113 *Environmental Health Perspective* 720

Coe, Andrew and Vaynman, Jane, 'Collusion and the Nuclear Nonproliferation Treaty' (2015) 77(4) *Journal of Politics* 983–97

Cohen, Miriam Alfie and Garay, Adrian de, 'Risk Society and the Precautionary Principle', in: Jamie Benidickson, Ben Boer, Antonio Herman Benjamin and Karen Morrow (eds.), *Environmental Law and Sustainability after Rio* (Cheltenham: Edward Elgar, 2011) 85

Coplan, Karl S., 'Inter-civilizational Inequities of Nuclear Power Weighed against the Intergenerational Inequities of Carbon Based Energy' (2006) 17 *Fordham Environmental Law Review* 227

Currie, Duncan E.J., 'The Problems and Gaps in the Nuclear Liability Conventions and an Analysis of How an Actual Claim Would be brought under the Current Existing Treaty Regime in the Event of a Nuclear Accident' (2006) 35(1) *Denver Journal of International Law and Policy* 85–127

Davie, Lincoln L., 'Beyond Fukushima: Disasters, Nuclear Energy, and Energy Law' (2011) *Brigham Young University Law Review* 123

Drell, Sidney D., Shultz, George P., and Andreasen, Steven P., 'Reducing the Global Nuclear Risk' (2012) *Policy Review* October–Nov 17

El-Hinnawi, Essam E., 'Review of the Environmental Impact of Nuclear Energy' (1978) 20(2) *IAEA Bulletin* 39–40.

Faure, Michael G. and Jing, Liu, 'Compensating Nuclear Damage in China' (2013) 11 *Washington University Global Studies Law Review* 781–816

Fuhrmann, Matthew and Lufu, Yonatan, 'Do Arms Control Treaties Work? Assessing the Effectiveness of the Nuclear Nonproliferation Treaty' (2016) 60 *International Studies Quarterly* 530, 537.

Gandhi, Sonal and Kang, Jungmin, 'Nuclear Safety and Nuclear Security Synergy' (2013) 60 *Annals of Nuclear Energy* 357–361.

Green, Harold P., 'Participation in Nuclear Power Plant Licensing: The Great Delusion' (1974) 15 *William and Mary Law Review* 503

Hagen, A., 'Nuclear Power, Man, and the Environment' (1982) 24(2) *IAEA Bulletin* 3

Hamada, Kazuko, 'Transparency and Nonproliferation in the Asia-Pacific Region: Enhancing Transparency, Strengthening the Nonproliferation Regime' (2008) 50 *Progress in Nuclear Energy* 660

Heffron, Raphael J., Ashley, Stephen F. and Nuttall, William J., 'The Global Nuclear Liability Regime post Fukushima Daiichi' (2016) 90 *Progress in Nuclear Energy* 4

John G. Palfrey, 'Energy and the Environment: The Special Case of Nuclear Power' (1974) 74 *Columbia Law Review* 1375, 1382

Joyner, Daniel H., 'Fundamental Rights of States in International Law and the Right to Peaceful Nuclear Energy' (2015) 4(3) *Cambridge Journal of International and Comparative Law* 661

Kamminga, Menno, 'The IAEA Convention on Nuclear Safety' (1995) 44(4) *International and Comparative Law Quarterly* 872–882

Kessides, Ioannis N., 'Powering Africa's Sustainable Development: The Potential Role of Nuclear Energy' (2014) 74 *Energy Policy* S57–S70

Kiss, Alexandre, 'State Responsibility and Liability for Nuclear Damage' (2006–2007) 35 *Denver J. Int'l l. & Pol'y* 67

Lamm, Vanda, 'The Protocol amending the 1963 Vienna Convention' (1998) 63 *Nuclear Law Bulletin* 14.

Lanni, L., 'Some Realities of Nuclear Power Plant Decommissioning' (1978) 20(6) IAEA Bulletin 25

Mannully, Yash Thomas, 'Law Relating to Nuclear Liability and Compensation in India' (2010) *International Journal of Nuclear Law* 112

McMillan, Karen, 'Strengthening the International Legal Framework for Nuclear Energy' (2001) 13 *Georgetown International Environmental Law Review* 983–1031

Molodstova, Elena, 'Nuclear Energy and Environmental Protection: Responses of International Law' (1994) 12(1) *Pace Environmental Law Review* 193

Molodtsova, Elena, 'Nuclear Energy Law and International Environmental Law: an Integrated Approach' (1995) 13 *J. Energy & Nat. Resources L.* 275–292

Nanda,Ved P. and Dyke, Jon M. Van, 'International Nuclear Law: An Introduction' (2006) 35(1) *Denver Journal of International Law and Policy* 47–65.

Paine, Christopher E., 'The Nuclear Fuel Cycle, Global Security, and Climate Change: Weighing the Costs and Benefits of Nuclear Power Expansion' (2009–2010) 44 *U. Rich. L. Rev.* 1047 1049

Partan, Daniel G., 'The Duty to Inform in International Environmental Law' (1988) 6 *B.U. International Law Journal* 43, 44

Reyners, Patrick, 'Underground Nuclear Repositories and International Civil Liability: The Time Factor' (2014) 17(1) *Journal of Risk Research* 133–143, 135

Rislove, Daniel C., 'Global Warming v. Non-Proliferation: The Time has Come for Nations to Reassert their Right to Peaceful Use of Nuclear Energy' (2007) 24(4) *Wisconsin International Law Journal* 1069–1098

Rodríguez-Rivera, Luis E., 'The Human Right to Environment and the Peaceful Use of Nuclear Energy' (2007) 35(1) *Denver Journal of International Law and Policy* 173–192

Saidi, Kais and Ben Mbarek, Mounir, 'Nuclear Energy, Renewable Energy, CO2 Emissions, and Economic Growth for Nine Developed Countries: Evidence From Panel Granger Causality Tests' (2016) *Progress in Nuclear Energy* 364–374

Sanders, Mark Callis; Sanders, Charlotta E., 'A World's Dilemma "Upon Which the Sun Never Sets": The Nuclear Waste Management Strategy (Part I): Western European Nation States and the United States of America' (2016) *Progress in Nuclear Energy* 69–97

Schulte, Gregory L., 'Strengthening the IAEA: How the Nuclear Watchdog Can Regain Its Bark' (March 2019) 253 *Strategic Forum* 4

Shiroyama, Hideaki, 'Nuclear Safety Regulation in Japan and Impacts of the Fukushima Daiichi Accident' (2014) *Reflections on the Fukushima Daiichi Nuclear Accident* 283–296

Sieg, Richard, 'A Call to Minimize the Use of Nuclear Power in the Twenty-First Century' (2008) 9(2) *Vermont Journal of Environmental Law* 305–370.

Silver, Joseph G., 'The Global Partnership: The Final Blow to the Nuclear Non-Proliferation Regime?' (2008) 21(1) *New York International Law Review* 69

Sprinz, Detlef F. and von Bünau, Steffen, 'The Compensation Fund for Climate Impacts' (2013) 5(3) *Journal of Weather, Climate and Society* 1–27

Stokke, Olav Schram, 'Nuclear Dumping in Artic Seas: Russian Implementation of the London Convention' in David G. Victor, Kal Raustiala and Eugene B. Skolnikoff, *The Implementation and Effectiveness of International Environmental Commitments: Theory and Practice* (Cambridge, MIT Press, 1998) 475–518

Sutaria, Ayushi, 'Placing the Indian Civil Nuclear Liability Regime in Context: The Extent of Supplier's Liability' (2014) 17 (1) *Journal of Risk Research* 97–113

Temple, Richard M., Penny, Christina and Sullivan, Mary Anne, 'Liability for Nuclear Incidents: Should the UK Now Follow the US Approach?' (2006) 18(3) *Journal of Environmental Law* 443–457

Toth, Ferenc L., 'Nuclear Energy and Sustainable Development' (2014) 74 *Energy Policy* S1–S4

Tully, Stephen R., 'The Contribution of Human rights to Universal Energy Access' (2006) 4 *Northwestern University Journal of International Human Rights* 518

Vadi, Valentina, 'Energy Security v. Public Health? Nuclear Energy in International Investment Law and Arbitration' (2015–2016) 47 *Georgetown J. of International Law* 1069, 1114

Walsh, Timothy J.V., 'Turning Our Backs: Kyoto's Mistaken Nuclear Exclusion' (2003) 16(1) *Georgetown International Environmental Law Review* 147–170.

Zakariya, Nasiru Imam and Kahn, M.T.E., 'Safety, Security and Safeguard' (2015) 75 *Annals of Nuclear Energy* 292–302

Reports

'Nuclear Energy in a Sustainable Development Perspective' NEA, OECD, 2000

'Nuclear Legislation in OECD and NEA Countries: USA' OECD, 2016

'Nuclear Site Remediation and Restoration during Decommissioning of Nuclear Installations', A Report by the NEA Co-operative Programme on Decommissioning, OECD 2014 NEA No. 7192

'Progress Towards a Global Nuclear Liability Regime', *Nuclear Law Bulletin* No. 93, OECD 2014 NEA No. 7181

'Safety Reassessment for Nuclear Fuel Cycle Facilities in light of the Accident at the Fukushima Daiichi Nuclear Power Plant', Safety Reports Series No. 90, (IAEA, Vienna, 2016) 2

'Stakeholder Involvement in Nuclear Issues', INSAG-20 A report by the International Nuclear Safety Group, (IAEA, Vienna, 2006) https://www-pub.iaea.org/MTCD/Publications/PDF/Pub1276_web.pdf

'The Regulatory Control of Radioactive Waste Management', Overview of 15 NEA Member Countries OECD 2004 NEA No. 3597

The Fukushima Accident, Current Status, http://www.iaea.org/newscenter/focus/fukushima/missionsummary010611.pdf

A guide to Nuclear Regulation in the UK, http://www.onr.org.uk/documents/a-guide-to-nuclear-regulation-in-the-uk.pdf

Anderson, Richard, 'Nuclear Power: Energy for the Future or Relic of the Past?' BBC News (27 Feb. 2015), http://www.bbc.com/news/business-30919045

Ashraf, S.A.H. and Chande, S.K., 'Decommissioning of Nuclear Activities: Indian Perspective', http://www.iaea.org/inis/collection/NCLCollectionStore/_Public/33/052/33052267.pdf

Atomic Energy and the Environment, Fact sheet of IAEA, Vienna

Basic Principles of Radioactive Waste Management, http://www.onr.org.uk/waste manage/basic-principles.pdf

Ben McRae, 'The Convention on Supplementary Compensation for Nuclear Damage: Catalyst for a Global Nuclear Liability Regime', https://www.oecd-nea.org/law/nlb/nlb-79/017-035%20-%20Article%20Ben%20McRae.pdf

Carrington, Damian, 'Unsure about Nuclear Power? Here are the Five Questions you must Answer to Decide', *The Guardian*, 21 April 2011

Climate Change and Nuclear Power, IAEA, Vienna, 2016

Donovan, Jeffrey, 'IAEA's Amano Calls for Strengthened Computer Security in a Nuclear World', IAEA Official Publication Information and Communication (June 2015).

Decommissioning of Nuclear Installations, IAEA, https://www.iaea.org/topics/decommissioning

Decommissioning of Nuclear Power Plants and Research Reactors Safety Guide, Safety Standard Series No. WS-G-2.1 IAEA, Vienna 1999

Drell, Sidney D., Shultz, George P. and Andreasen, Steven P., 'Reducing the Global Nuclear Risk', (2012) Policy Review, https://www.hoover.org/research/reducing-global-nuclear-risk, accessed 27 October 2017

Emmerechts, Sam, 'Environmental Protection under Nuclear Law: Still a Long Way to Go' in: International Nuclear Law: History, Evolution and Outlook, OECD, 2010

Environment Alert Bulletin, 'Nuclear Waste: Is Everything Under Control?' 2007, UNEP, http://www.grid.unep.ch/products/3_Reports/ew_nuclear.en.pdf

EPA, Radioactive Waste Disposal: An Environmental Perspective

European Commission, *White Paper on environmental liability* (Feb 2000) http://ec.europa.eu/environment/legal/liability/pdf/el_full.pdf

Financial Aspects of Decommissioning, IAEA-TECDOC-1476, 2005

Financing the Decommissioning of Nuclear Facilities, OECD 2016 NEA No. 7326

Future of Nuclear Energy, An Inter-disciplinary MIT study, Massachusetts Institute of Technology, Massachusetts, 2003, http://web.mit.edu/nuclearpower/pdf/nuclearpower-summary.pdf

'Government and Nuclear Energy' (NEA, OECD 2004)

Huges, Ross, 'Environmental Impact Assessment and Stakeholder Involvement', International Institute for Environment and Development, London, 1998

IAEA Safety Standards, Classification of Radioactive Waste, General Safety Guide IAEA Safety Standards Series no. GSG-1, IAEA, Vienna, 2009

IAEA Safety Standards: The Global Reference for Protecting People and the Environment from Harmful Effects of Ionizing Radiation (June 2009), http://www-ns.iaea.org/ downloads/standards/iaea-safety-standards-brochure.pdf

IAEA, Summary Report of the 5th Review Meeting of the Contracting Parties to the Convention on Nuclear Safety (4214 April 2011), http://www-ns.iaea.orgS at 3.

International Atomic Energy Agency, 'IAEA International Fact Finding Expert Mission of the Nuclear Accident Following the Great East Japan Earthquake and Tsunami: Preliminary Summary' 2011

'International Conference on Effective Nuclear Regulatory Systems: Sustaining Improvements Globally', Proceedings of an International Conference organized by the IAEA and held in Vienna, 11–15 April 2016, IAEA, 2017, 10–11.

International Atomic Energy Agency: Highlights of Activities 24 (1990)

International Problems of Financial Protection against Nuclear Risk, A study under the auspices of Harvard Law School and Atomic Industrial Forum, 1959, New York, Atomic Industrial Forum.

Liability for Nuclear Damage, World Nuclear Association, http://www.world-nuclear.org/information-library/safety-and-security/safety-of-plants/liability-for-nuclear-damage.aspx

Marcus, G.H., 'The NEA and the IAEA: partnering for progress' NEA News 2005 Volume 23, Number 2

'Nuclear Energy in a Sustainable Development Perspective' NEA, OECD, 2000

'Nuclear Legislation in OECD and NEA Countries: USA' OECD, 2016

'Nuclear Site Remediation and Restoration during Decommissioning of Nuclear Installations', A Report by the NEA Co-operative Programme on Decommissioning, OECD 2014 NEA No. 7192

Nuclear Energy in a Sustainable Development Perspective, NEA, OECD, 2000, 42.

Nuclear Safety & Security, Concepts and terms, IAEA 2007, http://www-ns.iaea.org/standards/concepts-terms.asp#3

OECD/NEA, Revised text of the *Exposé des Motifs* of the Paris Convention, approved by the OECD Council on November 16, 1982, para. 15, www.oecd-nea.org/law/nlparis_motif.html

ONR, Safety Assessment Principles for Nuclear Facilities, 2014 Edition

Opschoor, J.B. and Vos, Hans B., *Economic Instruments for Environmental Protection*, OECD, Paris, 1989

'Progress Towards a Global Nuclear Liability Regime', *Nuclear Law Bulletin* No. 93, OECD 2014 NEA No. 7181

Radioactive Waste, https://www.nrc.gov/reading-rm/doc-collections/fact-sheets/radwaste.pdf

Smies, Maarten, Geerling, Chris and Bie, Steven De, 'Environmental Impact Assessment for Oil and Gas in the Commonwealth of Independent States: Investor Objectives and National Ambitions, Investment and Finance for the Oil and Gas Industries', A Paper presented at a seminar of CEPMLP and Petroconsultants, 22–23 September 1994

'Regulatory Challenges of Decommissioning Nuclear Reactors', Nuclear Energy Agency, OECD, 2003, 7.

Regulatory Control of Radioactive Waste Management, Overview of 15 NEA Member Countries, OECD 2004

'The Regulatory Control of Radioactive Waste Management', Overview of 15 NEA Member Countries OECD 2004 NEA No. 3597

Smies, Maarten, Geerling, Chris and Bie, Steven De, 'Environmental Impact Assessment for Oil and Gas in the Commonwealth of Independent States: Investor Objectives and National Ambitions, Investment and Finance for the Oil and Gas Industries', a Paper presented at a seminar of CEPMLP and Petroconsultants, 22–23 September 1994

Soljan, Vedran, 'The New Definition of Nuclear Damage in the 1997 Protocol to Amend the 1963 Vienna Convention on Civil Liability for Nuclear Damage', in *Reform of Nuclear Civil Liability*, OECD Budapest Symposium, NEA, 2000

'Safety Reassessment for Nuclear Fuel Cycle Facilities in Light of the Accident at the Fukushima Daiichi Nuclear Power Plant', Safety Reports Series No. 90, (IAEA, Vienna, 2016) 2

'Stakeholder Involvement in Nuclear Issues', INSAG-20 A report by the International Nuclear Safety Group, (IAEA, Vienna, 2006) https://www-pub.iaea.org/MTCD/Publications/PDF/Pub1276_web.pdf

The Fukushima Accident, Current Status, http://www.iaea.org/newscenter/focus/fukushima/missionsummary010611.pdf

Tonhauser, Johan Wolfram and Wetherall, Anthony, 'Overview of the International Legal Framework Governing the Safe and Peaceful Uses of Nuclear Energy: Some Practical Steps' (2006) OECD Paper 13.

Vienna Convention on Civil Liability for Nuclear Damage 1997 and the 1997 Convention on Supplementary Compensation for Nuclear Damage- Explanatory Texts, IAEA International Law Series No. 3, IAEA, Vienna, 2007, 30

Websites

'Backgrounder on the Three Mile Island Accident', https://www.nrc.gov/reading-rm/doc-collections/fact-sheets/3mile-isle.html

'IAEA Milestones Approach: Developing the National Infrastructure for Nuclear Power' IAEA, https://www.iaea.org/sites/default/files/18/01/developing-the-national-nuclear-infrastructure-for-nuclear-power.pdf

Convention on the Prevention of Marine Pollution by Dumping of Wastes and Other Matter, IMO, http://www.imo.org/en/OurWork/Environment/LCLP/Pages/default.aspx

'Lessons Learned from the Fukushima Nuclear Accident for Improving Safety of U.S. Nuclear Plants', Nuclear and Radiation Studies Board, July 2014 https://www.nap.edu/resource/18294/fukushima-brief05-PDFfromNAP-LoRes.pdf 'Nuclear changes to the UK nuclear liability regime', file:///C:/Users/user/Downloads/NuclearBrochure.pdf

'Nuclear liability regime: major changes for the UK regime finalised - in force soon', http://knowledge.freshfields.com/m/Global/r/1545/nuclear_liability_regime__major_changes_for_the_uk_regime

'Radioactive Waste Disposal: An Environmental Perspective', EPA, https://www.nrc.gov/reading-rm/doc-collections/fact-sheets/radwaste.pdf

Changes to UK nuclear liability regime, http://www.world-nuclear-news.org/V-Changes-to-UK-nuclear-liability-regime-07031701.html

Chatzis, Irena, 'Solving the Back End: Finland's Key to the Final Disposal of Spent Nuclear Fuel', https://www.iaea.org/newscenter/news/solving-the-back-end-finlands-key-to-the-final-disposal-of-spent-nuclear-fuel

Emmerechts, Sam, 'Environmental Law and Nuclear Law: A Growing Symbiosis', https://www.oecd-nea.org/law/nlb/nlb-82/091_110_ArticleEmmerechtsSam.pdf

Environment Alert Bulletin, Nuclear Waste: Is Everything Under Control?

EURATOM Supply Agency, http://ec.europa.eu/euratom/mission.html

IAEA Action Plan on Nuclear Safety, https://www.iaea.org/newscenter/focus/nuclear-safety-action-plan

IEA, World Energy Outlook 2008 at 37, https://www.iea.org/media/weowebsite/2008-1994/WEO2008.pdf

Jaffer, Misam, 'Impact of Nuclear Power Plants', 26 March 2011, http://large.stanford.edu/courses/2011/ph241/jaffer2/

Jubin, Jean-Rene, 'Transparency and Openness' 7 (2011) IAEA, https://ansn.iaea.org/Common/topics/OpenTopic.aspx?ID=9087

Moens, John, US Energy Information, The Nuclear Power and the Environment, http://www.nuclearfiles.org/menu/key-issues/nuclear-energy/issues/health-environment/moens_nuclear_power_environment.html

Nuclear Reactors (Environmental Impact Assessment for Decommissioning) Regulations, http://www.onr.org.uk/eiadr.htm

Nuclear Safety and Regulation, https://www.oecd-nea.org/nsd/

Nuclear Technology Review 2016, IAEA, https://www.iaea.org/About/Policy/GC/GC60/GC60InfDocuments/English/gc60inf-2_en.pdf

Preparatory Commission for the comprehensive nuclear-test-ban treaty organization (CTBTO): An Overview, http://www.nti.org/media/documents/ctbto.pdf

Price-Anderson Act: Background Information, http://cdn.ans.org/pi/ps/docs/ps54-bi.pdf Public Engagement in the Nuclear Sector: A UK and EU Perspective, National Nuclear Laboratory, EU08051/06/10/01, Issue 3, 2016, http://s538600174.onlinehome.fr/nugenia/wp-content/uploads/2016/08/EU08051-06-10-01-Issue-3-Public-Engagement-in-the-Nuclear-Sector-A-UK-and-EU-Perspective.pdf

Radioactive waste management and decommissioning, https://www.oecd-nea.org/rwm/

Radioactive Waste, https://www.nrc.gov/reading-rm/doc-collections/fact-sheets/radwaste.pdf

Reducing Climate Change Impact, http://www.iaea.org/newscenter/news/2009/climatechange.html

Report to Congress on the Price-Anderson Act, US Department of Energy, https://www.energy.gov/sites/prod/files/gcprod/documents/paa-rep.pdf

Summary report of the 5th Review Meeting of the Contracting Parties to the Convention on Nuclear Safety, 4–14 April 2011, Vienna http://www-ns.iaea.org/downloads/ni/safety_convention/cns-summaryreport0411.pdf

Index

Made in the USA
Monee, IL
13 September 2026

62978982R10118